Longman Exam Guides
English as a Foreign Language
Intermediate Examinations

Longman Exam Guides

Series Editors: **Stuart Wall and David Weigall**

Titles available:
Bookkeeping and Accounting
Business Law
Economics
English as a Foreign Language: Intermediate
English Literature
Monetary Economics
Office Practice and Secretarial Administration
Pure Mathematics
Secretarial Skills

Forthcoming:
Biology
Business Communication
Business Studies
Chemistry
Commerce
Computer Science
Electronics
English as a Foreign Language: Advanced
English as a Foreign Language: Preliminary
French
General Principles of Law
General Studies
Geography
Mechanics
Modern British History
Physics
Politics
Principles of Law
Quantitative Methods
Sociology
Taxation

Longman Exam Guides

ENGLISH AS A FOREIGN LANGUAGE

Intermediate Examinations
Felicity O'Dell

LONGMAN
London and New York

Longman Group Limited
Longman House, Burnt Mill, Harlow
Essex CM20 2JE, England
Associated companies throughout the world

Published in the United States of America
by Longman Inc., New York

First published 1986

British Library Cataloguing in Publication Data
O'Dell, Felicity
   English as a foreign language: intermediate examinations.——
   (Longman exam guides)
    1. English language——Textbooks for foreign speakers
   I. Title
428.2′4   PE1128

ISBN 0-582-29679-X

Library of Congress Cataloging in Publication Data
O'Dell, Felicity, 1947–
   English as a foreign language intermediate examinations.

   (Longman exam guides)
   Bibliography: p.
   Includes index.
    1. English language——Examinations.   2. English language——
Text-books for foreign speakers.
I. Title   II. Series.
PE1114.O44   1986   428′.0076   85–25652
ISBN 0–582–29679–X

Set in 9½ on 11pt Linotron Times
Printed in and bound in Great Britain at
The Bath Press, Avon

Contents

Editors' Preface

Much has been said in recent years about declining standards and disappointing examination results. Whilst this may be somewhat exaggerated, examiners are well aware that the performance of many candidates falls well short of their potential. Longman Exam Guides are written by experienced examiners and teachers, and aim to give you the best possible foundation for examination success. There is no attempt to cut corners. The books encourage thorough study and a full understanding of the concepts involved and should be seen as course companions and study guides to be used throughout the year. Exminers are in no doubt that a structured approach in preparing for and taking examinations can, together with hard work and diligent application, substantially improve performance.

The largely self-contained nature of each chapter gives the book a useful degree of flexibility. After starting with Chapters 1 and 2, all other chapters can be read selectively, in any order appropriate to the stage you have reached in your course. We believe that this book, and the series as a whole, will help you establish a solid platform of basic knowledge and examination technique on which to build.

Stuart Wall and David Weigall

Acknowledgements

All the Examination Boards referred to in this book are thanked for their prompt and helpful replies to all my enquiries. I am particularly grateful to the following boards for giving me permission to reproduce previous questions:

ARELS Examination Trust
The University of Cambridge Local Examinations Syndicate
The University of Oxford Delegacy of Local Examinations
RSA Examinations Board
Institute of Linguists
Pitman Examinations Institute
Trinity College, London

I should like to thank the Cambridge Eurocentre for permission to reproduce a plan of the school and also to thank colleagues and students there who have helped me in many ways in the preparation of this book. I am particularly grateful to the Principal, Dr James Day.

Thanks are also due to Eddie Keeling who read the manuscript and made many helpful suggestions.

Grateful acknowledgement is also made to the following sources for permission to reproduce passages from previously published works.

B.T. Batsford Ltd for an extract from *British Woodland Trees* by H.L. Edin; Granada Publishing Ltd for an extract from *Word-Processing for Beginners* by Susan Curran, pub. Grafton Books; Hutchinson Publishing Group Ltd for an extract from *A Dictionary of British Folk Customs* by Christina Hole; Private Eye for an extract by Christopher Logue from *Bumper Book of True Stories*; Martin Secker & Warburg Ltd for an extract from *Small World* by David Lodge.

List of Abbreviations

ARELS Association of Recognised English Language Schools: a professional organisation which links the qualified language schools in the United Kingdom. One of its functions is setting and marking the ARELS Exams which are described in this book.

CUEFL Communicative Use of English as a Foreign Language. This term is used particularly about an exam produced by the RSA. It puts the emphasis on the student's ability to communicate rather than to use faultless grammar.

EFL English as a Foreign Language. This abbreviation is used to describe English as a subject studied by non-native speakers.

ELTS English Language Testing Service. This abbreviation refers to the English language tests produced by the British Council in collaboration with British universities.

ESB English Speaking Board. This examinations board exists to promote a high standard of English speaking. It administers exams for native speakers as well as for foreign learners.

FCE First Certificate in English. This is the name of the intermediate exam produced by the University of Cambridge Local Examinations Syndicate. It is the oldest and the most extensively used of the British EFL exams.

JMB Joint Matriculation Board. This board produces examinations for pupils leaving British schools. Its EFL exam is aimed largely at the foreign student who wishes to enter higher education in Britain.

RSA

Royal Society of Arts. This organisation is involved in, among many other things, various aspects of EFL, notably teacher training. It has also pioneered the communicative type of language exam.

TOEFL

Test of English as a Foreign Language. This is the major US exam for foreign learners of English. It is very extensively taken by students wishing to attend educational institutions in the USA.

Chapter 1

The Examinations

This book is for you if you are a student of English as a foreign language at an intermediate level and if you are thinking of taking an examination in general English. Most schools will be able to arrange a number of different exams for you and it is also possible for you to make independent arrangements to take all of the exams discussed in this book. The book will help you to choose which of the many exams available is best for you. Then it will show you how to prepare for the exam in the best possible way and it will also help you to do as well as you can on the day of the examination.

This first chapter describes the different exams which you can choose from. They all have their own particular characteristics and it is a good idea to select the one which is most suitable for your needs. When you have chosen your exam, you need to know how to prepare for it. Chapter 2 will be useful whichever exam you choose because it gives general advice on how best to learn English as well as guidelines which will help you to take any exam successfully. Chapters 3–17 look at different types of exam question. Which of these chapters are important for you depends on which exam you are taking. Table 1.4 at the end of this chapter shows you which chapters are particularly helpful for each examination at intermediate level.

There are a lot of general English examinations you can choose from. The most important of these are shown in Table 1.1. This table gives an indication of the levels of the different examinations but it is a simplification – it is not possible to say, for example, that the Cambridge First Certificate in English is exactly the same level as the RSA CUEFL Intermediate exam. This book concentrates on those exams in the middle group, those marked with an asterisk in Table 1.1 If you pass one of these exams you can feel that you are ready to begin a really advanced English course.

Do you already know which exam or exams you are going to take? If you do, turn to the part of this chapter on your exam and read it carefully, then look at Table 1.4 to see which of Chapters 3–17 are especially important for you. Study Chapter 2 and then work through those chapters indicated for you by Table 1.5.

Table 1.1 Comparison of Approximate Levels of General EFL Exams.

Elementary	Intermediate*	Advanced
University of Cambridge		
PET	FCE*	CPE DIPLOMA
Association of Recognised English Language Schools (ARELS)		
Prelim	Higher Certificate*	Diploma
University of Oxford		
Prelim	Higher*	
Royal Society of Arts (RSA CUEFL)		
Basic	Intermediate*	Advanced
Joint Matriculation Board	JMB test in* English	
TOEFL	All levels*	
British Council		
English Language Testing Service		All levels*
Institute of Linguists		
Prelim Cert Grade I Cert	Grade II Cert* Intermed Dipl.	Fin Diploma
Pitman Examinations Institute		
Elementary Intermediate	Higher Interm*	Advanced
Trinity College (Spoken)		
1 2 3 4 5 6 7*	8* 9* 10 11	12
Trinity College (Written)		
	Intermediate*	
English Speaking Board		Cert in
Foundation	Intermediate	Advanced English as an
1 2 3	1* 2* 3*	1 2 3 Acquired Lang
Associated Examining Board (AEB)	Test in English for Educational Purposes	

This table does not include specialist, professional exams organised by the London Chamber of Commerce and Industry, the General Medical Council, City and Guilds of London Institute and Pitman Examinations Institute for which the book will also be useful. Nor does it include exams which are also taken by native speakers of English.
(For further information about these exams, see *The Pitman Guide to English Language Examinations* by Susan Davies & Richard West, Pitman, 1984).

If you have not already chosen your exam, stop for a moment and note down on a piece of paper your reasons for wanting to take an exam.

- Do you need an entrance qualification for a college or university?

- Do you need an exam to help you do well in your present or hoped-for job? If so, which language skills are necessary for that job – reading, writing, speaking and/or listening?
- Do you just want to take an exam to help you discipline yourself to work hard?
- Do you simply want to test whether your English has, or has not, reached a good intermediate level?
- Do you have any other reasons?

Keep your reasons in mind as you read and we shall return to them later. In the next few pages you can read about the twelve different exams which could test your knowledge of general English at this level. As you read try to complete Table 1.2 which will then be a summary for you of the basic information about each exam. As an example, the Oxford Higher Exam has been partly completed for you.

Table 1.2 Comparison of Intermediate EFL exams by length, content and availability.

	How long does it take?	Would it test my				Where can I take it?	When can I take it?	Is there anything special about this exam?
		Rdg	Wtg	Skg	Lstg			
FCE								
ARELS								
OXFORD	6hrs 10m	yes		no		UK and abroad		Can use Eng-Eng. dictionary
RSA								
JMB								
TOEFL								
BRITISH COUNCIL								
INSTITUTE OF LINGUISTS								
PITMAN								
TRINITY COLLEGE spoken / written								
ESB								

UNIVERSITY OF CAMBRIDGE FIRST CERTIFICATE IN ENGLISH (FCE)

The Cambridge English examinations are probably the oldest and the best known of the exams for foreign students of English. In 1984 the Cambridge exams were changed a little to meet modern needs but they are still a traditional type of exam with a strong emphasis on accuracy in grammar and vocabulary.

The FCE has five papers:

Paper One	is a Reading Comprehension Paper which lasts one hour. All the forty questions in this paper are multiple choice – you have to choose from a set of four alternatives. The first twenty-five questions ask you to choose which word fits a blank in a sentence. Next you have to read three texts and answer fifteen questions on them.
Paper Two	is a Composition Paper lasting one and a half hours. You have to write two compositions of 120–180 words each and you can select your subjects from a choice of five. You will probably have to choose from a letter, a speech, a story, a discussion and a composition on a set literary text. Each year there is a choice of three literary texts. These change yearly and you can find out the current possibilities from the address at the end of this section.
Paper Three	lasts two hours and is called Use of English. It aims to test your knowledge of grammar. It has two sections:
	Section A asks you to do such things as fill in blanks in a paragraph and individual sentences, to reword sentences and to form sentences from given words.
	Section B asks you to do a piece of directed writing. You may have to read a text and then write a summary or you may have to reply to a given letter or advertisement.
Paper Four	is a test of Listening Comprehension and it lasts approximately half an hour. You listen to a tape recording and have to fill in answers in your exam book. Usually there are three passages and they are spoken slowly and clearly although you may have to cope with local accents and some background noise. You hear each recording twice.
Paper Five	is a speaking test and it is often called the Interview. It lasts about twenty minutes and has three sections:
	In Section 1 you look at a picture and have a conversation with the examiner based on this picture. At first you may simply have to answer questions about what you can see but then the conversation will become more general – from a picture of children you may start discussing the education system in your country, for example.
	In Section 2 you are given a few moments to read through a short text. You are then asked a few questions on the passage, such as 'Where do you think the text comes from?' You then have to read the text aloud.
	In Section 3 you have to use your English to explain something or to show how you would respond to a particular social situation.
	There are certain possible variations to Paper Five which you or your centre can choose. If you have decided to study one of the set literary books for the Composition Paper you can ask, if you like, to discuss this with the oral examiner. It is also possible for either the whole of Paper Five, or its third section, to be taken by three candidates together at the same time. This means that more realistic role-play of social situations can be organised.

With the FCE there are additional optional papers in Business, Science and Translation which you can choose to take if you wish. If you pass the basic FCE papers but not the options that you decided to take, you still get a certificate showing that you have passed the FCE. If you pass the options as well, your certificate will show that you have also passed additional papers in the relevant subjects.

You can take the Cambridge examinations in June or December and they can be taken all over the world. You must enrol very early. If you are going to take the exam in Britain, the enrolment dates are the same each year – 23 March for the June examination and 9 October for the December examination. The enrolment dates are even earlier if you are going to take the exam abroad. For further information contact:

> The University of Cambridge
> Local Examinations Syndicate
> 1 Hills Road
> Cambridge CB1 2EU
> United Kingdom
> Tel. Cambridge (0223) 61111

ARELS HIGHER CERTIFICATE

This is an exam which you take in a language laboratory and it tests how good you are at listening and speaking. It is a partner to the Oxford Higher Examination which tests reading and writing at the same level. The ARELS exams are highly respected by teachers and employers as they really test the listening and speaking skills which are needed in everyday working and social situations.

The ARELS Higher Certificate exam lasts about forty minutes and it is divided into six sections:

1. *Free expression*: In this section you talk for two minutes on a subject such as, 'Too much television is bad for family life.' You choose your subject from a set of five, which you are given fifteen minutes before the exam begins. You have time to prepare your talk but you are not allowed to use notes.
2. *Social responses*: For example, what do you say when your friend tells you that he has just failed an important examination?
3. *Pronunciation*: You read aloud one part in a dialogue.
4. *Listening comprehension*: You have to answer questions on several listening passages which are often taken from the British radio. Your understanding of English intonation is also tested.
5. *Sustained speaking*: You are given a set of pictures and have to tell the story which the pictures illustrate.
6. *Oral accuracy*: Here you have to do a series of exercises which test your grammatical accuracy.

You can take this exam in March, May/June and November and must enrol twelve days before the examination date. If you wish, your local centre may be able to organise an exam for you at another date.

Most schools which enter students for an ARELS exam also give some free lessons in preparation for the exam. You can take the exam in Britain and at accredited centres abroad. For further information contact:

The ARELS Examinations Trust
113 Banbury Road
Oxford OX2 6JX
United Kingdom
Tel. Oxford (0865) 514272

UNIVERSITY OF OXFORD HIGHER EXAMINATION

This examination is the partner of the ARELS Higher Certificate described above. It aims to test your ability to read and write English. Like the ARELS examinations, it aims to ask you to do only things which have a direct relevance to everyday life. You may use an English–English dictionary in the Oxford exams.

The exam has two papers:

Paper One (three hours) tests mainly writing and Paper Two (three hours plus ten minutes reading time) concentrates on reading. Each paper has five questions and you must do all the questions.

The kind of things you may be asked to write in **Paper One** include letters, reports, instructions, summaries and postcards. Often your writing is a response to a piece of reading – a reply to a letter or a comment on a newspaper article, for example. In your answers it will be necessary to show your understanding of register in English (i.e. the differences between writing to a close friend and writing to someone you have never met).

In **Paper Two** you have quite a lot of reading to do and you are expected to be able to read much more difficult things than you could write yourself. The passages you have to read are in everyday English and are neither too literary nor too technical. An important question in Paper Two is the dictionary question. This tests whether you can use an English–English dictionary.

You can take the Oxford Higher in May and November and must enrol three weeks before the date of the exam. It is possible to take the exam throughout Britain and at accredited centres abroad. For further information contact:

The University of Oxford
Delegacy of Local Examinations
Ewert Place
Summertown
Oxford OX2 7BZ
United Kingdon
Tel. Oxford (0865) 54291

ROYAL SOCIETY OF ARTS "CUEFL" EXAMINATIONS

"CUEFL" stands for Communicative Use of English as a Foreign Language which means that these exams – like the ARELS and Oxford exams – want you to show that you can communicate satisfactorily in everyday situations rather than merely to show how good your knowledge of English grammar is.

There are four CUEFL papers: writing; reading; speaking; and listening. These four papers can be taken at each of three levels, Basic, Intermediate and Advanced. You can take all four papers at the same level if you want to, or you can vary the levels. If you feel that your reading level is much better than your speaking, for example, you can take the reading paper at Advanced level, the speaking exam at Basic and the writing and listening papers at Intermediate level. If you prefer you can just do one or two papers. There is no need to try all four. In other words, you are free to choose the profile that is best for you.

1. *The Writing Paper* lasts one and a half hours but you are also allowed ten minutes' reading time. Dictionaries may be used. You have six questions to answer and must try them all. The questions are realistic and typically include filling in a form, writing a postcard, writing two or three letters, composing an advertisement and giving instructions or directions.
2. *The Reading Paper* lasts one hour and again you are allowed both ten minutes reading time and the use of dictionaries. In this paper you have a lot to read, perhaps a small magazine or several pages from a newspaper. It is very important, then, to be able to skim, choosing to read in detail only what is necessary for the question. Often the material that you have to read is the same as that used in the Advanced exam; it is the questions which are matched to an Intermediate level. You don't have to write much in this paper. You have to mark statements true or false, give one-word answers to questions or choose the correct answer from a selection of four or five.
3. *The Listening Paper* lasts half an hour. You listen to a tape recording and write answers in an answer book. Again at least some of what you hear is the same as that for Advanced students but the questions asked are not quite so difficult. What you hear is often taken from BBC radio programmes and other authentic off-air recordings.
4. *The Oral Interaction Paper* is quite different from other exams. Its aim is to make you feel as comfortable as possible so that you can really show how good your English is. You will be in the exam room for about fifteen minutes but you will probably find that you have to wait some time between doing the different parts of the test.

You will find that there are three important English speakers involved in doing the oral exam with you. There is the *Assessor*, the person who decides what mark to give you. The Assessor is present in the exam room all the time. Then there is the *Usher* who will probably be a teacher you already know. His or her job is to be with you in the preparation room and to explain anything about the tasks you have to do which you may not understand. Then there is a third person, called the *Interlocutor*, who will also probably be a teacher whom you already know. The Interlocutor will be in the exam room with you for much of the time trying to help you to show yourself to advantage.

There are three parts to the Speaking Paper. You have the chance to prepare for each part in a special preparation room with the Usher. In Part 1 you talk to the Interlocutor for about five minutes on a subject which is usually something quite everyday and personal – your experience of learning English, your country, your plans, for example. In Part 2, the Interlocutor is not present. Here you are in the exam room together with another student. You have to discuss a task, such as where to go for a class excursion, or how to improve facilities in your school. Part 2 also lasts for five minutes. In Part 3 the Assessor calls the Interlocutor back into the exam room and the Interlocutor asks the two students what they discussed in Part 2. The Interlocutor and the two students talk together about the same task for a further five minutes.

The RSA CUEFL examinations can be taken in Britain and in an increasing number of centres abroad. They are held twice a year – in June and November. It may be possible in future to take the exam at additional times. Enquire at your local exam centre or at the address below. You must enrol six weeks before the exam if you are taking it in Britain and eight weeks before if you are taking it abroad. For further information contact:

> The Examination Director
> RSA Examinations Board
> John Adam Street
> Adelphi
> London WC2N 6EZ
> Tel. London (01) 839 1691

JOINT MATRICULATION BOARD: TEST IN ENGLISH (OVERSEAS)

A major aim of this exam is to see whether your English is good enough to study a scientific subject at a British university or college. It tests your ability to understand the grammatical structures of English and to cope even when the vocabulary is comprehensible only to a specialist.

The exam has two elements – a written paper and a listening test. The written paper lasts two and a half hours (plus fifteen minutes reading time). The listening test takes forty minutes.

The written paper usually has three sections:

1. In the first section you have to write two or three compositions. These are based on charts or diagrams given in the examination booklet and you have to be able to describe, to compare, to show relationships and to explain processes and developments.

2. In the second section your grammar and vocabulary awareness are tested more precisely. You have to find where words are missing in a text and to insert them and you also have to match definitions to words in short passages.
3. The third section has some longer reading texts on semi-specialised technical subjects. You have to show your comprehension by, for example, marking a diagram, completing a table, labelling a drawing or ordering statements.

In the listening test you have to listen to passages of a type appropriate to further study – they may be from a lecture, a discussion or a set of instructions, for example. Again you must show your comprehension by labelling diagrams or completing tables.

You can take these exams in March and June at registered centres in Britain. You must enrol by mid-December for the March exam and by early May for the June exam. For further information contact:

Joint Matriculation Board
Manchester M15 6EU
Tel. Manchester (061) 273 2565

TEST OF ENGLISH AS A FOREIGN LANGUAGE (TOEFL)

A specific score in this exam is usually required by students who want to have some further eduction in the USA or Canada when English is not their first language. It is not a pass or fail type of exam. It is totally multiple choice and candidates are given their individual score. Different colleges have different entrance requirements. Some British universities, for example, recognise a score of 550 as being equivalent to a pass in the University of Cambridge Certificate of Proficiency in English and a score of 450 as equivalent to an FCE pass. (See Susan Davies and Richard West, *Pitman Guide to English Language Examinations*, p. 28.)

The test uses standard American English and is in three parts: listening (forty minutes); structure and written expression (twenty-five minutes); and reading comprehension and vocabulary (forty-five minutes).

In the listening test you have fifty questions and have to match sentences with similar meanings, to choose responses in a given situation and to answer comprehension questions. In the structure test you have forty questions and you must select the grammatical structures that fit particular contexts. You also have to recognise what is not standard English.

The reading comprehension and vocabulary test has sixty questions. Some of these ask you to choose the word or phrase that fits a particular sentence and some test your comprehension of short reading texts. The texts selected are usually on academic subjects.

The TOEFL exam can be taken every month at centres throughout the world. For further information contact:

Educational Testing Service
TOEFL
PO Box 899
Princeton
NJ 08541
USA
Tel. 609 921 9000

BRITISH COUNCIL ENGLISH LANGUAGE TESTING SERVICE

The British Council ELTS Exams are like the TOEFL ones in that they also aim to see if your English is good enough for a course of study in an English-speaking college or university. This exam is also not one where you pass or fail – you are given a grade out of a range from 1 to 9. Level 5 is intermediate and it may be enough for certain training courses in Britain although each institution or department decides on its own requirement.

The ELTS tests consist of five parts. The first two parts are general and the other three parts have variations depending on the subject you wish to study.

The general parts are a reading comprehension lasting forty minutes and a listening comprehension of thirty minutes. The special subject or 'modular' parts are study skills (fifty-five minutes), writing tasks (forty minutes) and an interview of ten minutes.

The general parts have only multiple-choice questions and you must be able to identify sentences with similar meanings, to fill in blanks in texts and to answer general comprehension questions. The listening test, which is on tape, may ask you to match a statement with a diagram and to choose responses in social situations.

The modular parts of the test give you a source booklet with texts relating to your field of study. The fields you can choose from are: Life Sciences; Medicine; Physical Sciences; Social Studies; Technology or, if none of these is quite right, General Academic.

The study skills part of the test includes reading comprehension questions on texts in the booklet. The writing tasks may ask you to explain texts in the booklet in your own words or to give your own opinions on topics discussed in the booklet. The interview may also refer to the booklet although the questions you will be asked will mainly be about your own study and future plans.

You can arrange to take the test through the British Council anywhere in the world at times which suit both the local centre and yourself. For further information contact:

The British Council
10 Spring Gardens
London SW1A 2BN
Tel. London (01) 930 8466

THE INSTITUTE OF LINGUISTS – GRADE II CERTIFICATE

Many British colleges and universities will accept this certificate as the equivalent of an A-level (English schools' final year exam). There are four parts to the exam: an oral; a listening comprehension; a translation paper; and a composition paper where you must answer questions on different aspects of British life and institutions. Dictionaries may be used in this examination.

The oral test lasts twenty minutes and you have to carry out three tasks:

1. Firstly you must give a three-minute talk on one of a choice of six topics. You are given the list of subjects twenty minutes before the exam and you may use brief notes when you give your talk.
2. Secondly, you must engage in a conversation with the examiner, developing from the subject of your talk to matters of more general personal interest.
3. Thirdly, you must read, summarise and answer questions on a text of about 200 words. You are allowed five minutes to study the text and to prepare your summary and you may look at the text while giving your answers.

The listening comprehension, which lasts thirty minutes, also tests your ability to summarise. You hear a passage of about 300 words twice and you must write a precis using about 200 words.

The translation paper lasts one and a half hours and you have to translate two passages of about 200 words each into your own language. The texts are on subjects of general interest and do not use specialist language. This is the only exam of all those described here in which you have to do some translation.

The composition paper tests both your ability to write good English and your knowledge of British life. Equal marks are allowed for both language and content. You have a choice of two syllabuses – A or B.

With syllabus A you have two hours to write three compositions of about 120 words each. There are a choice of six questions in each of three sections, and not more than two questions may be answered from any one section. The three sections are Geography, Institutions, and Life. With syllabus B you have two and a half hours to answer three questions, with about 200 words required for each answer. There is a choice of two questions on each of four sections and you must choose questions from three different sections. The four sections are Geography and Economics, Aspects of Public Life, the Social Situation and Cultural Life. The Institute of Linguists gives a reading list for syllabus B. This list changes every three years.

You can take this exam twice a year, in May and December, and enrolments must be made three or four months in advance. You can take the exam throughout the British Isles and at a number of centres abroad. For further information contact:

The Examinations Officer
The Institute of Linguists
Mangold House
24a Highbury Grove
London N5 2EA
Tel. London (01) 359 7445/6386

PITMAN EXAMINATIONS INSTITUTE – ENGLISH AS A FOREIGN LANGUAGE

The Pitman Institute organises a lot of examinations in typing, office skills and business English but they also have English language exams for people whose first language is not English. You can choose either of two syllabuses – syllabus L emphasises grammatical accuracy and syllabus C emphasises the ability to communicate in English.

The Higher Intermediate exam lasts for two and a half hours. In syllabus L you have to do four things – a dictation, a written summary of a passage read aloud twice, a composition of about 240 words and a set of twenty multiple-choice grammar questions.

The Higher Intermediate with syllabus C has two parts to the test: (a) reading and writing; and (b) listening, reading and writing. In both parts you must show you understand what you have read or heard by completing diagrams or forms and by writing letters, notes or advertisements. There are seven language areas covered by syllabus C and these are Domestic life; Buying and selling; Public and official services and information; Travel; Work; Entertainment; and Education.

You can take the Pitman exams at 4000 registered centres throughout the world. The centres themselves decide when the exams will take place. For further information contact:

Pitman Examinations Institute
Godalming
Surrey GU7 1UU
England
Tel. Godalming (04868) 5311

TRINITY COLLEGE LONDON: EXAMINATIONS IN SPOKEN ENGLISH

Trinity College organises exams in spoken English at twelve levels and we shall concentrate on levels 7–9 in this book. Grade 7 should not last longer than twelve minutes, Grade 8 fifteen minutes and Grade 9 twenty minutes.

Each grade has three sections:

1. In the first section you are given a dialogue to prepare before you go into the exam room. One of the parts in the dialogue is left blank. When you are in the exam room the examiner reads the given part and you have to say what you feel the other person in the dialogue would say.
2. In the second section you discuss a book you have prepared.

3. In the third section there is general conversation with the examiner.

You can take the exams at registered centres in Britain and abroad. The dates of the exams are arranged by agreement between the individual centres and Trinity College. Exams taken both in the UK and abroad are conducted by examiners from Trinity College. For further information contact:

Trinity College
11–13 Mandeville Place
London W1M 6AQ
Tel. London (01) 935 5773

TRINITY COLLEGE LONDON: WRITTEN EXAMINATION (INTERMEDIATE)

Trinity College provides a written examination at only one level. It is equivalent to about Grade 9 of the spoken exams. The exam lasts three hours and you have to do four sections.

1. The first section is a reading passage with open-ended comprehension questions.
2. The second section is a text with blanks – you have to choose the best word to fit each blank from a choice of three words.
3. The third section tests your grammar by asking you to complete sentences.
4. The fourth section requires you to write a composition of about 350 words – you are given a choice of topic.

You can take the exam twice a year in May/June and November/December, both in Britain and at registered centres abroad. For further information contact the address given for the Trinity College Spoken Exams.

ENGLISH SPEAKING BOARD (INTERNATIONAL)

The ESB gives exams in spoken English at ten levels. Three of the levels are intermediate. The exams last approximately fifteen minutes and have four parts. Often there may be several examiners present in the exam room – they may or may not join in with questions and comments.

You must prepare in advance for the first two parts.

1. In Part 1 you have to present a project to the examiner.
2. In Part 2 you have to read aloud a passage of prose or poetry which you have chosen yourself.
3. In Part 3 you are asked what you would say in particular social situations in English.
4. In Part 4 you have an open conversation with the examiner – this may deal with any area of your own experience or interests.

You may take the exams in Britain – and abroad by arrangement with the Secretary. Times for the exams depend on local requirements. For further information contact:

The Secretary
English Speaking Board Limited
32 Roe Lane
Southport
Merseyside PR9 9EA
Tel. Southport (0704) 34587

Which Exam?

Have you managed to complete Table 1.2? Check what you have done with the completed table on the next page.

Do you now have a better idea of which exam would best fit your circumstances? Let us go back to your reasons for wanting to take an English exam.

Do you need an entrance qualification for a college or university? If you want to study in the USA or Canada you need to take TOEFL. If you want to study in Britain you need to write to the department of the institution you are interested in and to ask them what they want. The exams they are at present most likely to accept are the University of Cambridge examinations, JMB, the British Council test and the Institute of Linguists exams.

Do you need an exam to help you do well in your present or hoped-for job? Which skills are needed in that job? Reading, writing, speaking and/or listening? Table 1.3 shows clearly which skills are tested by which exam. So, for example, if your job requires you only to read English, an ARELS exam would not be a good choice for you but an Oxford one would be. If you mainly need to speak English, then ARELS or a Trinity College spoken exam would be good for you.

Do you just want an exam to discipline yourself to work hard? If so, is your aim grammatical accuracy or just being able to communicate well in an English-speaking situation? If accuracy is your aim, try FCE, Institute of Linguists Grade II, Pitman Higher Intermediate Syllabus L or the Trinity College written exam. If competent communication is your aim try ARELS, Oxford, RSA, Pitman Higher Intermediate Syllabus C or an ESB exam.

Do you simply want to see whether your English has reached a good intermediate level or not? The times when you take the exam may be particularly important for you. Again Table 1.3 should help you to decide which exam is best for your circumstances.

If you have another reason for wanting to take an exam, or you still can't decide, perhaps Table 1.4 will help. It tells you how much it costs to take the exams discussed.

When you have decided which exam or exams you are going to take, look at Table 1.5. This shows you which chapters are particularly useful for you. Study Chapter 2 first and then work through the chapters relevant for you. Follow the advice in them and you should do well in your exam.

Good luck!

Table 1.3 Comparison of Intermediate EFL exams by length, content and availability.

| | How long does it take? | Would it test my | | | | Where can I take it? | When can I take it? | Is there anything special about this exam? * |
		Rdg	Wtg	Skg	Lstg			
FCE	5hrs 20m	yes	yes	yes	yes	UK and abroad	June & Dec	Very long-established well known exam
ARELS	40m	no	no	yes	yes	UK and abroad	Mar. May/ Jun. Nov	Take it in lang. lab.
OXFORD	6hrs 10m	yes	yes	no	no	UK and abroad	May & Nov	Can use Eng-Eng. dictionary
RSA	3hrs 25m	yes	yes	yes	yes	UK and abroad	May/Jun & Nov/Dec	Can use Eng-Eng dict. Profile of levels & skills
JMB	3hrs 10m	yes	yes	no	yes	UK	Mar & Jun	For people waiting to go to UK University
TOEFL	1hr 50m	yes	yes	no	yes	Worldwide	Any time	All multiple choice Score not pass or fail
BRITISH COUNCIL	2hrs 55m	yes	yes	yes	yes	UK and abroad	Any time	Score not pass or fail
INSTITUTE OF LINGUISTS	4hrs 20m	yes	yes	yes	yes	Mainly UK	May & Dec	Choice of syllabus Has translation
PITMAN	2½hrs	yes	yes	yes	yes	UK and abroad	Any time	Choice of syllabus
TRINITY COLLEGE spoken	12hrs 20m	yes	no	yes	yes	UK and abroad	By arrangm	Only spoken English
written	3hrs	yes	yes	no	no		May/Jun & Nov/Dec	Exam only at one level
ESB	c. 15m	yes	no	yes	yes	Mainly UK	Local arrangm	Several examiners present

* What you put in this column may vary according to your special interests.

Table 1.4 Comparison of Intermediate EFL exams by cost

This table shows how much it cost for a student in the UK to take one of these exams in 1985. Taking the exam abroad is often more expensive but it depends on where you wish to take the exam. This table gives an idea of how the costs of different exams compare with each other rather than an exact idea of how much it may cost to take a particular exam at any given time and place.

FCE	£28.30
ARELS	£21.50
OXFORD	£14
RSA	£5.75 for each of the 4 parts
JMB	£8.60
TOEFL	US $26 i.e. c. £20
BRITISH COUNCIL	£30
INSTITUTE OF LINGUISTS	£17
PITMAN	£2.75
TRINITY COLLEGE spoken	£8.20 (grade 7) – £11.80 (grade 9)
written	£6.60
ESB	£6.50

Table 1.5 Which chapters and topics are relevant for which exams

Chapter and topic	FCE	ARELS	OX-FORD	RSA	JMB	TOEFL	B.C. ELTS	INST. of LING	PIT-MAN	TRIN. Sp.	COL. Wr.	ESB
2. General Techniques	√	√	√	√	√	√	√	√	√	√	√	√
3. Grammar	√	√	√	√	√	√	√	√	√	√	√	√
4. Vocabulary	√	√	√	√	√	√	√	√	√	√	√	√
5. Conversation	√	√		√			√			√		√
6. Reading aloud and, Prepared Talks	√	√						√		√		√
7. Describing Pictures and Diagrams	√	√	√	√	√							√
8. Role Play and Social Situations	√	√		√		√	√			√		√
9. Reading Comprehension	√		√	√	√	√	√		√	√	√	
10. From Reading to Writing	√		√	√			√	√	√	√		
11. Blank-filling	√				√	√	√		√	√	√	
12. Listening Comprehension	√	√		√	√	√	√	√	√			
13. Presenting a Point of View	√	√	√	√	√		√		√	√	√	
14. Narrative and Dialogue	√	√	√	√				√	√		√	
15. Letter-writing	√		√	√					√		√	
16. Communicative Writing Tasks	√		√	√	√						√	
17. Checking and Correcting	√	√	√	√	√	√	√	√	√	√	√	√

Chapter 2

Chapter 2

General techniques

This chapter is going to look at different general techniques which will help you to do well in your English exam. The first part of the chapter, section A, considers techniques which will help you to learn English better. The second half of the chapter, section B, looks at techniques for the day of the exam itself.

A. TECHNIQUES TO HELP YOU LEARN ENGLISH

You will do best in your exam if you have a real understanding of English; hard work for two weeks before the exam will help a bit but it is much better to start developing good study skills as soon as possible. First of all try this quiz to see how good a student you already are:

1. How often do you do some work on your English?
   (a) A little every day?
   (b) A lot once a week?
   (c) A lot every day?
   (d) A little once a week?
2. Have you got:
   (a) a good bi-lingual dictionary?
   (b) a good English-English dictionary?
   (c) a grammar book that explains things clearly?
3. Do you think that these statements are true or false?
   (a) It is not a good idea to read magazines that are full of slang.
   (b) I must always try to avoid making mistakes in English.
   (c) I must write down all the new words I meet in English.
   (d) Watching American films will help my English.
   (e) I must know grammar perfectly in order to be able to speak good English.
   (f) It is useful to speak English with other people whose first language is not English.

Now mark yourself. Give yourself one mark if you answered (a) or (c) in question 1. Give yourself one mark for each of the books in question 2 which you have. Give yourself a mark for each of the statements in 3 which you marked like this:

(a) false
(b) false
(c) false
(d) true
(e) false
(f) true

If you got 10 out of a possible 10 you can feel pleased that you are probably a good student of English but, if you got much less than that, do not worry. It is never too late to start learning to be a good student.

In the paragraphs that follow we shall look at some of the points raised by the quiz in more detail.

The first question underlines the need to do your study regularly. When you are learning a language, it is much better to do a little every day than a lot once a week.

The second question highlights the need to have **three basic reference books** – a good bi-lingual dictionary, a good English–English dictionary and a good reference grammar. How can you decide whether the books that you use are good?

Let us look first at the **bi-lingual dictionary**. English is a language where one word often has a lot of different meanings and a good bi-lingual dictionary must be aware of this. How many meanings can you think of for the word 'service', for example? Look it up in your dictionary. Does it give a satisfactory translation for 'service' in all of these twelve sentences?

- My grandmother went into service when she was only 14.
- He saw service in both world wars.
- Can I be of service to you?
- They bought us a dinner-service as a wedding present.
- The waiter added 10 per cent to the bill for service.
- The local church holds three services every Sunday.
- The bus service in this town is very poor.
- You should have your car serviced every five thousand miles.
- These shoes aren't elegant but they're very serviceable.
- Her tennis is quite good but her service is still a little weak.
- These old climbing boots have seen some good service on my many holidays in the Alps.
- Work in the Civil Service is very secure.

A pocket dictionary may be useful when you're on holiday but it is not enough for studying purposes.

An **English–English Dictionary** is even more important for you than a bi-lingual dictionary. A good English–English dictionary – such as the *Longman Dictionary of Contemporary English* or the *Oxford Advanced Learner's Dictionary of Current English* – will tell you about:

meaning
spelling
pronunciation
verb forms
associated words
constructions used by verbs
comparative forms of adjectives
prepositions used by particular words
idioms
phrasal verbs
abbreviations
register
style

When you have your English–English dictionary look at the Contents page and try to answer these questions.

- Where is the International Phonetic Alphabet (the IPA)? What is the effect of ':' in the symbols used for vowels in the IPA?
- How is stress indicated by the IPA?
- Where is the list of abbreviations used by the dictionary? What abbreviations are used for noun, past participle, countable, slang, present participle, colloquial, female and look at?
- Where is the list of irregular verbs? Write down the three main parts of fall, feel and leave.
- What other interesting appendices or introductory articles does the dictionary have?

To illustrate the scope of the dictionary look up the word 'bug'. Do you understand the definitions? How is it pronounced? As a noun, is it countable or uncountable? Is there a picture of it? Where? What other words are often used with it? What colloquial meaning does it have? What slang meaning? Does it have any different uses in British and American English? When it's a verb is it regular? When it's a verb, does it double the 'g'? It should not be too difficult to answer these questions.

The third basic reference book which you need is a basic **reference grammar**. Good ones written in clear English are *Basic English Usage* and *Practical English Usage* both written by Michael Swan and published by OUP. *Basic English Grammar* by Eastwood, and Mackin and Cassell's *Student's English Grammar* by Jake Alsop, are also good and each have a companion volume of exercises which you would find useful.

Although you may find a good grammar with explanations in your own language as well, why not also buy one of the English ones recommended? I recommend them because they explain grammar very clearly and accurately. Reading them will also be extra practice for your English. Look up in your reference book something you have recently found difficult or made a mistake with? If you can't think of anything, look up, for example, the use of the articles in English. Is the explanation clear? Why do we say 'the USA' and 'the UK' but

'America' and 'Britain' without the article? Why do we say 'Life is short' and not 'The life is short'? Why do we say 'English weather is changeable' but 'The weather in England is changeable'?

Look up what it says about future time in English. Does it explain clearly when we say 'I'm doing it' or 'I'm going to do it' or 'I'll do it' or 'I'll be doing it' or 'I'll have done it' when we're talking about the future?

A good grammar will tell you about far more than just tenses and articles. Michael Swan's *Practical English Usage*, for example, tells you about taboo words in English, writing letters and British versus American English among many other interesting things.

Grammar is certainly not the only thing about learning a language. If you live a long time in a country you may learn its language very well without knowing anything about its grammar. To use a grammar book, however, you do need to understand some basic terms.

Do you know what these words mean?

noun
verb
adjective
adverb
preposition
pronoun
conjunction
article
phrase
clause
sentence

Can you give the grammatical names for all the words in the following sentence? And can you give an example of (a) a phrase and (b) a clause in the sentence?

A black cat sat by the fire and purred softly.

The answer is: article (indefinite), adjective, noun, verb, preposition, article (definite), noun, conjunction, verb, adverb. 'By the fire' is an example of a phrase (because it doesn't have a verb in it) and 'The black cat sat by the fire' is one of the two clauses in the sentence (there are as many clauses in a sentence as there are full verbs). We shall think about grammar a little more in Chapter 3 but it is a good idea to be clear about the ten basic grammar terms listed above from the very beginning.

The quiz at the beginning of the chapter highlighted another point: it is useful to do anything in English that you enjoy doing in your own language. What kind of things do you like reading in your own language? Make a quick note of these now.

Why not read similar things in English. If you like strip cartoons, get a Snoopy or Asterix book in English. If you mainly read newspapers, how about subscribing to the *Guardian Weekly* or another British or US newspaper? If you like magazines why not read the *Reader's Digest*? If thrillers or romantic novels are your taste, you will be able to find something you like in English. If you prefer reading classical novels you will find the English in these is harder; you could either try a simplified book or you could read something that you are already familiar with in your own language. Do not feel that you should only read intellectual or difficult books; you will learn most from reading what you enjoy.

Similarly try to bring English in to other things that you enjoy. Write down now a list of seven or eight things that you particularly like doing in your free time.

Is what you have written similar to the list made by a recent student of mine who wrote

- going to the cinema
- talking to friends
- listening to records
- writing letters
- listening to the radio
- aerobics
- pottery
- going out with my boyfriend?

Do you realise that you can bring English into all of these things too?

Your cinema or local television service probably sometimes shows films in English. Watch them if you can.

Perhaps you can talk to friends in an English club. If you can't find one in your area, you might start one.

Many popular songs are sung in English – if you can, find a singer you like whose words can be easily understood. If you listen often to songs that you like you will pick up quite a bit of modern English in a very pleasant way.

If you like writing letters it will not be difficult for you to find a penfriend to correspond with in English; you could ask for one through the pages of an English magazine you enjoy or you could ask the British Council office in your area to suggest the address of a school you could write to or write to the address given at the end of Chapter 15.

You can listen to the radio in English – either to broadcasts of the BBC World Service or to those of the Voice of America.

If you do aerobics regularly, you could get a record or cassette with instructions in English for you to work to.

With pottery or any other hobby, you should be able to find a specialist magazine or a book about your hobby in English.

Having an English boyfriend or girlfriend is perhaps the best way of all to learn English. Perhaps you yourself can think of a way to do something about that – if you are really dedicated to your study of English!

I make all these suggestions to point out that there may be all sorts of ways in which you can do what you like doing best and can also learn some English. Do not worry if you are practising speaking or writing English with people who are not native speakers: you will still benefit a lot. You will be learning how to communicate through English even if you and your friends are still making grammar mistakes.

Another point which question 3 of the quiz on p 17 highlighted was that it is not a bad thing to make mistakes. It really is true that you learn from your mistakes – or that you can do if you try. If you learn that you have made a mistake, do three things.

1. Firstly, make sure you understand what was wrong and why it was wrong. If you don't have a teacher, your dictionaries and your grammar books will help you with that.
2. Secondly, write out the correct word or sentence several times.
3. Thirdly, try and use the word or expression correctly in your next piece of written work.

Don't worry about making mistakes. If you are not sure if something is the right word or the right construction, try it. You will then learn if it is right or not. Deliberately try using new structures and vocabulary in your speaking and writing. Stretch yourself. Don't play too safe. In that way you will learn more – even if you may make more mistakes. On the day of the exam it is better to play safe, of course, but before the exam remember that you can learn a lot from your mistakes.

A last thing which we must discuss when thinking about study skills before the exam is how to learn vocabulary in an effective way. It is a good idea to have a separate notebook or a separate section of your file where you write down new vocabulary. But how much do you write down there and in what form should you put it? In the quiz at the beginning of the chapter (question 3 c) you lost a mark if you thought that you have to write down every new word that you meet. It is important to distinguish between words that you just want to recognise when you read or hear them and words that you may want to use yourself. Put another way, you must distinguish between your active and your passive vocabulary.

For example, can you divide these words into those which you need for your active vocabulary and those which you need for your passive vocabulary: come, frog, hope, broth, gipsy, sonnet, supersonic, oxygen, shorthand, conceited? There is no right answer here although basic words like 'come' and 'hope' are important for everyone. Your job or your interests will determine which other words are important for you.

When you write down new vocabulary concentrate on writing down those words which you want to be able to use in your own writing or speaking. You may want to write down also some of the words you need to know only passively but make sure that you highlight words that you think you need for your active use so that you can easily go back and revise them later. Why don't you turn now to the notebook where you write down your vocabulary and go through it, marking those words which you need to know actively?

How do you write down words in your vocabulary notebook? Do you write down just the word and its translation? Do you write down the verb in only its infinitive form (e.g. to do)? It won't take you long to give just a bit more detail so that you write down what will later help you to use the new words.

- With a verb – if it is irregular – write down its three basic parts, i.e. infinitive + past simple + past participle (for example, do, did, done). From these three forms you can make all the different possible forms of the verb.
- Then make sure you write down any related prepositions. Don't just write 'depend', 'interested' and 'consist', for instance, write 'depend on', 'interested in' and 'consist of'.
- With an adjective write down associated nouns. Don't just write down 'stale' and its translation, write down 'stale bread', or 'stale air' and 'stale jokes'.
- Some words have strong positive or negative connotations. If Mary is not fat we may call her 'thin', 'skinny' or 'slim'. 'Thin' is a neutral word and tells us nothing about the speaker's feelings towards Mary's appearance, 'skinny' is a negative word (the person who uses it feels Mary does not look good) and 'slim' is a positive word (the person who uses it thinks Mary looks good). Check whether the words you are writing down have positive or negative connotations and, if so, mark them with a + or a − in your notebook.

You can find all this information in your dictionary, of course, but writing it down will help you to remember it better.

B. GENERAL EXAMINATION TECHNIQUES

1. WRITTEN EXAMS

In this section we shall look at some of the basic rules of taking an exam. We shall look first at **general rules for taking written exams**. Much of what I say applies not only to English exams but also to maths, history and, indeed, to all exams. First of all, imagine that you are giving advice to a young brother or sister who is taking an important exam. Can you think of eight or nine general pieces of advice? Note down your ideas. When you've done this, turn to the next page and see if you have thought of all the nine rules that I give you. Perhaps you will think of some other important things too.

General rules for taking exams

1. Read the questions carefully.
2. Choose your questions sensibly.
3. Plan your answers.
4. Time your answers.
5. Keep to the point.
6. Show off what you know.
7. Hide what you don't know.
8. Check your work.
9. Write neatly.

Did you think of all these? Did you think of anything else? Let's look in a bit more detail at these rules.

1. Read the questions carefully

Spend time reading the questions so that you don't misread anything. The following two questions – 'Which of these four words is correct?' and 'Which of these four words is not correct?' – look very similar if they are read quickly!

2. Choose questions sensibly

In many English exams you will have no choice of questions. When you have a choice – for example, in the FCE composition paper – make sure you choose well. It is probably more interesting to write about 'The Advantages and Disadvantages of Television' than to write 'A First Letter to a Penfriend' but it is also much more difficult and you are taking more risks. Play safe and you will usually get more marks.

3. Plan your answer

Spend time thinking about what you are going to write and about the best way to present your answer. If you are writing a composition write down your paragraph headings and decide on their order **before** you start writing the composition itself.

4. Time your answers

Before the exam look at an old or a practice exam paper and decide how much time you can spend on each question. In the Oxford exam, the paper itself recommends how long to give to each question. Don't forget to allow time for planning and for checking as well as for writing. On the day of the exam, keep to the times you have decided. Even if you have not finished one question it is better to go on to the next one. Perhaps you will have time to finish an unfinished question at the end. You will almost certainly get better marks if you attempt all the questions than if you do one brilliant answer but do not have time to do the last question.

5. Keep to the point

In other words, answer the question asked. You may be able to write a beautiful description of, say, an English garden, but if you spend 60 words of a 150 word 'First Letter to a Penfriend' describing your garden you will lose rather than gain marks. If you bring irrelevant detail into your reading comprehension answers, you are only wasting time. It is important to follow the instructions given in the question. You will lose marks if you write 100 words when the question asked for 40 – even if your English is faultless.

6. Show off what you know

When you write, do your best to show the examiner how good you are. Use interesting expressions that you have learnt; show that you know how to use correctly things like 'look forward to + gerund', 'news +

singular verb' or 'suggest' with a correct construction. These points – and many others which are discussed in this book – are things that students often make mistakes with and you can be sure of making a good impression if you use them well. Be careful to keep to the point when you do this, of course.

7. Hide what you don't know	If you can't remember for sure whether, for example, 'news' takes a singular or a plural verb, avoid using it if possible. When you are studying for the exam, it is good to experiment but in the exam itself it's best to play safe. Write what you know is right. You will lose marks for making mistakes in intermediate EFL exams but you won't lose them for being unoriginal.
8. Check your work	It is so important to check your work carefully that we'll spend a whole chapter practising doing this. Make sure you allow enough time to do this well.
9. Write neatly	An examiner usually has hundreds of papers to mark and he or she is very happy to read one that is clear and neat. It may seem unjust but, if there are two identical pieces of work and one is written neatly and the other is difficult to read, the former is almost sure to get a better mark. If you want to make corrections do them so that it is still easy to read what you have written. You won't have time to do a first draft and then rewrite your answers. You may find it helps you to keep your work tidy if you write on alternate lines. Typing fluid can also help you to do neat work as can an ink rubber.

2. ORAL EXAMS

Now let us think about some **general rules for taking oral exams**.

In an oral exam it is really much more important to show that you can speak English reasonably fluently rather than to show that you never make any grammatical mistakes. Stop worrying about making mistakes and speak as much as you possibly can. You can't get any marks for silence, of course.

Many students lose marks by being nervous before an oral exam. This is understandable but a great pity as you have only a very short time to show what you can do and it is a shame to waste any of it unnecessarily. It is often helpful to calm yourself by taking ten deep breaths before going into the exam room. Other people relax by thinking of something nice that they are going to do when they come out of the exam. Perhaps you have some other relaxation technique of your own?

Just as writing neatly will help you to make a better impression on a written examiner, so impressions are important with an oral examiner too. When you come into the exam room, look straight at the examiner, smile and say 'Good morning' or 'Good afternoon'. Speak clearly and not too fast. And don't chew gum! Many examiners are older and find it a very off-putting habit.

Let's finish this chapter with a few hints on extra little things to remember **on the day of the exam itself**.

The night before the exam it's better to relax than to do last-minute preparation. If you feel you must work, just read something you enjoy in English or listen to your favourite English or American singers. I used to prepare myself the night before an exam by going to sleep with my most important textbooks under my pillow!

Make sure you know exactly what you need for the exam. Do you need pencils? You probably will if there are multiple-choice questions. If you need a pencil, you must have a rubber too. If you have to write your answers in ink, have some of that typing fluid or an ink rubber so that you can correct mistakes in a relatively tidy way. Highlighting pens are also a good idea; if you have to write a summary, for example, you can highlight the important points in the text. A ruler? A pencil sharpener? An identification card? A dictionary? Make a list of what you need and have everything ready the night before the exam.

Help yourself to be comfortable in the exam. Don't wear tight clothes. Have a sweater in case the exam room is cold. Perhaps a packet of peppermints will help you concentrate in a written exam.

In the exam concentrate all the time. Try not to notice the sunshine outside, the boy in front of you, the noises from the street. You don't really have very long to show how good you are and you must make use of every minute. You must try not to waste time by being careless which can easily happen if you are not fully concentrating.

This chapter covers the main points to remember about general exam techniques. In the last week before your exam read section B of this chapter again. Let's now move on to the rest of the book which will help you to answer all the different types of questions which you will meet in your exams.

Chapter 3   Grammar

A. GETTING STARTED

'Grammar' means the rules by which words are put together in a language. Thus, any piece of writing or speaking you do shows something about your grammatical ability in relation to the language you are using. Some exams test your grammar by asking you to do tasks which force you to use or to recognise particular structures. The **FCE, ARELS, TOEFL, Pitman (Syllabus L)** and **Trinity College** all include this kind of question. Other exams, however, simply get a picture of your knowledge of, or feeling for, grammar from the freer writing or speaking that you have to do.

In the previous sentence I said that you can have a knowledge of grammar or a feeling for it. If you are lucky, of course, you may have both. A knowledge of grammar means knowing exactly why, for example, a particular tense is the only possible one in the given circumstances. Teachers and textbooks will help you in all sorts of different ways to acquire this knowledge. It is almost certain that you do not have this kind of knowledge of your native language. If you were helping a foreigner to learn your language, you would instantly be able to tell him what is right and what is wrong in the language but you would probably find it extremely difficult to explain why. You have a perfect feeling for your native language rather than a grammarian's knowledge of it.

You can help yourself to get a feeling for a foreign language by surrounding yourself with it as much as possible, just as the child learning its mother tongue is surrounded by it. If you are lucky you may be able to spend some time in an English-speaking country. If this is not possible, you can still listen to English or American records and radio or even watch English or American films on video. Perhaps you can exchange letters with a penfriend. Maybe there is an English-speaking club in your area. Most important of all, you can read English as much as possible. By doing these things, you will become passively accustomed to the grammatical patterns of English and you will then automatically begin to write and speak accurately yourself.

Many teachers feel the methods described in the above paragraph give the best way to learn a language – it is, after all, most similar to the way in which we learnt our mother tongue. But to learn in this way can take quite a long time. Learning about grammar should provide a shortcut to being able to use a language well. It should help us to move more quickly from complete ignorance of a language to a working knowledge of it. After all, we are not exactly like little children acquiring a mother tongue; we already know something of the world and we can speak at least one language well and it seems sensible to make use of all the advantages we have at our disposal.

The important thing to remember is that learning grammar rules is not a goal in itself; it is just a method which should help you to achieve a working knowledge of a language more quickly. If it doesn't help you, if it confuses you, then there is little point in trying to learn the rules. Go back to reading and listening to English as much as is possible in your situation. After some time, you may find that the rules do begin to clarify things for you but, like the English child, you may begin to speak and write perfectly well without any understanding of the rules.

This chapter is for those of you who do find that knowing about grammar really does help you to use the language better. It will also help those of you taking any of the five exams named at the beginning of this chapter in that it gives some practice and guidance for the types of questions used by those exams.

B. ESSENTIAL PRINCIPLES

In this section we cover just some of the basic points that often cause problems for intermediate students. You will need a good reference grammar to help you with other problems. If you are lucky you will not be studying completely on your own but also have a thorough intermediate coursebook and a good teacher as well.

To find grammar rules helpful you need to be absolutely sure about the meanings of words used by grammarians. We looked at some of these in the previous chapter but now a few more have been added.

Can you understand all these terms?

1. Noun
2. Verb
3. Preposition
4. Adjective
5. Adverb
6. Conjunction
7. Pronoun
8. Article
9. Subject
10. Object – Direct
    Indirect
11. Gerund
12. Infinitive
13. Past participle
14. Auxiliary verb
15. Modal verb
16. Phrasal verb
17. Active and Passive
18. Countable
19. Uncountable
20. Phrase
21. Clause
22. Sentence

The following groups of words illustrate the categories listed above. Can you match them with the appropriate category?

(a) a, an, the
(b) can, may, must
(c) table, water, children, Paris
(d) to be, to live, to love
(e) in the garden, after leaving home, might have been
(f) because, while, as soon as
(g) happily, slowly, well
(h) have, do, be
(i) done, chosen, been
(j) We're working very hard at the moment.
(k) in, on, by, during
(l) to get up, to get rid of, to put off
(m) hoping, hopping, losing, finding
(n) she, we, they, I
(o) road, car, policeman
(p) I sent her a postcard. I posted a letter to Mary. I sent her a postcard. I love Mary.
(q) money, bread, butter, news
(r) good, bad, ugly
(s) unless you marry him; after he'd been to Australia; which I asked for.
(t) Janet and John left town quickly.
(u) produces and is produced
(v) would have done, to hear, listened, is coming

You will find the answers to this exercise at the end of this section.

TWELVE IMPORTANT RULES OF GRAMMAR

An English grammar book will have hundreds and hundreds of rules but here are twelve of the ones which are most frequently broken by students at your level. Make sure you understand these rules, check your work carefully always to see that you have not broken any of them and you will avoid many of the mistakes that other students will make.

1. **Every sentence in English must have a subject and a verb**. The verb must match the subject, i.e. it must be singular if the subject is singular and plural if the subject is plural. What is then wrong with these sentences?

> The child make a mistake.
> The news are good.
> The people is horrible.
> Is good here.

2. **A preposition in English is always followed by either a noun or the gerund** (which is the noun form of the verb, after all), e.g.:

I'm very interested in learning Japanese.
Before coming to England, she worked as an air hostess.
He did it by working hard.

The only problem here is 'to', which is sometimes a preposition and sometimes a part of the infinitive. In such expressions as 'look forward to', 'object to' and 'be *or* get used to', 'to' is a preposition. Thus:

I'm looking forward to seeing you soon.
She objects to smoking in the classroom.
They can't get used to living in a big city.

In the following sentences, however, 'to' is part of the infinitive:

I would like to go to China.
I want him to help me.
When he was a baby, he used to cry a lot.

N.B. The only present form of the latter is:

The baby cries a lot *or* The baby usually cries a lot.

Make sure you are quite clear about the difference in form and meaning between 'be or get used to' and 'used to'. The latter is simply a matter of habit, as in:

The baby used to cry a lot.

On the other hand:

I am used to the baby's crying a lot;

or: The baby's got used to feeding when it wants to,

suggest a mental acceptance of or adjustment to the situation.

3.   **Police and people are plural words**, i.e. English police are wonderful and so are English people.

4.   **These words are uncountable**, i.e. they can never take 'a' or 'an' (they use 'some' just like butter or milk). They also can never take a plural ending or a plural verb.

    news
    advice
    information
    weather
    progress
    luggage
    furniture
    knowledge
    research
    work

If you want to use them in a plural way, you have to say things like:

What were the main news stories on the radio this morning?
Can you give me a piece of advice (or information)?
Some of those items of furniture are really quite valuable.
He did a very original bit of research on the history of the haggis.
I've got masses of work to do today, including jobs both at home and at the office.

5. **Prepositions often are quite illogical and depend on the word which they follow**. Learn these common verbs and the prepositions with which they are associated. Make sentences using them to help you to learn them. Remember that 'something' can either be a noun or a gerund (see rule 2)

> to accuse someone of something
> to apologise for something
> to arrive at or in a place (never 'to')
> to be used to something
> to blame somebody for something or to blame something on somebody
> to depend on someone or something
> to get used to something
> to have difficulty in or with something
> to insist on something
> to be interested in something
> to look forward to something
> to object to something
> to participate in something
> to pay for something
> to prevent somebody from something
> to remind somebody of something
> to succeed in or at something
> to suffer from something
> to take part in something

Now look at these sentences using prepositions associated with particular nouns or adjectives. What are the prepositions and the words they are dependent on? When you have identified them, make sentences of your own.

> I wasn't very good at maths at school; in fact I was very bad at it.
> What's the reason for this terrible behaviour?
> She was always very kind to us but he was often a bit rude to my sister.
> There has been a huge increase in unemployment despite a decrease in the number of school-leavers this year.
> We were very shocked / surprised / astonished at the news.
> His parents are very proud of him.
> Has your teacher had much influence on you?
> She's living with a landlady but I'm staying at a hotel.
> I'm afraid of going to the dentist.

31

6. **Articles are big problems for speakers of some languages where there are no articles**, but even speakers of languages with articles still make mistakes over their usage in English. There are dozens of different rules but these five are probably those where foreign learners most often make mistakes.

   (a) Don't use 'the' when you're making general statements using uncountable or plural words. We say, for example: English people are interesting; or: Life is short, art is long.

   (b) Use 'a' or 'an' when saying what someone's job is.
   He's a dustman and I'm a brain surgeon.

   (c) Don't use 'the' with countries.
   I love France.
   Thailand is beautiful.
   The exceptions are those countries whose names are, or suggest, a plural:
   I like both the USSR and the USA.

   (d) Play. Use 'the' with musical instruments but nothing with games.
   She often plays the piano while they play chess.

   (e) Articles are usually used with the names of rivers, seas and theatres but are not normally used with lakes, continents or streets.
   I've swum in the Volga and the Pacific Ocean but never in Loch Ness. Have you ever been to Australia? The Queens Theatre is on Shaftesbury Avenue.

7. **Make and do**. Which of these you need to use may often seem illogical and there is really little alternative but to learn which is correct in a particular expression. Some points should help you though.

   - 'Make' often has a clear idea of creating something that can afterwards be held or seen. 'Do' is more general.
   - 'Do' is the word used with all kinds of work – homework, housework, gardening, washing, ironing and so on.

   Do these points help you to see the difference between?:

   Children make a lot of work.
   Mothers do a lot of work.

   The first sentence suggests that children create work, they make a mess etc. Their parents then have to do the work the children have created for them.

8. **Some verbs are followed by the gerund (or a noun).** Learn these verbs and make your own sentences using them. Remember that they can NEVER be followed by an infinitive.

   to avoid doing
   to enjoy doing
   to mind doing

to propose doing
to risk doing
to suggest doing
to be worth doing

9. **'Another' is one word, never two.**

10. **The verb to stop can sometimes be followed by an infinitive but it usually requires a gerund.** Can you see the difference in meaning which the gerund and infinitive give?:

Let's stop (working) now to have a cup of tea.
He stopped reading when I came into the room.
He was walking along the street when he suddenly stopped to look in a shop window.

In the examples with 'stop' the infinitive is an infinitive of purpose. It explains why someone did something and the infinitive is the shortest and easiest way of explaining someone's purpose in English, e.g.:

He came to Britain to learn English.
I wrote this book to help you pass your exam.
Note that 'for' is NEVER used in this kind of sentence.

11. **Verb and direct object**. In English the most common mistake of word order is to separate the verb and the direct object. They almost always need to be right beside one another. You must say, for example:

I like jazz very much; or (more emphatically):
I very much like jazz.
Nothing else is possible.

12. **One of the best** . . . Expressions like these must be followed by a plural noun. This is a little point but it is one of the most common mistakes which foreign students make in English.

VERBS

The twelve rules above do not deal with verb forms and tenses. This is perhaps the most complex part of English grammar. This section is just intended as a revision of the forms and meanings of the English tenses. If you do not understand anything, refer to your teacher or to a good English grammar book. Check that you are clear about all the forms of the English verb by making yourself a big table. Get a large piece of paper and write down the left-hand side all the names of the tenses like this:

Present simple
Present continuous
Present perfect (simple and continuous)
Past simple
Past continuous
Past habitual

Past perfect (simple and continuous)
'Going to' future
Future simple
Future continuous
Future perfect (simple and continuous)
Conditional (simple and continuous)
Past continuous

Now can you enter on your large piece of paper these forms of 'write' against the correct tense:

he is writing
he would write
he would be writing
he will write
he will have written
he will have been writing
he used to write
he is going to write
he would have written
he would have been writing
he wrote
he had written
he had been writing
he has written
he has been writing
he writes
he was writing
he will be writing

Notice that the continuous forms are all 'to be + —ing'; the perfect simple forms are all 'to have + the past participle'; the perfect continuous forms are all 'to have been + the past participle'. Can you make questions and negatives for each of these forms?

Now can you make the passive forms of all these tenses? Note that the passive is always the verb 'to be' in the tense you need plus the past participle, e.g. it was written (past simple passive) or it is being written (present continuous passive).

Now, most important of all, can you answer these questions about the significance of the different tenses? You will find the answers to these questions at the end of this section.

1. Which tense describes something that happened regularly in the past but no longer does?
2. Which tense describes a clear intention for the future?
3. Which tense describes something at one moment in the present?
4. Which tense describes something that happened before something else happened in the past?
5. Which tense describes something that began in the past and continued up to the present moment?
6. Which tense describes something that happens regularly?

7. Which tense is used to make a sudden prediction or decision about the future?
8. Which tense is used to look forward to a point in the future and then to look back from that point?
9. Which tense is used most of the time in telling a story about the past?
10. Which tense describes a situation at a particular moment of time in the future?
11. Which tense describes a situation at a particular moment of time in the past?
12. Can you explain the differences between the following sentences?

(A) The thief jumped out of the window when the police entered the room.
The thief was jumping out of the window when the police entered the room.
The thief had jumped out of the window when the police entered the room.

(B) I have been in Rio for three months.
I was in Rio for three months.

(C) I'm going to go to New Zealand next year.
I think I'll go to New Zealand next year.

(D) What'll you do when the train arrives?
What'll you be doing when the train arrives?

(E) A thief has stolen my bike.
My bike's been stolen.

(F) I used to play the guitar when I was a child.
I played the guitar when I was a child.
I have been playing the guitar since I was a child.

(G) I'll stay at home if it rains.
I'd stay at home if it rained.

(H) He'd do it if he had time.
He'd have done it if he'd had time.

Answers

Here are the answers to the exercises which were given earlier in this section.

PARTS OF SPEECH EXERCISES

1 (c);   2 (v);   3 (k);   4 (r);   5 (g);   6 (f);   7 (n);   8 (a);
9 (j);   10 (p);   11 (m);   12 (d);   13 (i);   14 (h);   15 (b);
16 (l);   17 (u);   18 (o);   19 (q);   20 (e);   21 (s);   22 (t)

TENSE QUESTIONS

1. Past habitual (Used to . . .)
2. 'Going to' future
3. Present continuous
4. Past perfect
5. Present perfect
6. Present simple
7. 'Will' future

8. Future perfect
9. Past simple
10. Future continuous
11. Past continuous
12. (A) In the first one the thief's jump coincides with the policeman's arrival and was probably caused by it.
In the second one the thief was already in the middle of jumping when the police arrived.
In the third one he was no longer there when the police arrived.

(B) In the first sentence I am still in Rio but in the second one I have already left.

(C) In the first sentence I have a definite plan but in the second one the idea has probably only just come to me.

(D) It's easiest to see the difference between these two tenses by answering the questions. The answer to the first one would be:

I'll get on the train.

The answer to the second one would be:

I'll be picking up my luggage.

(E) The second sentence is more natural. It emphasises the word 'bike' which is more important than the word 'thief'. Thief tells us nothing because only thieves steal. The passive is often preferred in sentences like this when we don't know the name of a person who did something or else it isn't really all that important. Thus the passive is particularly favoured in crime reports and in scientific writing.

(F) In the first one it is clear that I don't play any more. In the second one it isn't clear whether I still play or not. In the third sentence it is clear that I started playing when I was a child and am still playing now.

(G) In the first sentence, the speaker thinks that there is at least a fifty-fifty chance that it will rain.
In the second sentence, the speaker thinks it is not so likely to rain.

(H) In the first sentence, there is a chance that he will do it even if it is not very likely.
In the second sentence, it is quite impossible that he will do it. It is already too late.

C. EXAM QUESTIONS

Now here are some exam questions to practise. In section D, you will find some notes to help you answer each question and then the correct answers. I suggest you follow this procedure.

1. Read the question.
2. Read the notes on the question in section D.
3. Write your own answer.

4. Check your answer against that given in section D.

1.

These questions are of the type used in the FCE Use of English paper.

1.1.

Finish each of these sentences in such a way that it means the same as the sentence printed before it.

(a) I haven't seen her for ten years.
   I last . . .
(b) "Thank you, Mary. You bought my mother such beautiful flowers," said Jane.
   Jane thanked . . .
(c) "Shall we go to the theatre on Saturday?" said Frank.
   Frank suggested . . .
(d) The teacher made the little girl stand in the corner.
   The little girl . . .
(e) "Please, study hard," Jill's parents requested.
   Jill's parents wanted . . .
(f) After looking at the photographs, we had a cup of tea.
   When we . . .
(g) He didn't do much work, so he failed the exam.
   If . . .
(h) She's too tall to be a ballet-dancer.
   She isn't . . .
(i) "I saw your girlfriend last night," Jane said to her brother.
   Jane told . . .
(j) Bob's uncle asked him to write as soon as he got back home.
   "Please write . . .

1.2.

This is another kind of question which the FCE likes. Make all the changes and additions necessary to produce from the following sets of words and phrases some sentences which together make a complete letter. Note carefully from the example what kind of alterations needs to be made. Write each sentence in the space provided.

Example: I / wonder / why you / not reply / last letter.
Answer: I was wondering why you had not replied to my last letter.

Dear Bill,
(a) Thank you / your letter / tell us / your holiday plans.
(b) I wish / we can go / Greece / you.
(c) It be a long time / we last have / holiday abroad.
(d) We have / not enough / money / go abroad / July.
(e) I think / we probably go / Brighton / usual.
(f) Perhaps next year / we can afford / go / France / Belgium.
(g) I hope / you have / lovely time / island / you choose / the tourist brochure.
(h) We look forward / hear / your holiday / when you / return.
                    With best wishes,
                    Paul

2.

This is the grammar section of the ARELS exam AH35. In this exam, you would, of course, hear these prompts on a tape and not read them. The sentences in this question often relate back to the previous part of the exam. This is a picture story and the sentences you are asked to form make sense in the context of the picture story.

In this particular case the picture story showed an art student who, one afternoon, witnessed a car accident in which an old lady was knocked down by a car which failed to stop. The old lady broke her right arm and was taken to hospital in an ambulance. The art student sat on a nearby wall and drew a picture of the driver for the police. Because she could draw so well, the police were easily able to catch the man.

Now here are the grammar questions from the ARELS exam.

2.1.

You will hear some sentences about the picture story. Then you hear someone start the sentence in a different way. You must finish it so that it means the same thing. Listen to these examples.

(a) The car knocked down the old lady.
   The old lady . . .
   The old lady was knocked down by the car.
(b) Anne is a very good artist.
   Anne draws . . .
   Anne draws very well.

Now you do the same. Do the examples first for practice. Your answers to practice questions will not be recorded.

(c) The accident happened at four o'clock.
   It was . . .
(d) The driver looked at the woman, then he drove away.
   The driver drove away . . .
(e) "I'll draw a picture of the man," Anne said.
   Anne offered . . .
(f) The driver was going too fast to stop.
   Because . . .
(g) The police contacted the police station by radio.
   The police used . . .
(h) The man was caught in less than an hour.
   It took . . .
(i) Anne could draw the man because she was an art student.
   But if she . . .

2.2.

Now we want you to finish some sentences. Listen to these examples.

(a) The police wanted Anne . . .
   to draw the man.
(b) Anne quite enjoyed . . .
   drawing the man.

(c) Anne lost no time . . .
     in drawing the man.

So you complete each sentence using some form of 'draw the man'. Do the examples first for practice.

(d) Anne was very willing . . .
(e) The police thanked her . . .
(f) It only took her a few minutes . . .
(g) No one else there could . . .
(h) Anne was quite keen . . .
(i) She didn't object . . .
(j) She'll never forget . . .

2.3.

Anne and the policeman are at the police station. He agrees with everything she says. Listen to this:

(a) I'm worried about the old lady.
     So am I.
(b) I don't know her name.
     Nor do I.

Now you do the same. Agree with everything Anne says in this way. Do the examples first for practice.

(c) I hope she'll be all right.
(d) I'd like to visit her if possible.
(e) I was hoping the hospital would ring us.
(f) I should have asked them to.
(g) I shan't be home till late tonight.
(h) I'd better make a few phone calls.

2.4.

Now listen to Anne telling someone what happened at the police station. She tells her friend what the police asked her. We want you to say the actual questions the police asked her. Listen to these examples:

(a) They asked me how old I was.
     How old are you?
(b) They asked me where I lived.
     Where do you live?

Now you do the same. Say the questions the police asked. Do the examples first for practice.

(c) They asked me if I felt all right.
(d) They asked me if I'd seen the driver before.
(e) They asked me how tall he was.
(f) They asked me if I could remember his face.
(g) They asked me how long I'd been a student.
(h) They asked me if I'd seen the number of the car.
(i) They asked me to describe the driver.

2.5.

Listen to these sentences about the picture story. There is a mistake of fact in each sentence and you must correct it. Listen to these examples.

(a) A young girl was knocked down by a car.
       No, an old woman was knocked down.
(b) Anne studies music at college.
       No, she studies art.

You must correct the sentences. Do the examples first for practice.

(c) The old lady broke her left arm.
(d) They took her to hospital in a police car.
(e) Anne sat in the police car to draw the man.
(f) The accident happened early in the morning.

3.

This is a question from a past paper of the Pitman exam. The form and type of questions are the same as those used in the TOEFL exam except that in the TOEFL exam you are asked to put your answers on a form that a computer can interpret.

3.1.
If they (A) every
        (B) whenever   see you, you'll be in trouble.
        (C) ever
        (D) all ways

3.2.
When you arrived I was about to (A) left.
                                 (B) leave.
                                 (C) leaving.
                                 (D) be gone.

3.3.
Here is the letter which I (A) was supposed
                           (B) suppose
                           (C) was suppose   to bring yesterday.
                           (D) am suppose.

3.4.
Be here at (A) fifteen to eight
           (B) seven three-quarters   precisely.
           (C) a quarter to eight
           (D) seven hours and forty-five minutes

3.5.
Come back in (A) an hour time.
             (B) one hour about.
             (C) about one hour's.
             (D) an hour's time.

3.6.

I (A)   had to go
  (B)   have to go   to hospital last Saturday.
  (C)   had go
  (D)   have being

3.7.

People usually (A)   wake more
            (B)   stay waking   late to celebrate the New Year.
            (C)   keep wake
            (D)   stay up

3.8.

She is (A)   quiet
      (B)   complete   different from her sister.
      (C)   quite
      (D)   quit

3.9.

When I did wrong I (A)   got punishment
                (B)   got punish
                (C)   have punished   by my father.
                (D)   was punished

3.10.

That day I rose early, because I (A)   have invited
                            (B)   had invited
                            (C)   was invited   guests to the house.
                            (D)   have invitation

3.11.

The house was (A)   a
           (B)   in   fire, because the heater had overturned.
           (C)   on
           (D)   by

3.12.

My broken leg is (A)   wounding
             (B)   in pain by   me.
             (C)   hurting
             (D)   aching

3.13.

We are (A)   on vacation
      (B)   in vacation   next week.
      (C)   on holidays
      (D)   in holiday

3.14.

It would be pleasant if we (A)   known
                    (B)   know   where to go.
                    (C)   had know
                    (D)   knew

3.15

The sea is (A) besides
          (B) beside   the hotel.
          (C) nearby
          (D) at side of

3.16.

He promised me that he (A) would talk
                      (B) will talk
                      (C) have talked   to her last night.
                      (D) have to talk

3.17.

(A) At last
(B) Finally   of the story the man and the woman were married.
(C) At the end
(D) At the last

3.18.

The dog was (A) lain
          (B) lied
          (C) laying   in front of the fire.
          (D) lying

3.19.

At home we (A) use to
         (B) used to   exchange gifts on New Year's Day
         (C) used
         (D) have used to

3.20.

You must arrive early. Everybody else (A) does.
                                    (B) do.
                                    (C) don't.
                                    (D) are.

4.

This is a question from the Trinity College written exam of November 1984.

    Write down and complete the following sentences, using the appropriate form of the word given in brackets.

(a) "Do come to the disco with us." "Oh, yes, thank you. I   to. (like)
(b) February is   month of the year. (short)
(c) They said they'd come at 11.30. It's already 12 so they ought   here half an hour ago. (be)
(d) It was raining hard just now, but now it   . (stop)
(e) They carried on   even though I told them to stop. (write)
(f) The crowd gave the team a noisy reception. The team   a noisy reception. (give)
(g) If you   harder, you'd get better results. (work)
(h) I wouldn't have known unless you   me. (tell)

(i) We live in a house near the station. The house _____ is near the station. (live)

(j) She came to London last June. She _____ in London since June. (live)

In Chapter 11 you will find more exam questions with a strong grammar focus.

D. TUTOR'S NOTES AND ANSWERS

1.1

Read the initial sentence clearly and make sure you don't leave out any element of it in your transformation. You are given marks for each part of your sentence that is correct and it is silly to throw away marks by forgetting to include something. Also make sure that your transformation gives exactly the same meaning as the original sentence. The points covered by this exercise are points that are very often included in the FCE exam, i.e.:

(a) Past simple versus present perfect
(b) Constructions with verb + prepositions
(c) Construction with suggest
(d) To make someone do something versus to be made to do something
(e) Construction of verb + object + infinitive (to want, ask, advise, permit, request, invite etc.)
(f) Use of past perfect
(g) Conditionals
(h) Too and enough
(i) Construction with tell
(j) Reported speech

Look up any of these points in a good grammar book if you don't feel sure about them.

Answers

(a) I last saw her ten years ago.
(b) Jane thanked Mary for buying her mother such beautiful flowers.
(c) Frank suggested going to the theatre on Saturday / that they went / that they (should) go to the theatre on Saturday.
(d) The little girl was made to stand in the corner.
(e) Jill's parents wanted her to study hard.
(f) When we'd (had) looked at the photographs, we had a cup of tea.
(g) If he'd done more work he'd have passed the exam / he might have passed the exam.
(h) She isn't small (short) enough to be a ballet-dancer.
(i) Jane told her brother she'd seen his girlfriend the previous night.
(j) "Please write as soon as you get back home, Bob," asked his uncle.

1.2

Read the letter first and try to get an idea of what it must all be about.

Think about which tense is appropriate for each verb and make sure you put it in the right form.

Decide when articles are necessary and add them.

Think about which prepositions are needed.

Two particular problems that arise in this letter are the construction with wish and the future form of can. Check the use of these in your grammar book.

(a) Thank you for your letter telling us about your holiday plans.
(b) I wish we could go to Greece with you.
(c) It's a long time since we last had a holiday abroad.
(d) We haven't enough money to go abroad in July.
(e) I think we'll probably go to Brighton as usual.
(f) Perhaps next year we'll be able to afford to go to France or Belgium.
(g) I hope you'll have a lovely time on the island you've chosen from the tourist brochure.
(h) We are looking forward to hearing about your holiday when you return.

2

The ARELS grammar questions given here cover points that are frequently covered in this exam, i.e.:

Many of the same structures tested by the FCE in 1.1
Constructions with particular verbs
Agreement (So do I, etc.)
Question formation

Disagreement (No, he wouldn't etc.) is something that is also often tested by the ARELS exam and you can be pretty sure that there will be a third conditional somewhere.

For short agreement or disagreement it is often necessary to know that 'I'd rather' and 'I'd better' are the short forms of 'I would rather' but 'I had better'. Thus:

He'd better stay at home. Yes, he had.
You'd rather go to Spain, wouldn't you? No, I wouldn't.

Before you go into the ARELS exam, make sure you feel happy about the points listed above and then concentrate as hard as you can.

2.1
(c) It was four o'clock when the accident happened.
(d) The driver drove away after looking / after he had looked at the woman.
(e) Anne offered to draw a picture of the man.
(f) Because the driver was going too fast / very fast he couldn't stop.
(g) The police used (their) radios to contact the police station.
(h) It took less than an hour to catch the man.
(i) But if she hadn't been an art student she wouldn't have been able to draw the man.

2.2

(d) Anne was very willing to draw the man.
(e) The police thanked her for drawing the man.
(f) It only took her a few minutes to draw the man.
(g) No one else there could draw the man.
(h) Anne was quite keen to draw the man or on drawing the man.
(i) She didn't object to drawing the man.
(j) She'll never forget drawing the man.

2.3

(c) So do I.
(d) So would I. (So should I.)
(e) So was I.
(f) So should I.
(g) Nor shall / will I. (Neither shall / will I.)
(h) So had I.

2.4

(c) Do you feel all right?
(d) Have you / Had you seen the driver before?
(e) How tall was he?
(f) Can you remember his face?
(g) How long have you been a student?
(h) Did you see the number of his car?
(i) Will you / Could you describe the car?

2.5

(c) No, she broke her right arm
(d) No, they took her to hospital in an ambulance.
(e) No, she sat on a wall to draw the man.
(f) No, it happened in the afternoon.

3.

In multiple choice questions like these try to decide what fits the blank, if possible before you look at the choices given. In this way you are less likely to be distracted by what are in fact called the 'distractors'. In the exam questions given, it should be immediately obvious that some choices are completely impossible (3(D) or 3.6(D), for example). Ruling out these should make it easier for you to make a good guess, even if you don't know the structure being tested.

One of the most difficult points in this example of the Pitmans exam is the last question. Note that 'Everybody' (like 'everyone') is a singular word in English.

Answers

1 (c); 2 (b); 3 (a); 4 (c); 5 (d); 6 (a); 7 (d); 8 (c); 9 (d); 10 (b); 11 (c); 12 (c); 13 (a); 14 (d); 15 (b); 16 (a); 17 (c); 18 (d); 19 (b); 20 (a).

4.

Again this question tests lots of favourites like the present perfect, conditionals, passives and so on. Try first to understand what the sentence has to mean and then it should be easier to write correctly.

In some of these sentences you need several words to complete the blank and these are not necessarily just auxiliary parts of the verb. In (i), for example, you need a relative clause, consisting of a verb, its subject and a preposition.

Answers

(a) 'd like / would like
(b) the shortest
(c) to have been
(d) 's stopped / has stopped / 's stopping / is stopping
(e) writing
(f) was given
(g) worked
(h) 'd told / had told
(i) (which) we live in
(j) 's been living / has been living / 's lived / has lived

E. BEYOND THE COURSEWORK

Learn by your mistakes. Whenever a teacher corrects a piece of your work, make sure you understand what is wrong and, if possible, give yourself some practice in using the correct form. If you are not sure about something, do some extra practice on it from a grammar practice book. The practice books that go with Eastwood and Mackin's *Basic English Grammar*, Michael Swan's *Basic English Usage* or the *Cassell's Student's Grammar* could be useful for you. Also helpful are Fowler's *Practise Your English*, Books One, Two and Three.

When you read, you may find it useful to try to keep your eyes open for the grammar of what you're reading. If anything strikes you as strange make a quick note of it and then later look it up in your reference books or ask your teacher.

If learning grammar helps you, you may have an interest in language for its own sake and might be interested in reading one or two of the very readable English books on language like Simeon Potter's, *Our Language,* Anthony Burgess's, *Language Made Plain* or Brian Foster's *The Changing English Language*.

There are also magazines which are not too difficult and which deal with questions of interest to learners of English. You could subscribe to *English Today* published by CUP, for example, or to one of the BBC's magazines published to accompany the BBC's language broadcasts.

Chapter 4   Vocabulary

A. GETTING STARTED

Work through all this chapter no matter which exam you are taking. Every English exam tests your knowledge of vocabulary in some way and this chapter will help you:

1. To cope with words you do not know in a text.
2. To use words more effectively and accurately yourself.

The only types of exam question which are specifically covered here are the dictionary questions used in the Oxford exams and vocabulary questions of the type you will find in the JMB exam. Try these questions even if you are not planning to take either of these exams. They will help you to use your dictionary better and so you will become a much better student of English. You will find the other types of question which test vocabulary in Chapter 11. Work through the exercises in this chapter before you try these.

As we saw in Chapter 2, it is essential to have a good English–English dictionary and a good bi-lingual dictionary. You will need these beside you as you work through this chapter.

B. ESSENTIAL PRINCIPLES

PASSIVE AND ACTIVE VOCABULARY

Remember that it is necessary to distinguish between passive and active vocabulary. You can understand many more words in English – or indeed in your own language – than you yourself use. When you meet a new English word, decide whether you really need it for your active vocabulary. If you do, give it a * in your vocabulary notebook and make sure you practise using it in some oral or written work.

The first part of this section helps you to deal with words which you do not know when you meet them in an exam text. The second part of this section deals with your active use of vocabulary and how to improve it.

1. Passive vocabulary

There are thousands of English words which even well-educated English people do not know but it does not worry them if they meet an unknown word in a book. Usually the meaning is clear enough from the context. It is important for you also not to panic when you meet a word that you do not know in an exam. Keep calm and make a logical guess. You will probably be right. Do you know any of the words in the first column of Table 4.1?

Table 4.1

Word	Part of speech	Guessed definition	Dictionary definition
fumble			
reckless			
incite			
eclipse			
huff			
erratic			
willy-nilly			
castor			

You probably don't, but try to fill in the first two columns of the table by thinking about the meaning of the sentences below. Think about whether the word is a verb, a noun, an adjective or an adverb and then try to write a definition of the word. When you have finished, check your answers with those given at the end of section B or with your own dictionary. It is not necessary to be exactly right; it is important only to have an approximate idea of what the word means.

1. In the dark his hand fumbled to find the door handle.
2. It is reckless to drive too fast on narrow, mountain roads.
3. The soldier was shot because he incited his comrades to rise against their officers.
4. She was so beautiful that she eclipsed every other woman at the ball.
5. When she said that he was smoking and drinking far too much, he stormed out of the room in a huff.
6. He is a very erratic person – you never know quite what to expect from him.
7. It doesn't make any difference whether we invite her or not – she'll come willy-nilly.
8. There are castors fixed to the feet of the heavy armchair so that it can be moved easily.

Try to get into the habit of guessing words before you look them up in the dictionary. You will probably get quite good at it.

Sometimes the word itself helps you. Long words are often composed of two or three parts – a root with a prefix and or a suffix. For example, uneatable = un (negative prefix) + eat (root) + able (suffix of possibility). It is unfortunately not always possible to analyse words and to understand their meanings so easily but you will sometimes find it useful.

Prefixes, in particular, often clearly say something about the meaning of a word. How many of the prefixes in Table 4.2 are familiar to you? Complete the table. Use a dictionary to help you. The table gives you twenty of the most useful prefixes in English.

Check your completed table with that in section D and make sure you can use all the words given as examples. Now see if you can guess the meanings of the words underlined in this exercise. Look back at the table if necessary.

1. I've overeaten – I feel terrible.
2. This work is substandard.
3. I'd better post-date this cheque.
4. England is now a multi-racial society.
5. Try our superburgers with tomato sauce.
6. It's time we re-decorated this room.
7. Do you believe in predestination?
8. They say that mistranslation has led to some serious political situations.
9. The government has decided to hold an anti-smoking campaign.
10. I can't stand him – he's such a pseudo-intellectual.

Check your explanations of these words with the key at the end of this section.

Suffixes may also sometimes help you with the meaning of a word you have not met before. Look at the groups of words below and work out what the suffixes mean. Use a dictionary to help you if you wish. Can you think of any other words using the same suffix?

(a) dormitory, factory, laboratory
(b) booklet, leaflet, piglet
(c) waitress, goddess, lioness
(d) thoughtless, careless, hopeless
(e) purify, simplify, beautify
(f) childhood, sisterhood, boyhood
(g) westward, homeward, windward
(h) reddish, oldish, longish
(i) childlike, godlike, starlike
(j) thoughtful, careful, hopeful*
(k) waterproof, fireproof, rustproof
(l) employee, trainee, interviewee
(m) clockwise, crabwise, lengthwise.

* Note that there is only one 'l' in the suffix 'ful'

Table 4.2

Prefix	Meaning	Examples of words with this prefix
mis		
fore		
inter		
super		
trans		
over		
pre		
multi		
re		
sub		
post		
bi(s)		
un		
in, im		
in, im		
mono		
pseudo		
ante		
anti		
micro		

The **roots** of words can also, of course, help you to work out meanings. You are lucky if you speak a Romance language because you will find that the roots of many of the more literary words in English are familiar. This is because Latin and French have had a particularly strong influence on English.

Below are a few common Latin roots which have been used to make words in English. Try to explain the meanings of the words with these roots in the sentences which follow. Refer to the tables of prefixes and suffixes, if necessary. Check with your dictionary that you have understood correctly.

- pose, pone = place, put in position

  1. He superimposed a map of Britain on one of Siberia to show their comparative sizes.
  2. The composer decided to transpose his song to a different key.
  3. We postponed the football match because of the rain.

- port = carry

  1. Britain has to import all its tea.
  2. He transported all his furniture to his new house in a van.
  3. This sewing machine is called portable but I can't lift it.

- ven, vent = come

  1. Goodness knows how the fight would have ended if Fred hadn't intervened.
  2. Prevention is better than cure.

- scrib, scrip = write

  1. She decided not to re-subscribe to the magazine as she hadn't found it as interesting as she had expected.
  2. The most interesting part of his letter was the postcript.

You may also find that you can recognise a word you have not seen in English before from your **knowledge of another language**. Be careful, though. Words can look like old friends but occasionally have quite different meanings. Words have come into English from many different languages. Which ones can you think of from your language? Perhaps you can group the underlined words in the text below according to their language of origin. There are four words from each of ten languages.

The admiral was at the zenith of his career and so he had to travel incognito. He took his rucksack and his dachshund and left the yacht. He went to his favourite bistro, where, after consulting the menu, he ordered some spaghetti and a glass of brandy. While he was eating, he read in his newspaper about a new sputnik, about a war hero who had committed hara-kiri and about a guerrilla war fighting against an oligarchy. Then he read about two cousins who had had a vendetta for twenty years – one was now suffering from paralysis after the other had become a karate expert. At the back of the bistro, a man was playing a balalaika and a girl in a kimono was accompanying him on the piano. The atmosphere and the alcohol helped the admiral to forget both the angst and the mosquito bites from which he had been suffering in the morning. He sent his compliments to the <u>chef</u>, took a pinch of <u>snuff</u> and set off for the nearest <u>discotheque</u>. Meanwhile, back at his <u>ranch</u> in the <u>steppe</u>, his <u>au pair</u> decided to have a <u>blitz</u> on the housework. The admiral's little boy laid a <u>booby</u> trap for her and so she set him some extra <u>algebra</u> homework. When she had finished tidying the <u>patio</u> and arranging her <u>origami</u> she set off for the zoo to see the <u>buffaloes</u>, <u>flamingoes</u> and <u>walruses</u> which she really had quite a <u>fetish</u> about.

2. Active vocabulary

Let us now move on to your active vocabulary. In an exam it is important to use only that which you are sure is correct. This section deals with one or two ways in which you can make your use of vocabulary more impressive to an examiner. A first rule is not to over-use any word – particularly in written English.

If you come to Britain, you will probably hear people using some little words very frequently.

"Nice day, isn't it."
"She's such a nice person."
"We had a very nice meal last night."

Or

"Did you get my letter?"
"He got me a nice record for my birthday."
"I am getting used to living in London now."

Or

"The film yesterday was very good?"
"He isn't a very good teacher."
"It was good of you to help me."

Nice, get and **good** are often used in English conversation but they are weak words for written English. Try to avoid them – unless you are writing dialogue or an informal letter. Usually it is not difficult to find a more interesting word.

Write down all the alternatives you can think of for **nice** – most of the words you write will have a more precise, stronger meaning than nice. Think of words that could be associated with, for example, 'nice' weather, 'nice' clothes, 'nice' people, 'nice' books, 'nice' places and 'nice' food. When you have finished your list look at the list of alternatives for 'nice' which you will find at the end of this section. How many of these words did you find? Did you find any which are not included in the list?

Now give the next paragraph a better English style. Change all the 'nice's into more interesting words. There are lots of possible ways of doing this. You will find one suggestion at the end of this section.

I had a very nice childhood. I went to a very nice school in Scotland where the teachers were all nice to the children and the lessons were always nice. It was in a very nice part of the country and it seems to me now that the weather was always nice. I thought it was especially nice in winter when it was nice to play in the snow. Our school uniform was very nice and school dinners were always nice. I wonder if it was really as nice as I think now or if I am just becoming old?

You can also usually find a better alternative for **get** in written English. Can you find one for each of the uses of 'get' or expressions with 'get' in these sentences? Remember that there are a number of rather different meanings of get.

1. When a British citizen becomes 100, he or she gets a telegram from the Queen.
2. I suggested getting a new car but my husband said we could not afford it.
3. Pollution is getting a real problem today.
4. We are getting on well with our English.
5. It is hard to get all the words of a song when you listen to a record.
6. It is impossible to get him to understand what I mean.
7. Would you mind getting my coat from the cleaners when you are in town?
8. He can get Radio Moscow on his new radio.
9. I never get to see television these days.
10. He works so hard that he's sure to get ahead.
11. I wonder if I'll get through the exam.
12. Rain every day is bound to get you down.

You will find answers to this exercise at the end of this section.

Good is another word which students use too much. It is all right to use it occasionally in written English but, if you can think of a more interesting alternative, use it instead. Don't use it more than once in one paragraph.

Try to re-write the following paragraph. You may want to use some of the words you listed in the 'Nice' exercise or you may prefer to think of others. You may want to put in a different kind of expression rather than always replacing good with another adjective. You will find one possible answer to the exercise at the end of this section but there are plenty of other possibilities.

We had a very good evening on Friday. After a meal at a very good Italian restaurant we went to a good film. I liked it because the actors were all so good and the plot was a good one as well. Afterwards we were in such a good mood that we decided to visit some good friends of ours and tell them all about our evening. They were very good about our calling round so late and I was glad that I was able to do them a good turn by mending their clock while we were there.

COMMONLY CONFUSED WORDS

Under this heading we shall look particularly at some vocabulary points which often cause problems for foreign students. One way in which you can make a good impression on an examiner is by using correctly some of the words and expressions which students usually find difficult. If, however, you use these words incorrectly, you will certainly lose marks because examiners get tired of always seeing the same mistakes. So try hard now to understand how they are used and stop to consider carefully before you write them in an exam. Twenty of the most commonly confused sets of words are listed here. Learn two a day and you will have mastered them in ten days. Look them up in your Oxford Learner's or Longman Dictionary and practise using them. When you feel you understand the use of all the words on the list, try the exercise which follows.

1. rob/steal
2. bring/take
3. go/come
4. work/job/profession
5. travel/trip/journey
6. opportunity/possibility
7. economic/economical
8. agree
9. lend/borrow
10. lonely/alone
11. people/police (these are plural words)
12. news (this is uncountable, i.e. always needs a singular verb)
13. advice/advise
14. practice/practise

    (In 13 and 14 it may be helpful to remember that the word with 'c' is the noun and the word with 's' is the verb – just like 'rice' and 'rise' which you probably do not confuse.)

15. take/pass/fail an exam
16. experience/experiment
17. cry/shout
18. boring/bored
19. become/get/receive
20. technique/technology

Now try this exercise. The number of the question corresponds to the number on the list above. Fill the blanks with the necessary forms of the appropriate words.

1. I was   in London yesterday. My handbag was   .
2. When you come to see me,   your photo album with you. When you go and see her,   her some flowers.
3. When I   home to Italy, I shall speak perfect English. I hope I'll   back here soon.
4. She's finding it difficult to get a   . He's finding it difficult

to get   . Is teaching really a   or not? It is certainly
a very hard   but it is extremely interesting

5. I had a very difficult   when I came here. I love
Let's go on a day   to France. Tell me about
your   to Bangkok last year. She works in a
          agency.

6. I had the   to go to Japan when I was a student but there
was no   of my learning any Japanese because everyone I
met spoke very good English.

7. She is a very   housewife. Your car is much more
          than mine. I'm not keen on our government's
          policy. He's studying   history at university.

8. I   with what you say.
          you   with him?

9. A library   books to people. People   books from
libraries.

10. You can be   even when you are surrounded by other
people.
Everyone else left the room and I was at last   .

11. British people   very   .
I like people who   always sincere.
British police   guns.

12. The news today   very worrying.

13. Let me   you. I feel you need some   .

14. Do some   every day. The more you   , the better
you'll become.

15. When are you going   the exam? I hope you   . My
brother   it last year and I'm afraid he   .

16. Scientists in laboratories   . Living abroad is a very
interesting   even if you feel a bit lonely sometimes.

17. I think she   simply because she is so tired.
I saw him on the other side of the street and   to him but
he didn't hear me.

18. My mother always used to say that   people are
very   .
Are you often   ?

19. We   a little older every day.
What did you   for Christmas?

20. The industrial world should help the developing world
with   .
The school has lots of modern   – tape recorders,
computers and so on – but what do you think of the
teaching   ?

ANSWERS TO EXERCISES IN THE PRECEDING SECTION

Key to exercise on guessing words from context

Table 4.3 Key to exercise on guessing words from context

Word	Part of speech	Dictionary definition
fumble	verb	feel uncertainly with the hands
reckless	adjective	not thinking of the consequences
incite	verb	rouse, encourage
eclipse	verb	make someone seem dull by comparison
huff	noun	bad temper
erratic	adjective	irregular in opinion or behaviour
willy-nilly	adverb	wanted or unwanted
castors	noun	small wheels fitted to furniture so it can be moved

Completed prefix table

Table 4.4 Completed prefix table

Prefix	Meaning	Examples of words with this prefix
mis	wrongly	misunderstand, mispronounce
fore	in advance	Forewarned is forearmed
inter	between	international, inter-school
super	above	superstar, supernatural
trans	across	transcontinental, trans-Siberian
over	too much	oversleep, overwork
pre	before	pre-school, pre-wedding
multi	many	multi-national, multi-coloured
re	again	retell, rewrite
sub	under	subway, sub-committee
post	after	post-graduate, post-natal
bi (s)	two, twice	biplane, bi-centenary
un	not	unjust, unable
in, im	not	injustice, impractical
in, im	in, into	inhabit, impress
mono	one, once	monolingual, monotonous
pseudo	false	pseudo-scientific, pseudonym
ante	before	ante-room, ante-natal
anti	against	anti-freeze, anti-government
micro	small	microcomputer, microwave

Key to prefixes exercise

1 . . . eaten too much . . .   2 . . . not good enough.   3 . . . write a later date than today's on this cheque (perhaps I shan't have money in my bank account until next week).   4 . . . with people from many different races.   5 . . . our fantastically delicious beefburgers . . .

6 painted or wallpapered this room again.   7 Do you believe that fate – and not your own actions – determines what happens to you in your life?   8 . . . wrong translation . . .   9 . . . a campaign that will try to stop people smoking.   10 . . . he pretends to be such an intellectual although he isn't one really.

Key to suffixes exercise	Suffix	Meaning	Other examples
	(a) . . . ory	place where	observatory, lavatory
	(b) . . . let	small	playlet, starlet
	(c) . . . ess	female	actress, murdress
	(d) . . . less	without	penniless, faultless
	(e) . . . (i)fy	cause to be	horrify, solidify
	(f) . . . hood	state of life	manhood, motherhood
	(g) . . . ward	in the direction of	northward, upward
	(h) . . . ish	more or less	thirtyish, bluish
	(i) . . . like	in the manner of	warlike, doglike
	(j) . . . ful	full of	graceful, beautiful
	(k) . . . proof	able to resist	bulletproof, soundproof
	(l) . . . ee	person affected by action	divorcee, absentee
	(m) . . . wise	in the manner of or in connection with	crosswise workwise

Answers to origin of words exercise

Algebra, alcohol, admiral, zenith – **Arabic**.
Karate, kimono, origami, hara-kiri – **Japanese**.
Vendetta, incognito, spaghetti∗, piano – **Italian**.
Rucksack, dachshund, blitz, angst – **German**.
Guerrilla, mosquito, ranch, patio – **Spanish**.
Flamingo, booby, fetish, buffalo – **Portuguese**.
Yacht, brandy, snuff, walrus – **Dutch**.
Sputnik, steppe, bistro, balalaika – **Russian**.
Hero, oligarchy, atmosphere, paralysis – **Greek**.
Chef, menu, au pair, discotheque – **French**.

∗Note that spaghetti is an uncountable word in English, i.e. "Her spaghetti is delicious".

List of alternatives for "nice"

Fine, sunny, warm, pretty, smart, elegant, interesting, attractive, happy, pleasant, friendly, kind, enjoyable, exciting, marvellous, wonderful, beautiful, picturesque, delicious and tasty.

Suggested improvement of "nice" paragraph

I had a very happy childhood. I went to a very pleasant school in Scotland where the teachers were all kind to the children and the lessons were always interesting. It was in a very beautiful part of the country and it seems to me now that the weather was always fine. I thought it was especially enjoyable in winter when it was exciting to play in the snow. Our school uniform was very attractive and school dinners were always delicious. I wonder if it was really as wonderful as I think now or if I am just becoming old?

Answers to "get" exercise

1 . . . she receives . . .   2 I suggested buying . . .   3 . . . is becoming . . .   4 . . . are making good progress . . .   5 It is hard to understand . . .   6 . . . to make him understand . . .   7 Would you mind fetching . . .   8 He can receive . . .   9 I never have the

opportunity to see . . . 10 . . . he is sure to be successful. 11 . . . if
I'll pass the exam. 12 . . . is bound to make you feel depressed.

Alternative to 'good' paragraph	We had a very enjoyable evening on Friday. After a meal at a romantic Italian restaurant we went to a very powerful film. I liked it because the actors were so sensitive and the plot was an original one as well. Afterwards we felt so exhilarated that we decided to visit some close friends of ours and tell them all about our evening. They were very understanding about our calling round so late and I was glad that I was able to do them a favour by mending their clock while we were there.
Answers to exercise on commonly confused words	1. robbed, stolen. 2. bring, take. 3. go, come. 4. job, work, profession. 5. journey, travel, trip, journey (or trip), travel. 6. opportunity, possibility. 7. economical, economical, economic, economic. 8. agree, Do you agree. 9. lends, borrow. 10. lonely, alone. 11. are . . . nice?, are, do not carry. 12. is. 13. advise, advice. 14. practice, practise. 15. to take, pass, took, failed. 16. make experiments, experience. 17. is crying, shouted. 18. bored, boring, bored. 19. become (or get), receive (or get). 20. technology, technology, techniques.

C. EXAM QUESTIONS

A good learners' dictionary, as we saw in Chapter 2, will give you enormous help in your study of English – telling you about grammar and pronunciation as well as meaning. Doing the exercises in this section will help you with the vital study skill of using your dictionary well. Do these exercises whatever exam you are planning to take.

Use your dictionary when you are unsure about the meaning of a word but use it also when you want to check how to use a particular word. The Oxford exam places particular importance on using a dictionary and will always include questions which require you to use a dictionary. The first nine questions in section C are of the type used in the Oxford exam. Some are from previous exams – others are included to give you a full range of the types of question which a dictionary can help you to answer. The last two questions of this section are vocabulary questions of the type used in the JMB exam. Again these are useful practice for you even if you are not planning to take this exam.

Work through these questions. In section D you will find notes giving some guidance on how to do the question, followed by a tutor's answer. It is a good idea to do the questions in this way:

1. Read the question first.
2. Think about how you would answer it.
3. Read the introductory notes to the answer for that question in section D. .
4. Write your answer to the question.
5. Compare your answer with that given in section D.

1.

This question is from the Oxford Higher exam, May 1984. It shows that the dictionary gives you information about abbreviations.

Explain clearly what the following abbreviations mean in their contexts. Do not simply write out the abbreviation in full. The first one has been done for you.

   1. In applying for a job it is often necessary to write out a c.v. (A brief sketch of one's life and achievements.)

   2. It was an excellent PR exercise.

   3. The house had all mod cons.

   4. They gave him an IQ test.

   5. His job was to look after visiting VIPs.

   6. He wrote out an IOU.

   7. They bought it on HP.

   8. It was especially shocking that he should do such a thing as he was a JP.

   9. You ought to wear a DJ.

  10. He teaches PE.

  11. The letter had a PS.

2.

This question tests that you can use the dictionary to check the spelling of words. The question comes from the Oxford Higher exam, May 1984.

Study the following advertisement for a restaurant. There are some spelling mistakes. Underline each mistake and write the mis-spelt word correctly in the space to the right of the advertisement.

Andyras Restaurant

23 London Road
Tel. 76868

Wellcomes all visiters

All of you who like traditional
food will find it at
Andyras Restaurant

Andyras' especiality
is home-made casarole food
and freshley cooked vegetables.

We offer a glass of wine
free with each meal.

The propritor (Mr Andy) will give you
his personnel service, and show you
his skill after twenty years' experience
of the cataring bussines in London.

We hope to see you soon.

3.

This question tests your ability to look up words quickly and so understand the definitions given. It comes from the May 1984 Oxford Higher.

You should answer all sections.

(a) You are looking for the items listed below in a large department store. Give the name of the department where they could probably be found. (There may be several possible answers, give only one for each item.)

dishwasher	cheese-grater
tennis-racket	colour-film
zip	wheelbarrow
cushion-cover	dinner-service
teddy-bear	writing-paper

(b) Give examples of three things you would be able to buy in each of these departments.

Confectionery
Health Foods
Lighting
Footwear
Cosmetics

(c) Underline anything in these groups which would definitely not be found in the department given.

Furniture Department
Occasional tables Bedding plants
Press-studs   Dressing-table

Bureau | Toast-rack
Pouffe | Bedroom suite
Divan | Lentils

Handbags and accessories

Scarf | Mouth organ
Belt | Stole
Refuse-bag | Purse
Vanity-case | Mittens
Wallet | Flap-jack

Fancy Goods

Ashtray | Key-ring
China figures | Vase
Table mat | Cat-litter
Riff-raff | Disposable nappies
Coasters | Tray cloth

4.

This question tests that you can use the dictionary to find out the spelling of different parts of verbs. The question comes from the Oxford Higher exam, May 1983.

Use your dictionary to help you put the correct form of the verb in brackets into the following sentences. The first one has been done for you.

(i) (cancel)
Because of the weather the meeting had to be cancelled.

(ii) (appeal)
He was tried and sentenced in 1964 but the following year he successfully

(iii) (refer)
She gave an excellent lecture on Shakespeare, only occasionally   to her notes.

(iv) (handicap)
I don't know whether enough is done in this country to help disabled and   people.

(v) (further)
He always said that it was his godfather who had   his career.

(vi) (appal)
All the lower-paid workers were living in   conditions.

(vii) (detail)
He gave the police a very   account of his accident.

(viii) (deter)
The weather was getting worse but they were not   from driving into the country.

(ix) (worsen)
The situation   as the strike went on until many families were suffering real hardship.

(x) (develop)

The new process which the factory had   was a great
step forward.

(xi) (recur)

I try not to make mistakes when I am typing but they
keep

5.

This question tests that you can use your dictionary to work out the
pronunciation of words. It comes from the May 1983 Oxford Higher
examination.

Each of the words below has the same sound as one of the
headings below. Put the word under its correct heading. Use
your dictionary to find out the pronunciation. (For example,
'paw' would belong under the heading 'or' while the word 'low'
would belong under the heading 'so'.)

Words
draught, drought, owed, taught, owned, soul, snout, bough,
cough, wrought, dough, pawn, taut, paunch, soak, putt, tough,
coarse, comb, trough, cuff, lout, wan, won, gong, calf

Headings
COW   OR   SO   STOP   UP   CAR

6.

This question also comes from the Oxford Higher exam, May 1983
and it tests your ability to understand dictionary definitions and then
to use the words defined accurately yourself.

Use your dictionary to help you write sentences for the following
pairs of words to show that you fully understand their meaning.
The first one has been done for you. Do not copy any example
sentences from the dictionary.

1. pore/pour
   He poured out my coffee.
   I pored over my translation all evening.

2. beer/bier

3. pail/pale

4. bald/bold

5. stationary/stationery

6.　affect/effect

7.　loose/lose

The following three questions (7, 8, 9) are not from previous exam papers but they are of types that may well be found in the future and they also provide useful practice for all students in using the dictionary.

7.

This question deals with phrasal verbs and idioms. Use your dictionary to decide which expression based on the verb 'play' can be used to make a sentence with the same meaning as the sentence given. You may need to add a phrase to 'play' (e.g. 'play a big part') or you may need to add a preposition or particle to make a phrasal verb (e.g. 'play back'). The first one has been done for you.

(i)　The Prime Minister is minimising the importance of the strike.
　　The Prime Minister is playing the strike down.
(ii)　Children often behave mischievously with a new teacher.
(iii)　By continuing to use the stolen cheques, he gave the police an enormous advantage.
(iv)　He is thinking about starting his own business – but not very seriously.
(v)　The *Guardian* loves making puns in its headlines.
(vi)　He really doesn't mind being in a position of lesser importance.
(vii)　I wish he wouldn't always act so stupidly.
(viii)Surely those opinions are completely out-of-date now?
(ix)　When you've recorded your voice, listen to the tape and listen to your pronunciation critically.
(x)　My feet are hurting me again.

8.

This question tests whether your can understand the dictionary's categorisation of words according to their style. Put the words in the list under the appropriate headings. Note that some words may fit under more than one heading. For the words in the Slang, Colloquial and American categories, give the standard English meaning in brackets. The first one has been done for you.

Words
bread, Taffy, brass, faucet, ta, intern, loo, tuxedo, copper, tight.

Headings
SLANG COLLOQUIAL AMERICAN STANDARD ENGLISH
bread　　　　　　　　　　　　　　　　　　bread
(money)

9.

This question tests your ability to find the correct definition of a word in a particular context for words which have many different meanings. Write down an alternative for the underlined word in each sentence. The first one has been done for you.

(i) He gave a very impressive paper at the Royal Academy last year.
essay

(ii) The doctors cannot do more than stay the progress of the disease.

(iii) He got five years for a job he did in Birmingham.

(iv) The branches were bowed down by the weight of the snow.

(v) What are you going to plant in those beds over there?

(vi) Are pupils streamed in schools in your country?

(vii) He was booked for driving too fast down King Street.

(viii)Have you made a will yet?

10.

This question is of the type used in the JMB exam.

The following words and phrases can be substituted, without changing the meaning, for words or phrases in the passage below the list. In the spaces provided write the exact words from the passage.

burnt   . . . .

thrown   . . . .

trumpet   . . . .

wheel   . . . .

starts burning   . . . .

quickly   . . . .

beside   . . . .

allotted positions   . . . .

arrived at   . . . .

encouragement   . . . .

At a little before seven o'clock in the evening the Norse galley is brought to the starting-point of the procession and the torch-bearers take up their appointed places along the route behind it. The Guizer Jarl, in full Viking armour and flowing cloak, takes his place at the helm, with his own squad of Guizers lined up alongside the ship. At half past seven, the double ranks of paraffin-soaked torches are lit by flares and the procession moves briskly off. When the Burning Site is finally reached, the torch-bearers form a huge fiery ring around the galley, the Guizer Jarl leaves it and, at the sound of a bugle, all the torches are flung together into the ship, which at once bursts into flames. While it burns, ships in the harbour sound their sirens and a great noise of cheering goes up from the watching crowd. In less than an hour, the galley is totally consumed and nothing remains but ashes.

11.

This is another type of vocabulary exercise used in the JMB exam.

In the passage which follows the list below some words are underlined. Choose suitable dictionary definitions from those below and write, in the space provided, the appropriate word from the passage. Write X where a definition does not fit any of the underlined words in the passage.

rotten . . . .

likely to last for a long time . . . .

the regular coming round of events in succession . . . .

allowed to be seen . . . .

is cut down . . . .

growing strong and healthy . . . .

to become larger . . . .

one's native country . . . .

visible . . . .

types of upper layers of earth . . . .

very hard . . . .

making fewer in number . . . .

comes down freely by force of weight . . . .

typically . . . .

life-spans . . . .

Thriving larch plantations make rapid growth, and frequent thinning is necessary to prevent the young trees becoming too drawn-up. At every thinning, the crowns of the remaining trees must be left with ample room to expand. Thinnings are readily saleable from the smallest sizes for fence-rails, rustic poles and pickets, as they contain much heartwood and are durable out of doors. Larger sizes yield pitwood of the highest class, and still larger sizes provide satisfactory telegraph poles. Rotations for larch are fairly short, averaging around 80 years. It is not a long-lived tree and on many soils develops butt-rot at an early age. The decayed area lies in the centre of the trunk and is not revealed until the tree is felled.

D. TUTOR'S NOTES AND ANSWERS

For each question this section contains notes on how to answer the question followed by a suggested answer. It is strongly recommended that you read the notes before writing an answer to the question yourself.

ANSWERS TO QUESTIONS OF THE OXFORD HIGHER EXAM TYPE

Abbreviations

1.
If you have an *Oxford Learner's Dictionary*, note that there is a list of common abbreviations at the back of the dictionary. You will have to look at that first and then refer to the body of the dictionary if you do not understand the 'translation'.

Remember that you must not simply write out the abbreviation in full.

Be careful as some abbreviations, e.g. PM and DJ, have more than one possible explanation.

Answers

1. In applying for a job it is often necessary to write out a c.v.
   A brief sketch of one's life and achievements.
2. It was an excellent PR exercise.
   It distributed information about the organisation to the public.
3. The house had all mod cons.
   It had a shower, a modern kitchen and so on.
4. They gave him an IQ test.
   A test that aimed to measure his intelligence.
5. His job was to look after visiting VIPs.
   People who were considered to be very important.
6. He wrote out an IOU.
   A paper acknowledging that he owed money.
7. They bought it on HP.
   Buying something expensive by paying first a deposit and then monthly instalments.
8. It was especially shocking that he should do such a thing as he was a JP.
   A Justice of the Peace, a magistrate in the lowest level of court.

9. You ought to wear a DJ.
   A men's dark jacket for formal wear.
10. He teaches PE.
    Physical education, sport or gymnastics.
11. The letter had a PS.
    Something written as an afterthought, after the writer had signed his letter.

2.

Mark in pencil any word that you are not sure about and look it up.

Remember that a word may exist but that the spelling may be wrong for this particular context.

When you can't find a word as it is spelt in the text you may have to use a little ingenuity to work out what the right spelling should be. It may not begin with the same letter.

Answers

welcomes   visitors   speciality   casserole   freshly   proprietor
personal   catering   business

3.

If you can't find a compound word under its first part, look up its second part and the meaning should become clear.

Check everything that you are not sure about in section (c) of the question – remember that things with misleading names will deliberately have been included.

Answers

(a) dishwasher   electrical goods   cheese-grater   kitchen goods
     tennis-racket   sports   colour-film   photography
     zip   haberdashery   wheelbarrow   gardening
     cushion-cover   furnishings   dinner-service   china
     teddy-bear   toys   writing-paper   stationery

(b) Give examples of three things you would be able to buy in each of these departments:

     Confectionery   sweets, chocolate, cakes
     Health Foods   honey, lentils, brown rice
     Lighting   lamps, lampshades, light bulbs
     Footwear   shoes, sandals, boots
     Cosmetics   lipstick, mascara, eye-shadow

(c) These are the things which would definitely not be found in the department given:

     Press-studs   Refuse-bag   Riff-raff
     Bedding plants   Mouth-organ   Cat-litter
     Toast-rack   Flap-jack   Disposable nappies
     Lentils

4.

The first thing to do in this question is to make sure that you know which part of the verb is needed to fill the blank.

Is the last consonant to be doubled or not? The dictionary makes it clear. Look up 'offer' where the 'r' does not double and 'prefer' where it does and see how the dictionary shows this.

Answers

appealed referring handicapped furthering appalling
detailed deterred worsened developed recurring

5.

Inside the front cover of your Longman or Oxford dictionary you will find a copy of the International Phonetic Alphabet.

Look up the headwords first and write down their phonetic symbol beside them. Do this even if you are confident how to pronounce the words. It will make it much quicker to put the other words in the right places as you look them up.

Unless you are very short of time, look up all the words. The words are selected because they are not necessarily pronounced in the obvious way and it is most sensible to check them all.

Answers

COW drought snout bough lout
OR taught wrought pawn taut paunch coarse
SO owed owned soul dough soak comb
STOP cough trough wan gong
UP putt tough cuff won
CAR draught calf

6.

It is important here to make sentences which really illustrate the meanings of the words. 'The girl is very pale' will not get you full marks.

You are told not to copy any example sentences from the dictionary but use the examples to give you inspiration. Otherwise you can waste a lot of time trying to think of suitable sentences. For example, a dictionary example for 'affect' is 'Will the changes in taxation affect you personally?' Why not modify this to 'The change in government did not affect him at all.'

Keep your sentences simple. It is easy to make the mistake of writing something too complicated to be a natural sentence.

Answers

- Beer is probably the most popular drink in British pubs.
- The coffin lay on its bier until the end of the funeral service.

- When we were camping last year I used to get a pail of fresh milk from the nearest farm every morning.
- She was not hurt in the accident but she looked terribly pale for several days afterwards.

- Although he's only twenty he is already going bald.
- May I be so bold as to ask you how much you paid for your car?

- The lorry turned the corner too fast and bumped into a stationary car.
- Hotels often provide stationery for their guests to use if they want to write letters.

- I wonder how her job is affected by the management changes.

- I hope that giving her more responsibility will have a good effect on production.

- My skirt is loose – I must take it in a little.
- My skirt is tight – I must lose some weight.

7.

In a question like this make sure you do not overlook any entries for the word in question.

In rewriting the sentence be careful not to include anything that is not necessary. It is not necessary, for example, to repeat 'but not very seriously' in (iv).

Make sure you always put the expression into the form needed. You may have to put a verb into the past tense, for example.

Answers

(ii)   Children often play a new teacher up.
(iii) By continuing to use the stolen cheques, he played into the hands of the police.
(iv)   He's playing with the idea of starting his own business.
(v)   The *Guardian* loves playing on words in its headlines.
(vi)   He really doesn't mind playing second fiddle.
(vii) I wish he wouldn't always play the fool.
(viii) Surely those opinions are completely played out now?
(ix)   When you've recorded your voice, play the tape back and listen to your pronunciation critically.
(x)   My feet are playing me up again.

8.

In this question you must be careful to skim all the possible meanings of a word. Remember that a word may have several entries as well as several definitions under each entry.

Answers

SLANG:	bread (money)
	brass (i: high-ranking officer)
	(ii: money)
	(iii: impudence)
	copper (policeman)
COLLOQUIAL:	ta (thank you)
	Taffy (Welshman)
	loo (WC)
	tight (drunk)
AMERICAN:	faucet (tap)
	intern (houseman)
	tuxedo (dinner jacket)
STANDARD ENGLISH:	bread
	brass
	intern
	copper
	tight

9.

Here again you have to look through all the definitions of a word and you have to think very carefully about which one fits the given context.

(ii)	delay
(iii)	criminal act
(iv)	bent
(v)	garden plots
(vi)	divided according to ability
(vii)	charged by police
(viii)	document bequeathing property after death

10.

For questions in the JMB exam you are not allowed to use a dictionary.

The most important thing here is to be aware of what part of speech the words listed are. It is only possible to replace an adjective with an adjective. Similarly a verb in the past tense cannot be replaced by a verb in the present tense.

Sometimes the number of words in a phrase may not be the same as that in its equivalent. 'Arrived at' can replace a single word.

Answers

burnt	consumed
thrown	flung
trumpet	bugle
wheel	helm
starts burning	bursts into flames
quickly	briskly
beside	alongside
allotted positions	appointed places
arrived at	reached
encouragement	cheering

11.

Here also you must be aware of the part of speech which the dictionary definition represents and you must match this with an appropriate equivalent.

Do not be misled by definitions which may match other meanings of the words underlined. Check that the definition matches this particular context.

Answers

rotten   decayed
likely to last for a long time   durable
the regular coming round of events in succession   X
allowed to be seen   X
is cut down   is felled
growing strong and healthy   thriving
to become larger   expand
one's native country   X

visible   revealed
types of upper layers of earth   soils
very hard   X
making fewer in number   thinning
comes down freely by force of weight   X
typically   averaging
life-spans   rotations

E. BEYOND THE COURSEWORK

Both this chapter and Chapter 2 have given ideas for developing your vocabulary to a point beyond the limited needs of your exam. Let me just here re-emphasise some of the most important points.

1. Expand both your passive and active vocabularies by reading as widely as possible in English.
2. Always try to guess the meaning of a new word from its context before looking it up in a dictionary.
3. Write down your new words in a sensible way.
4. Exploit your teacher if you have one – ask him or her to correct any extra work that you do.
5. Experiment with words you are not sure of (except in the exam) and pay very close attention to any corrections.
6. Above all, make your dictionary a close friend.

Chapter 5   Conversation

A. GETTING STARTED

This chapter is different from many others in this book because the exact form a conversation may take in an exam varies so much from candidate to candidate. It isn't possible to give exact questions that have been asked in previous exams or to provide the precise answers wanted by the examiners. The examiners are not, of course, looking for precise answers. They just want to get an impression of the level that your English has reached. All we can do is to give some general advice for dealing with the conversation part of an exam and then to look at the kind of questions which you ought to be able to deal with confidently when you have reached an intermediate level in English.

B. ESSENTIAL PRINCIPLES

A first thing to remember when you go into an oral exam is to be friendly. When you enter the exam room, say 'Good Morning' or 'Good Afternoon' to the examiner and smile. Say 'Goodbye' (and possibly even 'Thank You') as you leave. Remember that the examiner only has time to get a quick impression of you. If you are polite and friendly, you are at once creating a good first impression.

Give full answers to the examiner's questions. Try to avoid just saying 'Yes' or 'No'. In written exams you should try always to keep to the point. An oral exam is much freer; the examiner wants to hear you speak English and, within reason, doesn't mind what you talk about. The examiner will probably be quite happy if you talk a lot and so save him or her from having to think up too many questions for you.

Remember that the examiner is probably seeing a lot of candidates and that it's quite tiring work. It'll be much more interesting for the examiner if you say something that makes you come alive for him or her. Don't be afraid to talk about yourself, to let the examiner know interesting personal details, to give stories about your own personal experience rather than to talk in very general terms. In doing this you will probably find it easier to speak in a more fluent way and you will also become an interesting individual for the tired examiner.

If you don't understand a question from the examiner, don't worry. Just ask him or her in good English to repeat the question. Say something like:

I'm sorry, I didn't catch what you said. Would you mind repeating the question?
or
I'm sorry, I don't understand the question. Could you possibly explain what you mean?

Try not to worry about making mistakes. The main thing is to communicate your meaning, and forgetting an occasional 's' is not too much of a disaster. Similarly, don't feel you have to speak too fast in order to sound English. In fact, quite the opposite is true. You will probably be far easier to understand if you don't speak too quickly. So take a deep breath before you begin, sit back in your chair, relax and don't worry. You know you can do well – all you have to do is to show this to the examiner.

C. QUESTIONS TYPICAL OF ORAL EXAMS

This section looks at twelve basic conversational areas and asks you five questions relating to each area. These are the kind of questions which you should be able to answer without too much difficulty in an intermediate exam. No exam will ask you so many questions, of course. Use them as a kind of checklist. Do you know all the vocabulary and structures you need to be able to answer them well?

I suggest that you follow these stages:

Answer the questions on your own.
Then have a look at the comments I make and the answers that I suggest in section D. Do my comments and answers give you any ideas about how you could give fuller or more natural answers of your own?
When you have thought about this, work through the questions in section C again.

1. Basic information about yourself

What's your name?
Can you spell it?
How old are you?
When's your birthday?
Where were you born?

2. Family and home

Have you got any brothers and sisters?
What do your parents do?
Where do you live?
Tell me about your house?
What about your own room?

3. English study

How long have you been learning English?
How have you learnt English?
What do you find most difficult about English?
Why do you want to learn English?
How are you going to continue learning English in the future?

4. Work or school

What do you do?
Describe your typical day.
What do you like and what do you dislike about your work or school?
Have you always done the same job? or Have you always been to the same school?
What do you plan to do in the future?

5. Leisure

What is your favourite sport?
How do you play your favourite sport?
Do you play a musical instrument?
What kind of music do you like?
What else do you like to do in your spare time?

6. Books and films

Who is your favourite author?
What have you been reading recently?
Do you prefer reading or watching television?
What kind of films do you like?
Tell me the story of a film that you've seen recently.

7. Holidays and travel

How did you spend your summer holidays last year?
Have you ever been to an English-speaking country?
Tell me about the most memorable holiday you have ever spent.
Tell me about your journey to work or school every day.
How did you come here today?

8. Food

What is your favourite meal?
What do you think of English food?
What is a typical meal from your country?
What do people drink in your country?
What did you have for dinner last night?

9. Weather

Lovely day today, isn't it?
What's the weather like today?
What's the weather like in your country?
What do you think of British weather?
What is your favourite season?

10. Describing people

Tell me about your closest friend.
Have you got a hero?
What does your mother look like?
What do you think an ideal teacher should be like?
What would your ideal husband or wife be like?

11. Your country or town	What's your home town like?
	What kind of agriculture does your country have?
	What does your country produce in its factories?
	Is your country a good one for tourists?
	What is the school system like in your country?

12. Opinions on topical subjects	Tell me about one story in the news just now.
	What are the main problems in your country at the moment?
	If you were the President or Prime Minister of your country, what would you do?
	What do you think of the current political situation in Great Britain?
	Do you think life is better now than it was a hundred years ago or not?

D. TUTOR'S NOTES AND ANSWERS

I have given suggested answers for all the questions above. Of course, you will answer them in very different, quite possibly better, ways. But I think my answers may give you some ideas about:

(a) appropriate tenses and structures to use when answering basic questions like these;

(b) how to avoid saying the minimum, to expand an answer so that it gives the examiner more to go on; and

(c) how to give an acceptable answer to the question when you don't really know what to say, in other words how to avoid the question in a not too obvious way.

When you read my answers look at them from the point of view of the three things listed above and think about these questions:

1. How do I do (a), (b) and (c) above in practice?
2. What other expansion and avoidance strategies can you think of?

1. BASIC INFORMATION ABOUT YOURSELF

Q. What's your name
A. Felicity O'Dell

Q. Can you spell it?
A. F-E-L-I-C-I-T-Y O-'-D-E-L-L

Q. How old are you?
A. I'm nearly 37.

Q. When's your birthday?
A. It's July the Fourth. American Independence Day.

Q. Where were you born?
A. I was born in Aberdeen in the north-east of Scotland. Now it's famous as the centre of the North Sea Oil industry but, when I was a child, it was just a quiet fishing port.

2. FAMILY AND HOME

Q. Have you got any brothers and sisters?

A. I've got one brother who's seven years older than me. He's a zoologist and works in London. He's married to a biochemist and they have two little boys.

Q. What do your parents do?

A. I'm afraid my parents are both dead now but my father was a professor of geography in the University of Aberdeen. My mother was a housewife after she was married. Before marrying she worked as a teacher. She also specialised in geography.

Q. Where do you live?

A. I live with my husband in a small house in Cambridge.

Q. Tell me about your house?

A. It's a small terraced house with a small garden at the front and a larger one at the back. On the ground floor, there is a sitting-room, a living-room and a large kitchen where we usually eat our meals. Upstairs there's a bathroom and three bedrooms. We use one of the bedrooms as a study. It's not a very big house but it always seems a happy little house and we are both very fond of it.

Q. What about your own room?

A. In a way I suppose all the rooms in the house are my own rooms and so let me tell you about my favourite room in the house which is the sitting-room. It's the one and only room in the house which is hardly ever untidy. So it's always quite a restful place to be. I like it especially because it has a coal fire, which I find much more cosy than central heating. There are lots of plants in the room and they also seem to do better in a room where there is an open fire rather than central heating. The walls of the room are white and the furnishings are either green or deep red. There isn't a lot of furniture in the room – just a table, a sideboard, a record-player, a pouffe, some chairs and, best of all, a chaise longue. It stands in the window bay and I love to lie on it, reading a good book and occasionally getting up to poke the fire or to change a record.

3. ENGLISH STUDY

Q. How long have you been learning English?

A. For about four years now although in the first year I had only one lesson a week.

Q. How have you learnt English?

A. In my first year I had a private teacher. Then I was able to join a course at my local college. I've been going to this course for two hours twice a week for the last three years. I've also learnt a lot by listening to the BBC World Service broadcasts in English and by subscribing to one or two magazines for foreign learners of English.

Q. What do you find most difficult about English?

A. I find a lot of things very difficult. I think prepositions are perhaps one of the hardest problems for me. Then spelling is dreadful too. I've learnt a lot of words by listening to the radio but then when I read those words I don't recognise them. G-A-O-L is a good example of a word I'd learnt by hearing it and then couldn't understand what it could be when I saw it in a newspaper. Also I never know when to use 'make' and when to use 'do'. In spite of all these problems, I still love English and want to learn it as well as I possibly can.

Q. Why do you want to learn English?

A. For lots of different reasons. I don't use English in my work now but I think I may need it in the future if I want to get a better job. Also I love travelling and today you can make yourself understood almost anywhere in the world with English. Through English you can get to know people from all over the world. I also love reading and have read quite a few English or American authors in my own language. I'd like to read them in the original too, if possible.

Q. How are you going to continue learning English in the future?

A. I'm going to continue going to classes twice a week but I'm also going to try to read a lot more English. We've got quite a good library near my home and it's got several shelves of English books which I can borrow. My aim is to read them all. I'm also saving as hard as I can and hope to have enough money to do a language course in England next year.

4. WORK OR SCHOOL

Q. What do you do?

A. I'm a teacher. I teach English to foreign students in a large new language school in Cambridge.

Q. Describe your typical day.

A. I generally get up at about seven and do some marking. Then I have breakfast and go to work. I walk to work and it takes me about fifteen minutes. I teach all day. Classes finish at a quarter past four. Then we sometimes have a staff meeting or often the teachers just sit in the staffroom chatting over a cup of coffee until five or so. In the evenings my husband and I often have friends round or go to visit people ourselves. We also often drive out into the country for a breath of fresh air and a little walk last thing at night.

Q. What do you like and what do you dislike about your work or school?

A. I very much enjoy meeting the students I teach. They are all adults and every class has a wide range of nationalities, occupations and attitudes in it. It means we can have very varied and interesting discussions in class and I feel that I learn a lot every day too. My students are almost always very keen to learn English and this makes teaching them a very pleasant job. I also enjoy the company of my colleagues. I don't like marking although I know it's important.

Q. Have you always done the same job? OR Have you always been to the same school?

A. No, although I've been in this job for seven years now. My first job after leaving university was in a boys' grammar school. I had to try to teach them French, German and Russian. German and Russian were all right because I had small classes of kids who were reasonably motivated to learn. French was dreadful, though. All the boys had to learn French and most of them thought it was a waste of time. The main aim of my lessons was to prevent the pupils from being so noisy that the teacher in the next room came in to complain. After that I worked as an auxiliary nurse in a hospital for a few months. That was a lot more peaceful than the school and I had almost decided to train as a nurse when I had a chance of a temporary research job at Cambridge University. When that came to an end, I found a summer job at a language school, enjoyed it very much and here I still am.

Q. What do you plan to do in the future?

A. It's difficult to say. Sometimes I think I'd like to write a great novel. Then I decide I'd prefer to write textbooks for foreign students. Often I feel I'd like to go and teach abroad. Probably, I'll just stay where I am for another year or two and then make a decision.

5. LEISURE

Q. What is your favourite sport?

A. I'm not very good at any sport because I'm very short-sighted. I always hated team games at school because I always let my team down by dropping the ball at the wrong moment. But I enjoy more individual sports like hill-walking or swimming.

Q. How do you play your favourite sport?

A. The most important thing for hill-walking is to have sensible clothing. You must have strong comfortable boots and warm, waterproof clothing. A padded anorak is a good idea because it is very light but still keeps you warm and dry. Then you must have good maps and you must know how to read them properly.

Q. Do you play a musical instrument?

A. No, I'm afraid I can't. I'd really like to learn how to play the flute now but I suppose I'm too old.

Q. What kind of music do you like?

A. I enjoy all kinds of music. There are lots of classical music concerts in the town where I live and I enjoy going to those. At home I like listening to records of folk music. I also like some pop music very much although I don't often buy pop records. I prefer to listen to them on the radio.

Q. What else do you like to do in your spare time?

A. Recently I don't seem to have had a lot of spare time but, whenever I do have any, I like spending it with friends at home. I enjoy cooking and trying out new recipes. I also read a great deal.

6. BOOKS AND FILMS

Q. Who is your favourite author?

A. I don't really have one favourite author. I like all kinds of different people, depending on my mood. I think there are a lot of good women writers in Britain at the moment. Margaret Drabble, Beryl Bainbridge and Iris Murdoch, for example. I particularly like Margaret Drabble because she writes about a world that I find familiar and she seems to describe it in just the right way.

Q. What have you been reading recently?

A. I've just finished a novel by David Lodge called *Small World*. I found it very amusing. It's about the life of university academics in the 1980s and it describes how they spend much of their time going from conference to conference around the world. David Lodge is a professor of English and so I suppose he knows the 'small world' he's describing. He writes in a very humorous and clever way, I think.

Q. Do you prefer reading or watching television?

A. I very much prefer reading. Television is good if I feel very tired and too lazy to pick up a book. That's when I watch soap operas and must admit that I quite enjoy them. I think there are quite a few good programmes on TV. Sometimes there are excellent plays or films. But on the whole reading is a much more satisfying thing to do.

Q. What kind of films do you like?

A. I like films that entertain me but which also have something to say. Good examples of that kind of film are, I think, *Gallipoli* and *Oh What a Lovely War*. I can't stand films that are full of pointless violence or films that are pretentious. I find cowboy films boring and I'm not too keen on science fiction either.

Q. Tell me the story of a film that you've seen recently.

A. The last film I saw was *The Killing Fields* which is about the war in Cambodia. It is an anti-war film showing the dreadful suffering of the ordinary Cambodian people. It is the true story of an American journalist and his Cambodian interpreter. The journalist is horrified by US involvement in the war and he tries to write the truth about what is happening. He helps his interpreter's family to leave the country just before the situation becomes very serious. Eventually he has to leave the country himself and he tries to take his interpreter with him. Their attempts fail but several years later his interpreter does manage to reach the USA and rejoin his family there.

7. HOLIDAYS AND TRAVEL

Q. How did you spend your summer holidays last year?

A. I spent my summer holidays with my husband in Scotland. We went up there by car and toured all round, going up the west coast right to the most northern point of the mainland. It was wonderful although our car was very old and only just made it up some of the very steep and narrow roads that we came across. The weather was perfect and we had magnificent views of mountains, lakes and islands. I hope we can go back there again soon.

Q. Have you ever been to an English-speaking country?

A. Yes, I've been both to Britain and the United States. I found it much easier to understand British English than American English but I enjoyed both places. I particularly liked the Lake District and Wales in Britain and in the USA I found New York a very exciting place to be.

Q. Tell me about the most memorable holiday you have ever spent.

A. That's a difficult question. I seem to have had a lot of memorable holidays. I suppose that one of the holidays I'll never forget was my first holiday abroad. We went to Iceland when I was just eight years old. It took two or three days to get there by ship and I loved the journey. Iceland was also a very exciting place for a child to visit. I remember the fields of lava, the geysers, the very smelly pools of boiling mud, the little ponies, the dried fish to chew and all sorts of other interesting things.

Q. Tell me about your journey to work or school every day.

A. I walk to work which gives me a chance to wake up properly and to get mentally prepared for the day. If I'm in good time I take a slightly longer route and walk through the Botanical Gardens. That is always a nice way to begin the day – particularly in spring when there are new things to notice every day.

Q. How did you come here today?

A. I came by bus. The bus was late and I was afraid that I wasn't going to get here on time but, thank goodness, it eventually came and I got here with a quarter of an hour to spare.

8. FOOD

Q. What is your favourite meal?

A. Without doubt, it's curry. I love Indian food and I could easily eat at an Indian restaurant every day – if I had enough money. My favourite meal starts with Shami Kebab, followed by Chicken Tikka and then, if I have enough room, a bowl of lychees.

Q. What do you think of English food?

A. It's very much better than I expected. English food is a joke in my country. Everyone always says it's terrible, quite tasteless. But my landlady makes very nice food and we have something different every day. The only thing I really can't get used to is a green salad without any dressing.

Q. What is a typical meal from your country?
A. My country is Scotland and a typical meal from there is soup with lots of meat and vegetables. It's such a filling soup that you don't have any room for anything afterwards except for just a piece of fruit or a light milk pudding.

Q. What do people drink in your country?
A. The national Scottish drink is whisky and Scottish people drink a lot of whisky. They drink it neat, not with water or ice as English people have it. They also drink a lot of beer. In a Scottish pub, you ask for 'a pint of heavy' rather than the English 'pint of bitter'.

Q. What did you have for dinner last night?
A. I had some fried rice with mushrooms and onions and some barbecued spare ribs. Afterwards I had an apple and a cup of black coffee. It was the first time that I'd tried to cook spare ribs and they tasted very good, though I say it myself.

9. WEATHER

Q. Lovely day today, isn't it?
A. Yes, isn't it beautiful!

Q. What's the weather like today?
A. It's quite chilly, much colder than yesterday. It isn't raining but the sky is covered in grey clouds and I'm sure it'll rain later on. Still, the weather forecast for tomorrow is good. They say it's going to get warm again.

Q. What's the weather like in your country?
A. It's a bit like the weather in England but a bit colder. It's very changeable. You never know for sure what the weather's going to be like from one day to the next. In winter we usually have snow which lies for about a month. It doesn't ever get really hot in summer but it can be very pleasant. We have quite a lot of rain all year round, particularly on the west coast.

Q. What do you think of British weather?
A. I quite like it particularly in spring and autumn. I'd prefer it if it were a little hotter in summer and a little colder in winter but at least it's never boring. You never know quite what to expect.

Q. What is your favourite season?
A. I like autumn best of all. It's so beautiful watching the trees gradually changing colour and I love shuffling through a carpet of autumn leaves. Mind you, other seasons are good too. Winter is nice when there's snow. Spring is beautiful with its wonderful fresh greenness and new flowers. And summer is a lovely relaxing time of year with marvellous long evenings when you can sit outside until quite late at night.

10. DESCRIBING PEOPLE

Q. Tell me about your closest friend.

A. I have several close friends but one of them is an Australian girl who has spent quite a lot of time in this country but has now unfortunately gone back home. We keep in touch by letter and I hope she'll come back here soon. She is a very pretty girl, with dark curly hair, fair skin and big grey eyes. She's one of the kindest people I know and she'd do anything to help anyone else. She also has a very strong sense of fun and somehow always manages to bring a room to life whenever she's in it.

Q. Have you got a hero?

A. I don't know if hero is the right word but I admire my mother more than anyone else I know. She is totally unselfish and always loving and giving to all around her. She is often in considerable pain but never complains and always manages to find the good side of a situation. She supports me in everything I do and I am very grateful to her for all she's done for me and the rest of our family.

Q. What does your mother look like?

A. She's a little bit taller than I am and a little bit plumper. Her hair is darker than mine is but when she was my age she was also blonde. She has a very beautiful and kind face; this is not just a biased daughter speaking – other people also often comment on her beauty too.

Q. What do you think an ideal teacher should be like?

A. I think the ideal teacher must like and respect all his (or her) students. If he doesn't like a particular student, he must be very careful not to let this show. He must be able to explain things very clearly and mustn't lose patience when students find things difficult. He must enjoy teaching and must be interested in trying new ways of helping his students to learn. A sense of humour is quite a useful quality for a teacher too, I think.

Q. What would your ideal husband or wife be like?

A. He'd be understanding, considerate, intelligent, dependable and pleasant to be with. He'd accept me for what I am with all my faults. He doesn't have to be handsome or rich although I suppose that I wouldn't mind if he were!

11. YOUR COUNTRY OR TOWN

Q. What's your home town like?

A. It's a beautiful city in the north-east of Scotland. Most of the buildings are made of granite and they sparkle in the sunlight – although I must admit they also look rather grey and depressing in the rain. We have a marvellous beach there – it's long and sandy. If only the climate were better, we'd be a major international holiday resort. There are about two hundred thousand inhabitants in Aberdeen. Many of them are now employed in the oil industry but fishing is also still fairly important. There is also a very old university in Aberdeen and a very good teaching hospital.

Q. What kind of agriculture does your country have?
A. We grow wheat and other cereals. Soft fruit are important too. We also grow vegetables like potatoes and carrots. We also have a lot of animals on our farms, particularly cattle and sheep. The cows give very good beef and the sheep are used for both meat and wool.

Q. What does your country produce in its factories?
A. Whisky is probably our most important export and we have lots of whisky distilleries in Scotland. Woollen goods are another big export. Most Scottish industry is in the south of the country and there are all sorts of factories there, producing cars, machine tools, furniture, food products and all sorts of other things.

Q. Is your country a good one for tourists?
A. Yes, it's a very popular country with tourists. It's not so good for people who like nightlife and expensive restaurants, but it's ideal for those who enjoy magnificent scenery and a chance to get right away from it all.

Q. What is the school system like in your country?
A. It's quite complicated as it varies very much from region to region. Throughout the country, however, children start school at five and must stay there until they're sixteen. Usually children go to primary school until they're ten or eleven and then they go on to a secondary school. In secondary school they usually specialise quite a lot. At about thirteen, for example, a child has to choose whether he or she wants to concentrate on science or arts subjects. It's possible but quite difficult to change courses later on. To go to university involves staying at school until you're eighteen and taking exams in the three or four subjects that you've specialised in.

12. OPINIONS ON TOPICAL SUBJECTS

Q. Tell me about one story in the news just now.
A. One story we've been reading a lot about recently is the case of a mother who agreed to give birth for a couple who desperately wanted a child but the wife was unable to have a baby. An agency organised things and both the agency and the mother received a lot of money from the couple. Some people argue that it is totally unethical for a baby to be born in this way and they feel the couple should not be allowed to take the baby. I feel very sorry for the couple and think they should be allowed to keep the child. But it does seem wrong that an agency should make a lot of money out of such a situation.

Q. What are the main problems in your country at the moment?
A. I'm afraid we have a lot of problems in our country at the moment. Unemployment is probably the most serious one. More and more people are unable to find work. This is giving rise to all sorts of other social problems. Crimes of theft and violence are increasing at a very rapid rate. More and more people have

problems with drugs or drink. I don't think that these problems can possibly be solved until there is work for everyone who wants it.

Q. If you were president or prime minister of your country, what would you do?
A. I think I'd probably resign immediately. I really would hate to be actively involved in politics although I love talking about current affairs. It's very easy to say what's wrong but quite a different matter to find a solution.

Q. What do you think of the current political situation in Great Britain?
A. I think Britain is facing a particulary difficult time at the moment. The country has very serious economic and social problems, not to mention the political problems of Northern Ireland. I think that there have to be a lot of changes in the organisation of the country before the situation can improve significantly.

Q. Do you think life is better now than it was a hundred years ago or not?
A. Yes, I do. I think it's very easy to romanticise life in the past and to imagine that everything was peaceful and carefree a hundred years ago. But in fact life was very hard then for the majority of people. Work conditions were bad for many people. Medicine wasn't as advanced as it is now and life expectancy was very much shorter. Cultural and travel opportunities are far greater now than they ever used to be. Of course, we have problems now that were undreamt of in the past, but, all things considered, I think life is very definitely better now than it used to be.

E. BEYOND THE COURSEWORK

There are two aspects of being good at English conversation. The first is to feel confident using English; in other words, not to feel nervous or embarrassed if you have to speak it. The second is to know what is an appropriate thing to say in a natural English conversation.

Try to get practice in speaking English so that you feel at ease using it. Is there an English-speaking club in your area? Perhaps you can find a native speaker of English who lives in your area and would be happy to talk to you. Failing that, perhaps you can agree to talk only English with someone else who is trying to learn the language. At least that will give you good practice in using the language even if you don't get the good model of spoken English that you would get from a native speaker. Lots of students even say that they find it useful to talk to themselves in English, having little conversations inside their heads in English.

You can help yourself to learn what is an appropriate thing to say in a natural English conversation by listening to radio broadcasts in English, by watching films with an English soundtrack and by working with cassettes. Lots of textbooks now have cassettes which practise conversational English as well as traditional grammar drills, e.g. the *Strategies* series by Brian Abbs and Ingrid Freebairn published by Longman. Reading widely will also help your conversational skills.

Remember that outside the exam room the aim is not necessarily to say as much as possible. Listening well, smiling in the right places and asking apt questions are the sort of things that may give you more of a reputation for being good at English conversation in 'real life'.

Chapter 6

Reading aloud and prepared talks

A. GETTING STARTED

Reading aloud is a part of only three exams – the **FCE**, **ARELS** and **ESB**. Prepared talks are also part of only three exams – **ARELS**, **Institute of Linguists** and **ESB**. The exact form that these two skills take varies from exam to exam.

In the **FCE** you have a few moments in the exam room to look at a short text and then you have both to read it aloud and answer a few questions on it. In **ARELS** you have two minutes to prepare to read one part of a dialogue. In the **ESB** exam you choose the passage that you want to read yourself. You may choose prose or poetry and your reading should not last longer than two minutes.

The nature of the prepared talks also varies. In the **ARELS Higher Certificate** you are given a list of five topics about fifteen minutes before the exam begins. You choose one topic and prepare to speak on it for two minutes. You may not use notes during the exam. The **Institute of Linguists** exam is similar in that you have twenty minutes to prepare a talk from a choice of six subjects. Your talk should last about three minutes and you may use brief notes (of a heading type). In the **ESB** you must present a project. You may use brief (heading) notes and you must use visual aids. Your talk should last from three to five minutes depending on the Stage at which you are taking the exam.

Reading aloud is not something that most of us need to do very often in our own language or in any other. It is only really useful for actors or people who work in radio or television. To read aloud well you need some of the skills of an actor. It is quite likely, however, that in "real life" you may need to give a prepared talk and so you may find it useful to look at part of this chapter at least, no matter which exam you are taking.

B. ESSENTIAL PRINCIPLES

Even when you are using your own language it can be difficult to read aloud or to give a prepared talk well. Most people speak better when they are speaking freely and spontaneously. When something is planned or read, it often sounds flat and uninteresting for listeners. How can you avoid sounding flat?

1. If at all possible, take a couple of deep breaths before you begin to read or speak.
2. Take care not to read or speak too fast. Speaking fast doesn't make you sound more like a native speaker. It just makes you more difficult to understand.
3. Remember to make your voice go up and down in a natural way. English speech is not naturally flat. You can do this best if you decide what mood you as the speaker should be in – enthusiastic, questioning, angry etc. – and try to convey that feeling in your voice.
4. Imagine that you are reading the information to a friend or relative over the telephone. Try to forget that the examiner is there.

It is very important that you know how to pronounce numbers and letters. This is often necessary when you have a text to read aloud and it may also be useful in a prepared talk.

Why are these letters grouped together like this?
A   H   J   K
B   C   D   E   G   P   T   V
F   L   M   N   S   X   Z
I   Y
O
Q   U   W
R

Can you read these sentences aloud?
I was born in 1958.
His phone number is 210664.
Take a 25 bus or a 181.
The population of the village is 2369.
It costs £29.50.
It's 2½ hours' walk from here.
The picture is 7¾″ × 1′.
Profits have increased by 15.7%.

Answers

The letters are grouped together because of how you say the letters. All the letters in each group have the same sound as each other.

*   I was born in nineteen fifty-eight.
*   His phone number is two one oh, double six four. (Note how we divide the numbers into groups of three when we say them.)
*   Take a twenty-five bus or a one eight one. (Note how two figure numbers are said as a complete number but three figures are said

as three individual numbers – the same happens with road numbers, e.g. Take the A eleven and then the B one four two nine.

- The population of the village is two thousand three hundred and sixty-nine. (Don't forget the 'and'.)
- It costs twenty-nine pounds fifty.
- It's two and a half hours' walk from here.
- The picture is seven and three-quarter inches by one foot.
- Profits have increased by fifteen point seven per cent.

C. EXAM QUESTIONS

I suggest you approach each of these questions in the following way.

1. Read the question and think about how you would answer it.
2. Read the notes for that question given in section D.
3. Prepare your own answer, recording your own voice if possible.
4. Compare your answer with the suggested answer given in section D.
5. Answer the question again if necessary.

1.

Here are three texts of the FCE type. You would only be asked to read and discuss one of these in the actual exam but practise all three of them now.

Read aloud and answer the question "Where would you find this text?"

(a) This is a problem-solving program which provides the complete beginner with instant answers to the questions of what to plant and where. Simply tell the computer whether you prefer a shrub or a flower, the type of soil, light and shade conditions and required flowering time and the computer will come up with a selection of possible plants. The program comes complete with databases containing full information on 55 flowers and 47 shrubs. You can add to these and save them on cassette to build up your own library of garden and household plants.

(b) Dear Miss Manners,

I hate it when animals jump on me but other people's pets are always doing so. Dogs, particularly, always ignore the guests who are trying to pet them and throw themselves at animal haters such as myself. I'm not above kicking a pet when the owner isn't looking but what can I do to get rid of it when the owner is looking right at me?

Gentle Reader,

The most tactful thing to do would be to announce an allergy. This is not strictly a lie if you define 'allergic' loosely, the way sophisticated children have learned to do so, as in "I think I'm allergic to vegetables."

(c) On the last day of the year Percy MacGarrigle flew into Heathrow on a British Airways jumbo jet. Having only hand-baggage with him, he was one of the first of the passengers to pass through customs and passport control. He went straight to the nearest British Airways Information desk. The girl sitting behind it was not Cheryl. "Yes?" she said. "Can I help you?"

"You can indeed," he said. "I'm looking for a girl called Cheryl. She works for British Airways. Can you tell me where I can find her?"

"We're not supposed to answer that sort of question," said the girl.

"Please," said Percy. "It's important."

2.

This is an example of a dialogue from an ARELS Higher Certificate exam. It comes from exam no. AH 35.

You are telephoning Bob to tell him about a home computer that you know is for sale. You will hear Bob's voice on the tape and you must read the part marked CANDIDATE.

You have two minutes to study the passage before you start reading. You may write on it if you like. Remember, you will have to read the part marked CANDIDATE.

Bob: 31625
CANDIDATE: Hello, Bob. It's me. Sorry to disturb you at this time of
            night but I'm sure you won't mind when you hear what I've got to
            tell you.
Bob: Oh, what's that then?
CANDIDATE: Well, you've been talking about getting a home
            computer for months now, haven't you?
Bob: Well . . . yes.
CANDIDATE: Oh no! You haven't already got one, have you?
Bob: No, not yet.
CANDIDATE: That's good, because I've got details of one here that
            you'll absolutely love. It's got 16K ROM with microsoft colour
            BASIC.
Bob: Hold on – 16K RAM was that?
CANDIDATE: No, ROM – that's R. O. M. "Read Only Memory", I
            think it means.
Bob: 16K ROM. OK.
CANDIDATE: And listen to this from the leaflet:

Screen resolution of 320 × 200 with text and graphics or 160 × 102 individually addressable pixels in four colours.

Bob: Uh huh. Individually addressable what?
CANDIDATE: Pixels. It's spelt P-I-X-E-L-S. They're the things for
            plotting and generating solid shapes.
Bob: OK. OK. Don't go mad. I can tell you now. I can't afford
it.
CANDIDATE: That's just it. You can. You see, although it usually costs
            at least £168 in the shops, you can have this one for £128.

Bob: Really? It sounds a bit fishy to me.

CANDIDATE: There's nothing fishy about it at all. It's my friend Rudi's. You remember Rudi, don't you? The consultant for ALFAMAX who was staying at the Albany. He's going home and he's selling his computer. It's almost brand new. So, are you interested, or not?

Bob: What do you think? I'd better ring him right now. Have you got his number?

CANDIDATE: Yes, it's 338 3980. And I told him you'd probably be ringing. Good luck!

Bob: Thanks. Bye.

CANDIDATE: Bye.

3.

Here is a second ARELS reading passage. This one is from AC 29.

Your friend Bob is ringing you to ask your advice. You will hear Bob's voice on the tape and you must read the part marked CANDIDATE.

Bob: Hello there. Bob here.

CANDIDATE: Oh hello, Bob. What can I do for you?

Bob: Well, do you remember when you sent your camera through the post?

CANDIDATE: I'll never forget it. What a business it was sending it off to the maker's. I've got it back, by the way, and it's fine.

Bob: Good. The thing is. I'm in the same situation. The shutter's jammed and I need it for my holidays. Do you remember what you did about packing yours?

CANDIDATE: Yes, I got a couple of leaflets from the Post Office. One of them – "Wrap Up Well" – had a diagram in it with very clear instructions and I just did what they said.

Bob: Can you remember what it said?

CANDIDATE: Of course. In fact, the leaflets might be right here. Hang on a second, will you? Yes, I thought they'd be here. That was lucky. Now what was it you wanted to know?

Bob: Mainly about wrappings and things like that.

CANDIDATE: Right. I'll read out what it says. Here we are:

"You can use crushed newspapers, kitchen roll, tissue paper and corrugated cardboard. Also sawdust, foamed plastics, such as polystyrene, or wood wool."

Bob: I've got the box my tape recorder came in and there's a lot of polystyrene stuff in that.

CANDIDATE: That should be all right. Listen to the wrapping instructions. I'll dictate them, shall I?

Bob: Yes, good idea. OK. Fire away.

CANDIDATE: OK. Here goes. There are just two bits. Here's the first.

"Pack wrapped items in centre of carton and pack material around and over. Pack cushioning material in bottom of carton. Wrap each item separately."

Bob: OK so far. Should I tie it with string or use sellotape?
CANDIDATE: Oh, yes. That's the bit just below. It says:

> "Boxes should be firmly sealed along all seams with a good quality adhesive tape. It is recommended that the tape should be at least 1½″ wide."

> And I'd strongly advise you to put big FRAGILE WITH CARE notices all over it. You know what postmen can do with parcels.

Bob: Good idea. What about insuring it?
CANDIDATE: That's in the other leaflet. Hang on, yes, here it is. You have to use the Registered Post System.
Bob: Does it say how much it costs?
CANDIDATE: Yes, it says:

> "The amount of compensation payable depends on the fee paid.
>   For compensation up to £500 – 90p.
>   For compensation up to £750 – 95p.
>   For compensation up to £1000 – £1."

> That's not bad, is it?

Bob: No. In fact, it's very cheap. Right, thanks a lot. I'll start packing it right away. 'Bye.
CANDIDATE: Good luck. 'Bye.

4.

Here think about what *you* would choose to read for the ESB exam. First of all think about what kind of things would be suitable. Remember that you are going to read in front of an audience who will not have a copy of what you are going to read. What would they enjoy hearing?

The next three questions are about preparing talks. You will find more suggestions which will help you do this in Chapter 13, Presenting a Point of View.

5.

Here are five topics from the ARELS AH 35 exam. Choose one of them and prepare a talk. You have only two minutes for your talk.

- Strikes lead to less money and less work for everyone.
- The person I admire most is . . .
- Every young person should do one year's voluntary social work.
- Wives can't really choose to stay at home.
- Doctors prescribe too many drugs.

6.

Here are the topics which were given to some candidates in the Institute of Linguists Grade II Certificate exam in the winter of 1982.

- Reasons for enjoying a particular television programme.
- Law and order.
- North Sea Oil.
- A plan for making the most of a first short visit to London.

- The British car industry.
- The North of England.

7.

Now think about what project you could present in the ESB exam. What would interest your audience? Plan an outline for your talk. Look at Chapter 7 for advice about illustration of your project. What illustrations would you use?

D. TUTOR'S NOTES AND ANSWERS

As suggested at the beginning of section C, it is a good idea to read the notes which introduce each answer before you try to answer the question yourself.

1.

The first question an FCE examiner will ask you about any reading text will probably be "Where do you think this text comes from?" Could you answer that question for each of these three passages? What sort of mood do you think is appropriate for the speaker of thesc texts? Imagine yourself in that mood, take a deep breath and begin.

The first text (a) is from an advertisement for some computer software. The tone to read it in would be enthusiastic.

The second text (b) is from a book of advice about how to behave. The letter-writer is exasperated. The answer is slightly ironic.

The third text (c) is from a novel. Percy is anxious.

Record your voice, if possible, when reading these texts. Try to judge your recording yourself – or ask a teacher or a friend. Is your reading clear? Have you conveyed the necessary mood?

2. and 3.

You have two minutes to prepare these texts. You will read them best if you understand more or less what they are about. So, the most important thing is to read the whole text through for its gist. As you do so mark any words which you think need a particular emphasis because of the meaning of the text. If you have extra time:

(a) work out how to pronounce any numbers;
(b) decide whether any tag questions should be pronounced with a rise or a fall. (It'll be a rise if it's a real open question but a fall if the speaker is just expecting the other person to agree with him.)

The person marking your text will not be correcting every single word or phrase, s/he will be listening for about twenty different points. You can't know exactly what these are but you can be fairly sure that numbers and intonation of tag questions will be individually marked.

When you have prepared your reading, record yourself on tape if possible.

Answers

2.

When the examiner marks your tape s/he will be looking at a sheet like this:

1. Sorry to disturb you at this time of night   rhythm and catenations
2. a home computer   pronunciation and stress
3. months   pronunciation
4. haven't you   fall
5. already got one   stress (on got)
6. have you?   rise
7. 16 K ROM (R-O-M or Rom)   pronunciation
8. That's R-O-M   stress on O
9. And listen to this from the leaflet   weak forms of 'to' and 'from'
10. 320×200 pronunciation of numbers (three hundred and twenty, two hundred); pronunciation of $\times$ (by or times)
11. addressable   pronunciation
12. pixels   spelling out
13. generating   pronunciation
14. You can   stress on 'can'
15. although it usually costs at least   catenations
16. £168 in the shops   pronunciation of figure (a hundred and sixty-eight pounds); rhythm and intonation
17. £128   contrastive stress on twenty
18. There's nothing fishy about it at all!   rhythm and catenations
19. consultant   pronunciation
20. who are staying at the Albany   rhythm and catenations (ignore pronunciation of Albany)
21. . . . are you interested, or not?   rise, then fall
22. 338 0980   phrasing and pronunciation (double three eight, oh nine eight oh)
23. Impression mark 0–8

In the impression mark you will not lose points for having a foreign accent as long as what you say has natural English phrasing and intonation and can be easily understood.

Catenation means not pronouncing the words separately but linking them together in naturally connected phrases.

If you are unsure about the pronunciation of any of the words noted above, check in your dictionary for the correct way to say them – make sure you notice where the stress is as well as seeing how the syllables are pronounced.

Ask a teacher, if you can, to listen to your recording or to listen to you speaking the dialogue. Ask them to be critical – particularly about the points listed above. If you have no convenient teacher, try to listen to yourself critically.

3.

These are the points listed in the examiner's key for this dialogue.

1. I'll never forget it   rhythm
2. sending it off to the maker's   rhythm
3. had a diagram in it   unstressed 'it'
4. Hang on a second, will you?   catenations; rise
5. I thought they'd be here   stress on thought
6. What was it you wanted to know?   rhythm; catenations
7. crushed newspaper . . . cardboard   list intonation
8. sawdust   pronunciation and one stress (on saw)
9. I'll dictate them, shall I?   rise
10. Pack wrapped items   separate stresses
11. items   pronunciation
12. cushioning   pronunciation
13. a good quality adhesive tape   rhythm
14. adhesive   pronunciation
15. recommended that the tape   unstressed 'tape'
16. 1½"   pronunciation (one and a half inches)
17. And I'd strongly advise you to   rhythm and catenations
18. That's in the other leaflet   stress on 'other'
19. registered   pronunciation
20. £750   pronunciation (Seven hundred and fifty pounds)
21. That's not bad, is it?   fall
22. Overall impression 0–8 marks

Follow the same procedure as that suggested for the previous question.

4.

The two most important criteria in choosing your passage are:
(a) Will it interest your audience?
(b) Do you enjoy it yourself?

If it interests your audience, you will sense it and it will encourage you to read well. If you like it yourself you are more likely to read it well.

What kind of thing then would interest your audience? Something that is complete in itself – a short story, for example, or a newspaper article.

It is probably easier to read something well if it has a dramatic story content rather than being very descriptive. You can choose to read a poem but poetry reading is quite a specific skill. Do it only if you love poetry and feel that you can read it clearly and well.

Now, do you feel you can select something good?

Practise your reading plenty of times so that you know the passage very well. Work out where the natural places to take a breath are and mark them if you like. If possible ask an English person to record the passage for you and listen to this recording as often as possible so that the pronunciation becomes second nature for you.

When you read it to your audience, try not to have your head in your copy all the time. Look up at your audience as much as possible. It will then be much easier for them to follow you and to find you interesting.

It is not, of course, possible to give a 'tutor's answer' for this question.

5.

Don't spend too long selecting your topic. Choose one that you feel you can speak happily on for two minutes and then start thinking about what you are going to say.

Note down headings for your talk and make sure these are in a logical order.

When you give your talk, expand your headings. Explain what you mean. Give examples.

I choose the third topic and my headings are the following:

- Modification of statement
- Benefits to young
- Benefits to society
- Conclusion

Answer

Every young person should do one year's voluntary social work.

This statement is a little extreme. I do not think that it should be compulsory for every young person to do a year's voluntary social work. However, both society and the young person could get a lot of benefit from this. Moreover, I think it would be a lot more useful for both society and the individual than compulsory military service which many young men have to do for a year.

Young people would benefit because it would give them broader experience of life. It could help them to decide what kind of work they wish to do in the future. It would give them an awareness of social problems. It should teach them some useful practical skills. It would help them in their relationships with other people too. In short, it should help them to become mature.

Society would benefit because many useful jobs could be done very cheaply by these young people. Parks could be made more beautiful. Schools and hospitals could have extra auxiliary staff. Old people could be helped. All sorts of services, that are otherwise too expensive, could be provided. Surely all these things are more useful than teaching people how to kill and how to fear other countries.

Yet, I think anything that is compulsory can quickly start to have a negative effect. Most people do not like being forced to behave in a particular way and so many of the advantages of the idea might be lost. Why not just encourage young people to do a year of voluntary social work if it appeals to them?

6.

Again don't spend too long choosing your topic. Choose the one that seems easiest to you. Notice that these topics mostly relate to aspects of British life. Don't forget that you need to know about British life and institutions for this exam. You can only use headings when giving your talk. Here are my headings for the London talk. Could you talk for three minutes using these headings? How would you approach the subject yourself?

- Johnson quote
- Bus tour
- Art gallery
- Theatre + meal
- Walk
- Hydrofoil
- Parliament
- Hyde Park Corner
- Serpentine
- Shopping
- Other things – conclusion

Answer

A plan for making the best of a first short visit to London.

Samuel Johnson said that the person who is tired of London is tired of life. London is so big and so varied that you can spend years there and still find things that are new and exciting.

It is a problem if you are going there for only a short time? How can you get a feeling of London in just a few days? On your first morning I would suggest going on a bus tour round the city. This would show you all the main sights of the city and give you some idea of where you might like to return to. The tour also gives you a feel of the layout of the city.

Spend the afternoon in an art gallery. Go to the Tate if you like modern painting and sculpture or to the National Gallery if you prefer classical art. Buy a magazine called *Time Out*. This lists everything that is on in London that week. You may find that there is a special art exhibition on somewhere that is particularly interesting for you.

London is famous for its theatre. Use *Time Out* again to help you to choose a show that appeals to you. Many of the theatres are near Soho. Why not go there for a meal after the performance. You will find lots of good Italian, Indian and Chinese restaurants there.

Spend the next morning just walking around getting the feel of London. I suggest starting from St Paul's and walking down Fleet Street, the lively centre of the newspaper industry. Go also into the Inns of Court. They are a complete contrast to the noise of Fleet Street. They are quiet and peaceful courtyards. Have lunch in one of the interesting old pubs in Fleet Street.

In the afternoon take a hydrofoil down the river to the Tower of London. There are lots of interesting things to see there including the Crown Jewels. The hydrofoil will take you back to Westminster and then I suggest trying to get into the House of Commons to listen to a debate. It's cheaper than going to the theatre and it can be just as entertaining.

If you're in London on a Sunday, you mustn't miss Speakers' Corner. This is a corner of Hyde Park where anybody who wants to say something to an audience can get up on a soap-box and say it. You can hear people talking about all sorts of things – politics, religion, social problems – or just making jokes. If it's a nice day perhaps you might also take a boat out on the Serpentine, a little lake in the middle of Hyde Park. If you don't feel all that energetic, just have a picnic beside the lake and watch the other people boating.

You're sure to want to spend some time shopping. Harrod's is very famous and it's interesting to have a look at but it's terribly expensive. Unless you're very rich you may find it more sensible to do your shopping in more humble places. Oxford Street is generally thought of as one of the best shopping streets in London.

There are lots of other things to do in London. There are dozens of beautiful parks. There are masses of museums of all kinds. There are all sorts of entertainments available. There are all kinds of interesting places to explore. I have just suggested a few places for a first short visit but I am sure you will want to return later and to see more another time.

7.

You will not find a 'tutor's answer' to this question but here are a few ideas for you to consider when planning your ESB project. The most important thing is that you should present a project on something that you know a lot about and are enthusiastic about. In this way you should be able to make your project interesting for your audience. What do you know about? How do you spend your free time? What makes you feel excited? Something that makes you feel angry would also be a suitable topic.

Here are some specific ideas:

- A favourite writer or musician
- Your home town or any place you love
- A favourite sport
- Your hobby
- A social issue

When you have chosen your topic plan your presentation carefully. Work out your headings. Try to have five or six of these and make sure you can expand each of them fully. Try to have one visual aid for each heading and make sure that you will really use the visual aid.

Give your talk to a friend. Ask them to tell you if anything isn't clear. Also ask your friend to tell you honestly what was interesting and what was not interesting. Change what you say according to your friend's advice.

E. BEYOND THE COURSEWORK

You can buy cassettes and records of good actors reading short stories, poems and plays in English. Just listening to these can give you a feel for the sounds and patterns of the language when it is read well.

Try to get a cassette with a good native speaker on it reading a text of which you have a copy. Try not only to listen but also to speak with the speaker. You can only do this if you:

(a) take breaths in the natural English places;
(b) group words in the correct way and only stress the important words;
(c) make your voice go up and down as the speaker's does.

Practising doing this should help you develop natural English rhythms of your own.

Chapter 7

Describing pictures and diagrams

A. GETTING STARTED

There are a number of different things which you may be asked to do with pictures and diagrams in EFL exams.

In the **FCE** you will have to look at a picture in the oral exam. Then you will have a conversation with the examiner about the picture; first you will have to describe what you see and then the conversation will move to a topic relating to the picture. If, for example, the picture shows a family watching television you may have to talk about your own favourite television programmes.

In the **ARELS Higher Certificate** you have to look at a series of pictures which illustrate a story. Then you have two minutes to tell the story shown in the pictures.

In the **Oxford Higher** exam, pictures are used in different ways. You may, for instance, have to match pictures with the pieces of text which relate to them or you may have to label a diagram using information given in a piece of text.

In the **RSA CUEFL** exam, advertisements and maps are often used as the basis of written work.

In the **JMB** exam you often have to label diagrams from a text which you may have to read or listen to; you also have to describe a process that is illustrated by a picture; you also have to be able to describe pictures that are similar, categorising the differences between them.

The **British Council English Language Testing Service** also occasionally makes use of pictures. You may, for example, be asked to match pictures with text.

In the **ESB** exam, you have to present a project of your choice to the examiners. It is a good idea to illustrate your project and to make use of the illustrations when talking about your project.

In exams, then, you may have to talk about pictures or you may have to write about pictures. Or you may have to understand when other people talk or write about pictures so that you can mark a picture accordingly. This chapter deals with three of the four skills – speaking, writing and reading – and the way that they can relate in EFL exams to pictures and diagrams.

B. ESSENTIAL PRINCIPLES

It is very important here to be able to understand and to use prepositions of place and expressions which describe where things are. Do you know the meanings of all the prepositions or phrases of place below?

> opposite
> near (to)
> beside
> next to
> on or to the left
> on or to the right
> on or to the left-hand side
> on or to the right-hand side
> on top of
> under
> above
> in the corner
> in the middle
> between
> about a metre from
> in front of
> at one end
> at the other end

Let me describe where I am working now. Try to **draw** the room from my description. I am sitting at a table in a square room with my back to the door. In front of me and about a metre from the end of my table is the door of a wall cupboard. To the left of the cupboard is an open fireplace. There is an armchair in front of the fireplace. Opposite me on the wall to my left there is a window. There is a bed along the fourth wall on my left with its head along the wall with the window. There is a standard lamp beside the bed. There is a small table in the middle of the room with a radio on it. Between me and this small table there are a lot of papers on the floor.

Check your drawing with the one you will find at the end of this section.

Wall
cupboard

Fireplace

Arm chair

Window

Table

Table

Papers
on floor
Radio

Me

Bed

Door

My Room

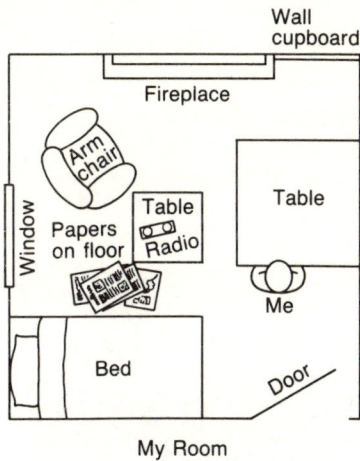

I wonder where **you** are reading this chapter? Look around you and try to describe where you are, if possible using all the words listed above. If you need any other place expressions use your teacher or your dictionary to find out what they are.

Now choose a picture and try to describe it. Many of the prepositions and phrases listed earlier will be useful but you may also need:

- in the foreground
- in the background
- in the distance
- in the top right-hand corner
- in the bottom left-hand corner

These are some general points useful for **all** exams but you will find a lot more advice specific to the types of questions used in your exam in section D.

C. EXAM QUESTIONS

This section is divided into four parts: talking about pictures (qs 1–3), writing about pictures (qs 4–5) and reading about pictures (qs 6–7). In many ways the questions are good practice for you all but these are the ones you should pay particular attention to if you are taking one of the exams listed in section A. First try the questions relevant to you, then try the others.

FCE	qs 1–2
ARELS	qs 1–2
OXFORD	qs 4–7
RSA CUEFL	qs 6–7
JMB	qs 4–7
ESB	qs 1–3
BRITISH COUNCIL ELTS	qs 4–7

Although the questions suggested above sometimes include questions that are a little different in type from those used by the exam named, they are all practising language in a way that will help you prepare for that exam.

1.

This is a question of the type used in the FCE. Look at the picture and answer the questions underneath.

What can you see?
What do you think the people are doing?
Have you any idea where these people are?
How do you feel about queues?
Have you ever belonged to any children's organisation?

2.

This is a set of pictures which has been used in a previous ARELS Certificate exam. You have two minutes to look at the pictures and to think about how you are going to tell the story. The story shows how John saw someone snatch a woman's handbag at a market one day. Begin your story. "One day John was doing some shopping at the market when . . ."

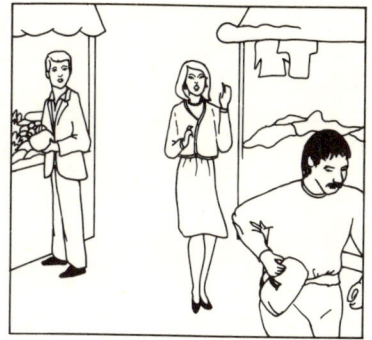

3.

Here we are just going to ask you to think about the visual part of the project you need to do for the ESB exam. Chapter 4 dealt with other aspects of preparing a talk – and you should find that Chapters 13 and 14 also help you with useful language for your talk.

Here you can imagine that you are going to present projects on these three subjects:

- your favourite sport
- your favourite writer
- a town or country

Decide on a set of visual aids which would help you give a good presentation. How would you relate them to your talk? Remember that you have to use time well – there are three intermediate stages of the ESB exam and you have three minutes for your presentation at Stage One, four minutes at Stage Two and five minutes at Stage Three.

4.

This is a question of the type used in the JMB exam. Here you have a diagram of a modern language school. Write a detailed description of it for an English friend who is an architect. Use only the information that you can see in the plan. Write about a page.

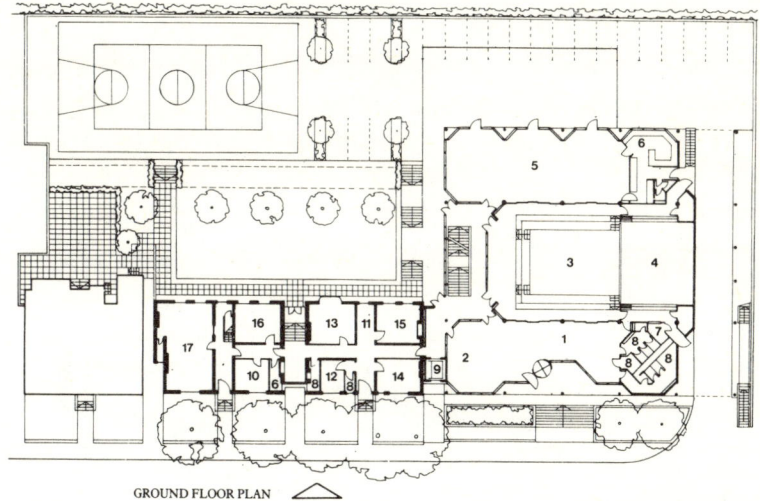

GROUND FLOOR PLAN

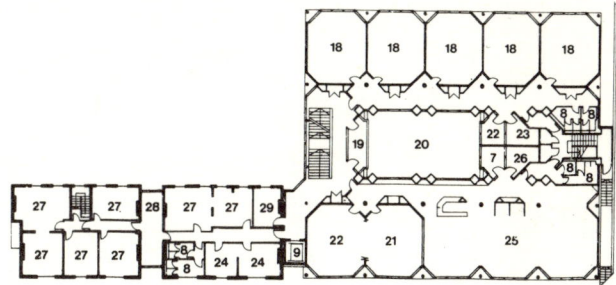

FIRST FLOOR PLAN

1 entrance	11 photocopying	21 language laboratory
2 reception	12 sick room	22 computer studies room
3 hall	13 principal	23 teacher
4 lecture room	14 accommodation secretary	24 teacher resources
5 dining area	15 principal's secretary	25 multi-media study centre
6 kitchen	16 travel secretary	26 librarian
7 projection room	17 meeting room	27 staff room
8 wc	18 class room	28 lockers
9 lift	19 balcony	29 video
10 store	20 void	

5.

It is useful for 'real life' as well as for exams like the JMB and the British Council ELTS to be able to interpret diagrams. Look back at Table 1.1 in Chapter 1 and write about 200 words explaining what it shows.

6.

These next two questions use pictures to check that you have understood the reading text. This example comes from the Oxford Higher exam of May 1983.

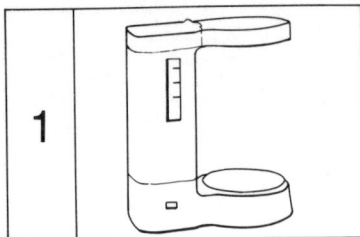

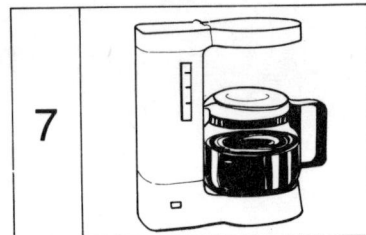

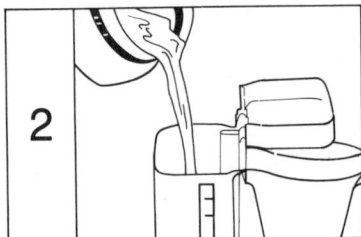

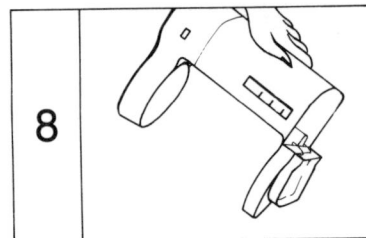

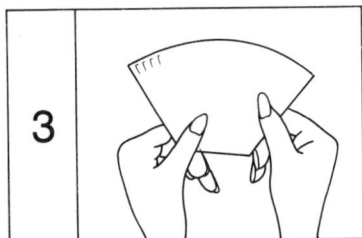

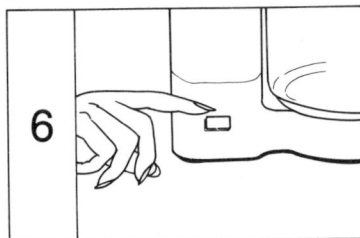

(a) Measure in the required amount of finely ground coffee – one measuring spoon (approx. 6g.) per cup. More will be required if you use regular or drip grind coffee. Tea brewing instructions. Measure in your favourite loose tea – one heaped measuring spoon for 4 cups. Shake filter top gently to settle tea leaves before inserting filter top into the unit.

(b) Fold over the bottom seam of a filter bag and place in the filter top.

(c) Enjoy your coffee. The hot plate will remain on until you turn the switch off.
Please do not keep coffee hot for too long. For optimum flavour and aroma, it should be consumed as soon as possible after making.

(d) Slide the filter top into position. Place the heat resistant glass jug with lid on hot plate.

(e) If you do not intend to use the coffeemaker for some time, remove the electric plug from the socket and drain out any remaining water by tilting the unit.

(f) Pour the required amount of water into the water tank by using the level indicator on the coffeemaker.

(g) Before using your coffeemaker for the first time, wash the filter top and glass jug. Then pour cold water into the water tank, place the heat-resistant glass jug on the hot plate and switch the coffeemaker on. This ensures that any dust inside the coffeemaker is filtered away, and you can get perfect coffee from the very first drop.

(h) Turn on the switch. The pilot lamp will light up and your coffee is ready in a few minutes.
If another jug of coffee is desired turn the switch off and wait 10 minutes between brews.
Otherwise the second jug may take several minutes longer.

(a) The eight pictures are in the correct sequence and they show how to use a coffee-maker. The instructions, **not** in their correct sequence, are given below the pictures. Write beside each instruction the number of the picture it applies to.

(b) Now, using the information given in the instructions opposite, answer these questions.

(i) What part of the machine shows you how much water to put in the coffee machine?

(ii) You should wait ten minutes before drinking the coffee. True or false?

(iii) You cannot use drip grind coffee in this machine. True or false?

(iv) The pivot lamp tells you the coffee is ready. True or false?

(v) It is necessary to empty the machine if you use if often. True or false?

(c) Using the information and the pictures write the names of the parts of the coffee machine on the diagram alongside. One has been written in for you.

7.

This is a question of the type used in the JMB exam. The following words are used to describe certain parts of the Soviet education system. Read the definitions and label the parts numbered in the diagram with the letters **a** to **h**. Write X if there is no suitable definition.

a – **vuz** – higher educational establishment: students go there for 5 years after general school or after ptu or sptu

b – **sptu** – technical college for students who have not completed ten years at the general school; they can complete their secondary education there as well as learn a trade

c – **ptu** – technical college offering one-year courses for students who have already completed ten-year secondary education

d – **yasli** – creches for the very youngest children

e – **special schools** – schools for the specially talented; secondary schools attended by a minority of Soviet children

f – **detskie sady** – pre-school institutions for children from three years old

g – **aspirantura** – post-graduate facilities, the highest level of education

h – **nepolnoe srednee obrazovanie** – secondary schools which do not offer the last two years of the compulsory course

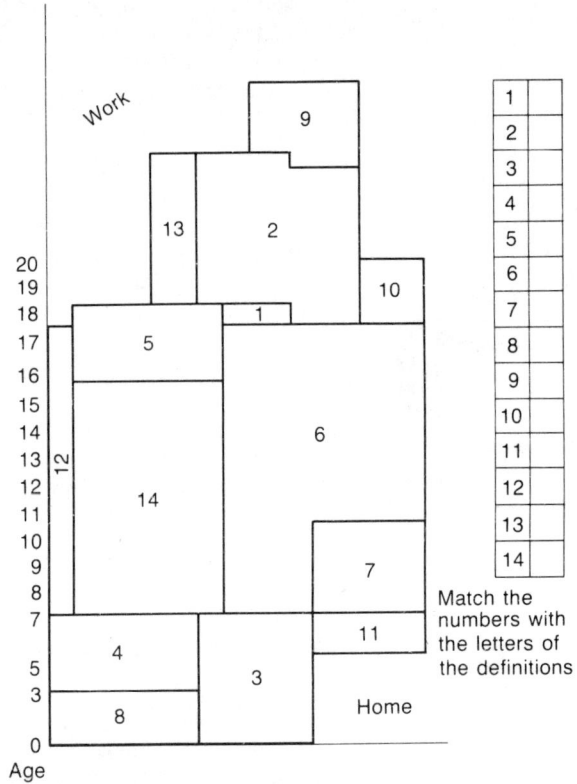

Work

20
19
18
17
16
15
14
13
12
11
10
9
8
7

5
3

0

Age

9
13   2
10
1
5
6
12
14
7
11
4
3
8

Home

1	
2	
3	
4	
5	
6	
7	
8	
9	
10	
11	
12	
13	
14	

Match the
numbers with
the letters of
the definitions

D. TUTOR'S NOTES AND ANSWERS

Read the notes introducing each answer before you prepare your own answers. Then compare your own work with the answers suggested. Do the suggestions give you any ideas for modifying your own work. If so, prepare an improved answer of your own.

1.

The pictures used by the FCE exam are often not very clear and so you will probably find it useful to know language like this:

> The picture isn't very clear but I think the person on the left is probably a tramp.
> The object on the right might be a briefcase.
> I think the people could be kicking a ball.
> I can't quite make the picture out but I think the child is probably holding a kitten.
> It looks as if the woman is carrying something heavy.
> The building in the background looks like some kind of palace.

I think they must have just missed a bus or something like that.
I would guess that she's English.
Judging by the puddles, I would say that there must have just been
heavy rain.

The examiner is more interested in your English than in your
ability to distinguish pictures and so do not worry if you are not sure
what the picture shows. Just make a guess – and do so as fully as
possible.

Remember to use the present continuous when describing what
you can see in the picture. It is as if a picture captures one moment of
time and so the natural tense to use is the present continuous.

When the conversation moves away from the picture to a related
topic, again remember to speak as much as possible. The oral exam is
short and so don't waste time in silence. The examiner will be grateful if
you talk without him/her having to make efforts to draw you out.

You could answer the examiner's questions like this.

What can you see?
I can see a large open space with a building in the background. In front
of the building, there's a high wall with a tower. It isn't very clear but
there seem to be trees in front of the wall and it looks as if there are a lot
of people standing in front of the trees. In the foreground there are a
few children looking across the space to the wall and the people.
They're wearing shirts and caps and the tallest of the children, the one
on the left, is wearing a scarf round his neck.

What do you think the people are doing?
I have really no idea but perhaps the people in the background could be
standing in a queue. The building behind the wall looks large and
important – perhaps it's a museum and the people are waiting for it to
open. The children at the front look as if they're wearing some kind of
uniform. They could belong to some kind of children's organisation.

Have you any idea where these people are?
I'm afraid I don't know where it is although it looks a bit familiar. It
must be somewhere quite hot, judging by the way the children are
dressed. And the building in the background looks important, as I said,
so I would guess it's a capital city somewhere.

How do you feel about queues?
I hate standing in queues. If there's a queue at our local shop I always
prefer to go away and come back later. But I know that English people
like queues and I suppose that they are a good idea at bus stops in the rush
hour. It must make things easier for old people.

Have you ever belonged to any children's organisation?
No, never. When I was about seven I very much wanted to join our local
children's group but my father wasn't keen. I was terribly disappointed
and I can still remember crying my eyes out. Lots of my friends had joined
and were going off to summer camp. When I was older and my father was
prepared to let me join, I had lost interest and no longer wanted to.

The candidate above would have got very good marks even though he or she didn't know very much about what the picture showed and had never been a member of a children's organisation.

Did you recognise the scene in the photograph? It shows Red Square in Moscow with the Kremlin in the background. The people are queuing to go into the low building in front of the wall which is the Mausoleum where Lenin, the leader of the Russian Revolution, lies.

2.

The ARELS picture stories give you the beginning of the story and tell you which tense to use. The tense will almost always be the past as this is the most natural tense to use when telling a story.

Two minutes is not a long time but you will have to tell the story quite fully or you will come to the end too early. When you are practising for the exam, practise looking at your watch and speaking for two minutes so that you get some idea of how much you need to say. It is a good idea to take your watch into the exam with you and to look at it as you start to tell the story. If you are able to do this, you will find it helps you to balance the story well. (You will find that your watch will also come in handy in section 6 of the ARELS exam.) You will not lose marks if you have not finished the story when the time is up but it is not a good idea either to be at the very first part still or to have finished too early.

You will get marks for three things:

1. pronunciation, stress, rhythm and intonation;
2. appropriate and varied use of vocabulary and dialogue;
3. appropriate and varied use of structure.

Fill the time and gain marks by remembering to introduce dialogue into the story where possible. You will also gain marks by remembering to use expressions like 'First . . .' 'Then . . .', 'In the end . . .' Give variety of structure by saying 'When he had done that, he . . .' or 'While he was doing that, she was doing . . .'

Don't be afraid to use your imagination and to add details to the story that can't be seen from the pictures.

Suggested answer

It takes me about two minutes to tell the story like this:

One day John was doing some shopping in the market when he noticed a beautiful young woman there. She was very smartly dressed and he watched her as she walked from stall to stall looking at the fruit and vegetables which were for sale. The market was very crowded but this woman was so elegant that she stood out in the crowd. "She looks like a film star," thought John to himself. Suddenly a thief ran through the crowd and snatched the woman's handbag. She screamed but the man disappeared with the bag before anyone could stop him. John wanted to help the beautiful young woman and so he ran as quickly as he could to the nearest phone box. Thank goodness, it was free! Then he dialled 999. "Please, come to the Market Square at once," he asked the police. "A thief has run off with a lady's handbag." John then returned to the market to try to calm the young woman. He had only just got back when the police arrived. However, the thief had also already returned and was quietly chatting to the young woman. They explained to John and the police that they were only making a film and they pointed to the cameras which John hadn't noticed before. There were cameras on the roofs of several buildings round the Market Square and all the cameramen were looking at John and laughing. Everyone – even the policemen – thought it was very funny except for John who felt dreadfully embarrassed. "That's the last time I try to help women who look like film stars," he thought and he walked away, blushing.

3.

In the ESB exam pictures will help you to present a project that is much more interesting for the examiners and much less nerve-racking for you. Some of this language should be useful for you:

This picture shows . . .
Here you can see . . .
This is an illustration of . . .
This is a typical example of . . .
This diagram represents . . .
This table shows the trend towards . . .
As you can see here . . .

Choose visuals which illustrate your talk clearly and can be easily seen by the examiners. You will not be able to hand your visual aids to the examiners during the presentation as this distracts their attention. Don't forget to refer to them fully. It is better to have three or four really good ones and to use them well than to have a lot more but not to deal with them properly.

Suggestions

If I were going to talk about a sport I would have a clear picture of someone dressed to play this sport and I would also bring in any necessary equipment, for example a tennis racquet or ball. Then I would have a diagram of the place where it is played, for example, the tennis court. Then I would have a chart illustrating the scoring system. Next I would have a picture of a famous person or team playing the sport. The plan of my talk would thus be:

1. Introduction – briefly what my favourite sport is and why I like it.
2. What you need to play this sport.
3. How to play it.
4. Great players and what makes them special.
5. Conclusion.

In talking about my favourite writer I would bring in:

- a large portrait of him
- a chart showing the major events of his life – including the main things he wrote
- a photograph of him and his family or of the place where he lived

- an illustration from one of his books or a still from a film of one of his books

The plan for my talk would be:

1. Introduction – my favourite writer, who he is, what his face reveals about him.
2. A brief description of his life showing how aspects of his biography relate to his writing (e.g. the influence of his wife or of the surroundings he lived in).
3. My own favourite work of his and why I like it so much.
4. Conclusion.

For a talk on a town or a country I would have:

- a map
- one or two photos clearly showing famous sights in this place
- a picture showing a typical person from this place
- two or three objects that are typical products of or souvenirs from this place

The plan for my talk would thus be:

1. Introduction – what I am going to talk about and where it is (the map will be useful here and throughout the talk).
2. What you can see here.
3. What the people are like and how they live.
4. What this country produces and/or what the tourist can buy there.
5. Conclusion.

In all these talks the visuals are spread throughout the presentation in a balanced way. They are varied in type and they can be produced so that they can be easily seen.

4.

Spend plenty of time looking at the plans and making sure that you understand exactly what they show.

Organise your answer systematically. Decide where you are going to begin your description – the entrance hall would be a logical place to start and take it from there. Don't forget to divide your writing into paragraphs. One paragraph per corridor would be a convenient way to organise your description.

One page is only about 250 words at most and so you will not have space to describe everything that is shown in the plan. Choose what is most important. Clearly the classrooms are more important than the sick room, for example.

Suggested answer

You come into the school up a flight of steps and you find yourself at first in a large reception area. Straight ahead of you there is a big central hall with a lecture hall on the right. There is a large dining area on the other side of the hall with doors opening out into the garden.

To the left of the reception area there is a door into the wing of the building where you will find most of the administrative offices. The accommodation and travel secretaries, for example, have their offices off this corridor. At the end of this corridor there is a large meeting room. The rooms on the right-hand side of this corridor look out over a garden and, beyond that, a volleyball court.

Next to the meeting room there is a flight of stairs which leads up to the first floor. On the corridor above the administrative offices you find a number of rooms for teachers. In this part of the school there is also space for teachers' resources.

Leaving this part of the school and returning to the body of the school, you find that there is a corridor of five identical octagonal classrooms on the side of the building above the canteen.

On the other side of the school, above the entrance hall, there is a multi-media study centre which is the size of three of the classrooms. Next to this study centre, there is a language laboratory and a computer studies room.

5.

The difficult thing about doing a good answer here is that you have not very many words with which to summarise a lot of information. Spend plenty of time looking at the diagram and making sure that everything is clear in your own mind. Then ask yourself what the most important information is which you have to get across.

Organise your information into a logical sequence. It is probably a good idea to start from a general description of what the table shows and to go from there to more specific information. Remember to organise your information into logical paragraphs.

Be careful to keep to information that you can gain from the table and not to add anything that you know from your own experience.

Suggested answer

Table 1.1 shows the exams that are available for testing knowledge of English as a Foreign Language. It considers only general English exams and does not look at specialist exams in, for example, commercial or medical English. It compares the general exams by level, showing which are elementary, which are intermediate and which are advanced.

There are twelve different boards organising examinations in English as a Foreign Language. Some of them offer exams at all levels and some only deal with one level. The University of Cambridge, for example, has four different levels of exam whereas The Associated Examinations Board has only an advanced exam.

Boards that cater for the full range of ability do so through a varying number of tests. The Trinity College Spoken exam can be taken at twelve different levels, for instance, while the British Council and TOEFL exams cover all levels with one exam.

Table 1.1 also indicates which exams are covered by this book. Twelve exams are indicated and they are all more or less at an intermediate level although the ARELS Higher Certificate, the Oxford Higher and the JMB seem to be rather harder than some of the other intermediate exams, like the ESB Intermediate Grades.

6.

Read the instructions carefully before you start to number them. Look up anything that isn't clear in your dictionary but do not waste unnecessary time on this. Only look up those things which are really important for answering the question. The most important words are the verbs. Most of the nouns describing the different parts of the machine should be clear from looking at the picture as long as you understand the verbs.

Answers

(a) Matching pictures and text.
1 (g); 2 (f); 3 (b); 4 (a); 5 (d); 6 (h); 7 (c); 8 (e).
(b) (i) the level indicator; (ii) false; (iii) false; (iv) false; (v) false.
(c) 1. level indicator; 2. switch; 3. filter top; 4. glass jug; 5. hot plate.

7.

It is worth spending time looking at the diagram to make sure that you understand what it shows before you start to read the definitions. It should then be much easier to pick out the important parts of the definitions. Mark first the ones you are sure about. At least that will narrow the choice left for those that you find very difficult.

Answers

a:2; **b:**5; **c:**1; **d:**8; **e:**12; **f:**4; **g:**9; **h:**14.

E. BEYOND THE COURSEWORK

When you read a newspaper look at any information which is given in pictures or table form. Compare what you see with what is written in the text. How does a journalist refer to figures which are shown in a table? What do captions under photos say? Notice the kind of language that is used as you may find it useful for answering this kind of question.

If you like looking at more beautiful pictures, you might find it interesting to look at a book in English about your favourite painter or sculptor and to think about the kind of language that is used there to describe art. Many art galleries publish books about art that are in three or four languages. Perhaps you can find such a book that is in both your own language and English.

Scientific textbooks often use English in this way. Do you specialise in any particular technical or scientific subject? If you do, find a textbook on your specialism in English. Pick out the language that is used there to describe diagrams and tables. If the textbook is about your special area, it should be relatively easy for you to understand what is being said and so you can focus on how it is said.

A good way to practise describing pictures yourself is to work with a friend. Draw a picture each without letting the other see what you have drawn. Then in turn describe your picture while the other person tries to draw it. At the end, compare drawings and think about how you could have improved your description so that your partner could have drawn a more similar picture to yours.

Chapter 8

Role play and social situations

A. GETTING STARTED

This chapter deals with a common element of oral exams in EFL. In many exams you are asked what you would say in English if you were in a given situation. For example, you might be asked, 'You have just arrived at London Airport and want to find out about cheap hotels. You go to the Tourist Information Counter. What do you say?'

In the **FCE** this is one possibility for the third part of the oral test (coming after the picture-based conversation and the text for reading aloud). In the **ARELS** exam the second of the six sections asks you to say what you would say in twenty different situations. The whole of the **RSA CUEFL** Oral examination is role play. There is no spoken part of the **TOEFL** exam but some of the multiple choice questions test social situation responses. The same kind of multiple choice question may also be found in the British Council **ELTS** Test. Trinity College tests your ability to say the right thing in a given situation by asking you to complete a passage of dialogue in which one part has been left blank. The **English Speaking Board Oral** exam also asks you to act out social situations.

This chapter deals with these questions from an oral point of view. The practice done will also be useful for the exams which test your ability to give the right response in a social situation through multiple-choice questions.

B. ESSENTIAL PRINCIPLES

The most important thing about this kind of test is to use your imagination and really to try to put yourself in the situations given. You will then find it much easier to give a natural answer and to get good marks. You mustn't say, "If I were in this position, I'd ask where the cheapest hotels are"; you should say something like, "Excuse me, can you give me any advice about where I might find a hotel that isn't too expensive?" Don't be shy. Act.

In all these intermediate social situations and role plays the examiner wants to see whether you can communicate satisfactorily in English. In other words, it is not so important to be totally grammatically correct as it is to speak in a way that is **socially appropriate** for a particular situation.

An important aspect of this is always to be **polite** – especially when you are talking to anyone who is not a close friend. When you are speaking to a stranger, begin with 'Excuse me'. Don't forget 'please' and 'thank you', 'would you mind' and 'could you possibly'. It may sound exaggerated and insincere to you but it will sound polite and friendly to a native English speaker. It isn't possible to be too polite but it is very easy to be rude.

Another aspect of being polite is to give a **reason** why you can't do something when you are refusing an invitation or a request. This is necessary if you want to be polite in English – and it is more important in this kind of situation to be polite rather than to be truthful.

The **way in which you speak** is important in all oral exams. Remember to give a full answer. If you don't say much, you are making it much more difficult for the examiner and he cannot give you any marks for silence. Don't speak too fast – this will make it harder for you to be understood.

C. EXAM QUESTIONS

It is a good idea to approach the questions in this chapter in the following way:

(a) Read the question.
(b) Look at the notes relating to it in section D.
(c) Answer the question, recording your voice if possible.
(d) Compare your answer with those given in section D, remembering that the tutor's answers here are only a suggestion and there are often other possibilities which are just as appropriate.

1.
These are the twenty social situations which were used in the ARELS Higher Certificate exam AH35.

First you will hear six remarks which might be made to you when you are using your English. Some are questions and some are comments. After each one reply in a natural way. (The first one or two situations are done for you in the actual exam to make it absolutely clear what you are expected to do.)

(a) Do you mind if I use your phone?
(b) Sorry I can't shake hands. I've hurt my hand.
(c) About that 50 pounds you lent me last week. Here's thirty of it back.
(d) Do be careful if you're going upstairs.
(e) You know that girl over there, don't you? Do you think you might introduce me?

(f)   Well, what sort of place would you like for a summer holiday?

Now you will hear fourteen situations in which you might find yourself. Say what it seems natural to say in each situation.

(g)   You've just heard that John has lost his job. What do you say to him?

(h)   You're giving a party. You've just noticed that one of your guests is standing all alone looking rather lost. What do you say to him?

(i)   You see a young boy taking photographs outside Buckingham Palace, but he's forgotten to take the cap off the lens of his camera. What do you say?

(j)   Walking home one evening you see a woman trying to push her car off the road. What do you say?

(k)   An English friend tells you that her son has just been accepted for Cambridge University. What do you say?

(l)   You see a friend who never has much money getting out of a chauffeur-driven Rolls Royce. What do you say to him?

(m)   An old friend, Mary Brown, is in hospital after an operation. You ring the hospital to find out where she is and when you can visit her. What do you say?

(n)   You see something in the window of an antique shop. You would like to buy it but you don't know what it's called in English. What do you say?

(o)   Your neighbour has just come back from a holiday abroad. He now has his leg in plaster. What do you say?

(p)   Your car breaks down on a country road. You walk to a nearby house. What do you say to the woman who comes to the door?

(q)   Some friends have asked you to babysit for them. Their children are not very well-behaved. Say no, but nicely.

(r)   You are watching television with some friends. You go to the kitchen to make coffee for them. When you come back, they've changed over from the programme you wanted to see. What do you say?

(s)   You know your neighbours are on holiday. In the middle of the night, you hear noises coming from their house. You ring the police. What do you say?

(t)   You're in a plane sitting in a NO SMOKING area. The man in front of you lights a cigarette. What do you say?

2.
This is the RSA CUEFL Oral exam of June 1984.

Part I

You must talk with a teacher for about five minutes.

While you are talking, an Assessor will be listening to what you and the teacher say.

You have made an application for a grant/scholarship to continue your English studies and you have been invited to attend an interview.

In a few minutes your teacher will talk to you about your application and help you to prepare for your interview.

Part II/III	For Part II of the examination you must do this task on this sheet with a fellow-student. When you have completed the task, a teacher will come into the room. You must explain to him/her what you have discussed in your task and what you have decided to do. This is part III of the test.
Task	At your school or college/ your work place/ local club there is a social programme three evenings a week. You have been asked to make some suggestions for activities.

In a moment, the Examiner will give you a list of five activities but if you wish you may make other suggestions. Discuss each of the activities with your partner and make three choices. You do not have to agree with each other but you must be prepared to give reasons for your choice. In part III try to persuade your teacher to accept the ideas.

The list which the assessor provided was:

- a disco
- an evening of international food and songs
- a debate on nuclear disarmament
- a table tennis tournament
- film

3.

Here are two examples of the kind of things you could be asked to do in either the FCE Interview or the ESB.

(a) You are interested in courses at an English language school and go there to make enquiries. What do you say?

(b) An American or English friend asks whether your home town is a good place for tourists to visit. What do you say?

4.

Our last question is an example of the dialogue which you have to complete in the Trinity College Spoken exam (Grade Nine).

The candidate is given time to prepare his own part and is allowed to keep his copy of the partial dialogue during the examination. Candidates who are able to amplify their own parts rather than simply offering the bare minimum will score higher marks.

Jane: You're looking very unhappy. What's the matter?
JOHN: . . .
Jane: Then you'd better visit the dentist.
JOHN: . . .
Jane: Why not? Are you afraid?
JOHN: . . .
Jane: You want to go to the swimming pool? How can you go swimming with toothache?
JOHN: . . .
Jane   It's no good leaving it until tomorrow. It'll be far worse tomorrow.
JOHN: . . .

Jane:	Yes, of course it may get better, but is it likely to? I think you should do something about it today.
JOHN:	. . .
Jane:	Probably because you don't look after your teeth properly.
JOHN:	. . .
Jane:	I don't think you do. You don't clean them twice a day, for example.
JOHN:	. . .
Jane:	Oh no, you don't. Not every day.
JOHN:	. . .
Jane:	Well, if the dentist can't fill the tooth, that's what he'll have to do. I had one out last month.
JOHN:	. . .
Jane:	No, not much. I hardly felt it.

D. TUTOR'S NOTES AND ANSWERS

1.

In answering these situations always try to say something, even it it is "I'm sorry, I didn't catch what you said." It isn't necessary to give lengthy answers as long as you reply in a way that is clear, polite and natural. Read again all the advice in section B of this chapter before you attempt these situations.

Answers

The answers suggested here are good possible answers to these situations. There are usually other possibilities that are just as good.

(a) Do you mind if I use your phone?
    Not at all. Use the bedroom one. It's more private.
(b) Sorry I can't shake hands. I've hurt my hand.
    Oh, dear. What happened?
(c) About that 50 pounds you lent me last week. Here's thirty of it back.
    Thanks very much. When do you think you'll have the other twenty?
(d) Do be careful if you're going upstairs.
    Why? What's the problem?
(e) You know that girl over there, don't you? Do you think you might introduce me?
    Yes, of course. I work with her. Her name's Liz Sim.
(f) Well, what sort of place would you like for a summer holiday?
    I'd really prefer to go to Spain for a change this year.
(g) Sorry to hear about your job, John. Still, I'm sure you'll find something else soon.
(h) Mary, come and meet Peter. He used to work in your school.
(i) Careful, you've forgotten to take your lens cap off.
(j) Excuse me, can I give you a hand?
(k) Congratulations. You must be very pleased. What's he going to study?

(l) Goodness me! Where on earth have you been? Have you just come into some money?

(m) I'm enquiring about Mrs Mary Brown who had an operation yesterday. Can you tell me, please, which ward she's in and when I can visit her?

(n) Excuse me, can I have a look at the little wooden thing on the table in the window? Can you tell me what it's called in English?

(o) Hallo. Did you have a good holiday? What's happened to your leg?

(p) Excuse me, my car has broken down about a quarter of a mile down the road. Would you mind if I used your phone to ring the AA?

(q) I'm terribly sorry but I've already promised to go and visit John's mother that evening. Perhaps Jill could do it for you.

(r) Hey, what's happened to the other programme? I was watching it.

(s) I'm ringing from 12 Smith Street. I can hear noises coming from no 14 and I know the people there are on holiday and won't be back for another week. Can you come and investigate, please.

(t) Excuse me but this is a NO SMOKING area. Would you mind not smoking?

2.

Remember that you have time to prepare a little for the RSA CUEFL Oral and that you have a chance to ask if you do not understand anything in the tasks.

These tasks are fairly realistic but you still do not have to tell the truth. You may find it easier to find a lot to say if you act a role. In **Part I**, for example, think of a good reason why you need a scholarship and explain this as fully as you can to the teacher. The teacher who will speak with you is free to take the conversation into a number of different directions. He or she might ask about your previous experience of learning English, about what you find difficult in English and about your future plans, for example. Feel free yourself to guide the conversation into the direction you would like it to go. What you say is not so important as the way you say it. So, for example, if you would feel happy talking in detail about the kind of course you would like to follow, make sure that you help the discussion to go in that way.

In **Parts II** and **III** you are together with another student and it is important that you give each other fairly equal chances to speak. Try to interact with each other rather than just make individual statements. Disagree with each other, ask each other questions, comment on each other's points. If you can, forget that you are in an exam and try to act as if the situation were a real one. You should find the phrases given below useful.

> Good idea.
> I agree (with you).
> I don't agree (with you).
> So do I! So am I! etc.
> What do you think?
> How about . . .?
> Why don't we . . .?

Read the instructions carefully and do everything that is asked. Pay especial attention if something is underlined on the task sheet.

Try not to come to a decision too quickly. Examine each of the items on the lists in some detail and try to weigh up the advantages and disadvantages of each fairly fully. It is not at all important if you do not come to any final decision but it is awkward if you feel too soon that you have made your choice and there is nothing left to say.

In Part III your teacher returns to the room (when summoned by the examiner) and you tell him or her what you have been discussing. Report back fully on your discussion. Again make sure that you both have a fair turn to speak. The teacher will ask you further questions and you may, of course, add things that you did not talk about in Part II.

Answer

Here the tutor's answer gives you just some parts of a good RSA CUEFL Oral. There are lots and lots of ways in which the tasks can develop and what I suggest is just one of many possibilities.

Part I

TEACHER: You've made an application for a grant to go on with your English studies. What exactly do you want to do?

STUDENT: I'd like to spend a year studying in England. I think that's the only way to become really fluent. After I've finished studying I want to become a teacher in my own country and I don't think I can be a really good teacher unless I can speak well. I can learn the grammar and read lots of literature at home but I can't get enough speaking practice.

TEACHER: Do you want to spend your year at a school in Britain?

STUDENT: Yes, I'd like to find a school where I could be in class for about three hours a day. Then I'd have the chance to find some part-time work as well. I think you can learn some useful things at school and other useful things by working in an English environment. I know it could be very difficult for me to find work but I'd be prepared to do anything. If I got this scholarship I'd be able to do voluntary work which would be just as good for my English, of course.

TEACHER: What aspects of learning English do you find most difficult?

STUDENT: Well, it's hard to say. Sometimes everything seems very difficult. I suppose pronunciation is one of my biggest problems. And I find it quite hard to understand when people speak very fast. That's why I feel I really need to spend a long time in Britain.

Part II

STUDENT A: Well, as we're at a school where there are lots of different nationalities, I think an evening of international food and song would be a very good idea.

STUDENT B: So do I! It'd be really interesting to try food from Japan and Saudi Arabia and Zisan's Turkish songs are wonderful. Let's organise that for a Friday and then we can go on quite late.

STUDENT A: Good idea! What do you think about the other suggestions? How about a disco?

STUDENT B: I don't think we should hold a disco. If people want discos there are lots of other places they can go.

STUDENT A: I don't agree with you. There are only two or three places in town and they're terribly expensive. School discos are nice too because everyone knows everyone else.

STUDENT B: Perhaps you're right. Anyhow, let's look at the other ideas. How about a table tennis tournament?

STUDENT A: We had one only a month ago. Let's try and think of something a bit different. Why don't we have a chess tournament instead?

Part III

TEACHER: Well, what have you been discussing?

STUDENT B: We've been thinking about possible evening activities for school.

TEACHER: What have you decided on?

STUDENT A: We're sure that an international evening would be very successful but we can't agree about whether we should have a disco or not. I think it'd be a good idea but Beat doesn't.

STUDENT B: No, I think people can go into town or even up to London if they want discos. Anyhow I don't like discos!

STUDENT A: Don't you? Why not?

STUDENT B: They're noisy and smoky and I don't enjoy modern disco music very much.

STUDENT A: Still, it's a good way to meet people. But to get back to the task, we thought a chess tournament would be a nice change from a table tennis one.

STUDENT B: Yes, and lots of people like Scrabble too. Perhaps we could have different kinds of games going on at the same time.

TEACHER: That wouldn't be very interesting for the students who aren't playing though, would it?

STUDENT A: Well, lots of students enjoy games and I'm sure we can collect quite a few boards so that plenty of people can play.

STUDENT B: Yes, and we can have records and coffee available so that people who aren't playing can sit and talk in a relaxed way.

3.

Again the important thing here is to try and act. If you can really imagine yourself in these situations, you will find them easier to do well. The examiner may help you by participating in the role play but, if he or she doesn't, don't worry. Go on speaking as much as you feel is appropriate. Think of lots of different questions that you could ask about courses – costs, hours, numbers of students, accommodation, facilities, social activities and so on. Talk about all sorts of things that are important for tourists – sights, entertainment, hotels, food, sport, souvenirs, countryside nearby and so on.

Answer

I'd like to make some enquiries about courses at your school, please. How many hours a week do students do? Could I enrol at the beginning of next month? What are the fees? Does the school arrange accommodation with English families? Do you have other Danish students? What social activities does the school organise? Do you do any courses in business letters? Do you have courses preparing for particular exams? Have you got a language lab? I'm sorry to ask so many questions but there's such a lot I'd like to know.

It's not really very good for tourists as it's quite an industrial town but quite near to us there's a marvellous village up in the mountains which tourists love. It's about twenty kilometres from my town and it's a village on the edge of a small mountain lake. You can sail and waterski on the lake and, if you don't mind quite cold water, you can swim there. They catch delicious fish in the lake and the restaurants in this village are famous both for their fish dishes and for the local wine. Tourists often like to visit the local vineyard. They also go on sightseeing tours to an old monastery up in the mountains. It's very picturesque.

4.

When deciding what to say in the blank space, remember to look both at what goes before and at what comes afterwards. Both the preceding and the following statements limit what you can say.

In the dialogue, you will probably have to do most of these things:

- ask some questions
- give short answers
- agree and/or disagree
- make suggestions
- express hopes and wishes

Make sure you can do all these things.

Remember you will get extra marks if you say more than the bare minimum. When you look at my answer, think about what I've said that was not strictly essential. What other ways could the dialogue be filled out to make it better?

As extra practise with this question, look at the answers given below. Can you now remember what the other person in the dialogue said?

Practise with dialogues from your textbook. Write out one half of any dialogue. A few days later look at what you have written and try to reconstruct the whole dialogue. Check what you do with your textbook.

Answer

I feel dreadful. I've got terrible toothache.

I know I should but I can't go today.

Of course not, though I used to be terrified of the dentist when I was a child. No, I've already arranged to go swimming with Mary and Sue.

I promised I'd go swimming and I don't suppose it'll do my tooth any harm. I'll go to the dentist tomorrow.

It might not be. It could even be better tomorrow.

I really can't do anything about it today. Oh, how unfair it is. Why does it have to happen to me?

But I do look after them.

Oh yes I do.

I clean them twice almost every day. Oh dear, I hope he won't take my tooth out.

You poor thing! Did it hurt?

E. BEYOND THE COURSEWORK

If you have the chance to watch films in English notice what people say in social situations in the film. Do they behave in the same way as people from your country? Of course, people in films don't necessarily behave like people in real life. You can also think about what people say in the books that you read.

One of the best things that you can do beyond the coursework for this part of the exam is to join a drama group. Even practising role plays in your own language will help you to get used to imagining yourself in all sorts of different – possibly sometimes quite strange – roles.

If you can't find a local drama group, why not start one in your school or college.

If you have a friend to work with, you could find two unusual sets of books useful for practising the kind of English discussed in this chapter. These books are *Pair Work A and B* (published by Penguin) and *Partners 2 and 3* (published by Language Teaching Publications). These books each give roles for two students working together – each knows something the other does not and they have to follow instructions in order to solve a puzzle or to role play a situation.

Chapter 9

Reading comprehension

A. GETTING STARTED

All English exams either directly or indirectly test your reading comprehension. Even the **ARELS** exam asks you to read a text aloud and you cannot do this well unless you understand what you are reading. This chapter, however, is about the more direct tests of reading comprehension, those which are found in written exams. It deals with questions where your written answers are fairly short. In Chapter 10 we look at questions where you have to read and then write a long answer based on your reading.

Some reading tests, particularly those in the **Oxford** and **RSA CUEFL** exams, give you very long pieces of English and you have to skim through them quickly, picking out only what is important. More traditional exams, like the **FCE** or the **TOEFL**, ask you to look at shorter texts and to answer questions which involve an understanding both of the whole passage and of details within it.

An important way in which exams check your reading comprehension is through your understanding of the questions asked. It is very important to read the question as carefully as you read the text and to make absolutely certain that you answer the question that was asked.

B. ESSENTIAL PRINCIPLES

In a reading question the most important thing is to read through the text quickly to get an approximate idea of what it is about. In the **Oxford** and **RSA** exams you are allowed ten minutes to read before you start answering any questions. This should be long enough for you to get a rough idea of what the reading material you have been given is about. Don't spend too long on this stage. It isn't necessary to get a complete picture of the texts.

If you are taking an exam where you are allowed to use a dictionary, don't waste time looking up words. It is very easy to waste valuable time by checking things that you really knew or by finding out meanings that do not relate to the questions.

Then look at the questions. Find the part of the text which gives the answer. Read both the question and this part of the text very carefully. Then answer the question. It is very important in all reading comprehension questions that you answer the question by looking at the text and not by giving your own opinion or thinking about something else you have read on the same subject. If you don't think about what is written in the text itself you will probably choose the wrong answer.

Many exams test your reading comprehension by asking multiple-choice questions where you have to choose the correct answer out of a set of four alternatives. Here it is a good idea just to read the basic part of the question first, without looking at the alternatives offered. Look at the text. Decide what you feel fits the basic question. Then look at the alternatives given. Is there one which matches your own answer? If so, that will be the correct answer and you hardly need to think about the other suggestions made. If in the end you cannot decide what the right answer is, don't just leave a blank. Make a guess. You have a reasonable chance of making the right choice even by just guessing, especially if you can eliminate one or two of the alternatives available.

C. EXAM QUESTIONS

In this chapter I suggest you:

(a) Read each question
(b) Look at the notes on it in section D
(c) Do the question in accordance with the notes
(d) Check the answers in section D.

1.

In the **FCE** and the **TOEFL** the parts of the exam called Reading Comprehension consist of two sections. The first focuses on vocabulary and the second on the understanding of texts. In each case the questions are multiple choice. In the vocabulary questions of the **FCE** you choose which word out of four alternatives given fits a blank. There is practice of this in Chapter 11.

The following question is of the type used in the **TOEFL** exam where the form is slightly different. Here you are given a set of sentences where one word or phrase is underlined. Then you are given four other words or phrases and you have to decide which would best keep the meaning of the original sentence if it were substituted for the underlined word or phrase.

1. Johnny's mother scolded him this morning.
    (a) burnt   (b) played with   (c) reprimanded   (d) smacked
2. I can't put up with his behaviour.
    (a) understand   (b) tolerate   (c) have in my home   (d) control

3. The news eventually <u>filtered through</u> to the kitchen staff.
   (a) made its way to (b) was known by all   (c) surprised
   (d) burst through to
4. They <u>settled</u> in Germany five years ago.
   (a) stayed   (b) made their home   (c) got married   (d) started a
   business
5. The accused was <u>discharged</u> at the end of the trial.
   (a) dismissed from his job   (b) sent home   (c) put on
   probation   (d) allowed to go free
6. His poor health is the main <u>stumbling-block</u>.
   (a) obstacle   (b) worry   (c) danger   (d) disaster
7. Her money turned out to be a <u>curse</u> to her.
   (a) an enormous benefit   (b) a natural way of life   (c) a source
   of problems   (d) a mixed blessing
8. Your advice has been <u>invaluable</u> to me.
   (a) worthless   (b) very precious   (c) of little importance
   (d) misleading
9. He <u>pretended</u> it was his car.
   (a) claimed   (b) insisted   (c) said falsely   (d) denied
10. She has <u>a great repugnance</u> to writing letters.
    (a) a strong dislike of   (b) an enthusiasm for   (c) a longlasting
    habit of   (d) no talent for
11. He does seem <u>to fritter away</u> his money.
    (a) to use his money well   (b) to give away a lot of money
    (c) to spend his money on food   (d) to waste his money
12. Could I have my hair <u>trimmed</u>, please?
    (a) styled fashionably   (b) cut a little   (c) washed and
    dried   (d) tinted slightly
13. The match has been <u>postponed</u> till next Saturday.
    (a) put off   (b) put out   (c) put down   (d) put by
14. Does that word have a <u>pejorative</u> meaning?
    (a) figurative   (b) subjective   (c) negative   (d) ambiguous
15. He's <u>hardly</u> learnt the basic English verbs.
    (a) with difficulty   (b) only   (c) scarcely   (d) cleverly
16. Would you like to live in such <u>bleak</u> countryside?
    (a) windswept   (b) white   (c) hilly   (d) dramatic
17. The treasurer <u>misappropriated</u> the society's funds.
    (a) put in the wrong place   (b) took for his own use
    (c) lost   (d) wrongly calculated
18. Their aim has always been to <u>diffuse</u> learning.
    (a) spread   (b) simplify   (c) complicate   (d) encourage
19. Do tell us about any <u>incidental</u> expenses you have incurred.
    (a) chance   (b) large   (c) ongoing   (d) additional
20. The singer was <u>hissed</u> at by the audience.
    (a) asked to be quiet   (b) encouraged to sing more   (c) noisily
    disapproved of   (d) loudly clapped
21. Robert the Bruce is famous for his <u>perseverance</u>.
    (a) unceasing efforts   (b) fearless loyalty   (c) brave
    fighting   (d) ruthless behaviour

22. That argument is based on a fallacy
    (a) an imaginative idea   (b) a mistaken belief   (c) an error of judgement   (d) a doubtful theory
23. She sees him every now and again
    (a) frequently   (b) occasionally   (c) rarely   (d) daily
24. Mary's dog went for her
    (a) loved   (b) travelled with   (c) shopped for   (d) attacked
25. He has been a mentor to me on financial matters for many years
    (a) a liar   (b) a trusted advisor   (c) an interpreter   (d) an experienced teacher
26. People are starving throughout the world.
    (a) dying of poverty   (b) working hard   (c) dying of hunger   (d) working on the land
27. I dread his arrival.
    (a) long for   (b) worry about   (c) expect   (d) fear
28. She went on working, nevertheless.
    (a) just in case   (b) in spite of everything   (c) just as much   (d) regardless of the consequences
29. The firms were amalgamated last year.
    (a) started doing business   (b) became friendly   (c) were united   (d) were split
30. Hurry up, or else you'll be late.
    (a) otherwise   (b) however   (c) therefore   (d) at least

2.

The second part of the reading comprehension in the **FCE** and the **TOEFL** exams tests your understanding of texts through multiple-choice questions. Here is a set of questions in the style of the **TOEFL** where you have rather shorter passages than those used in the **FCE**. The skills necessary to do well in these exams are identical, however.

After switching on the computer and the VDU, type *W and you will be able to start word-processing. Press ESCAPE and begin typing. If you make a mistake, press DELETE and the preceding letter will disappear. When you are ready to print what you have typed, press ESCAPE to return to the menu, check that your printer is connected and press 6. You should then have a perfect version of what you typed.

1. This text has been written to:
    (a)   encourage people to use a word-processor;
    (b)   give basic instruction in how to use a word-processor;
    (c)   explain how a word-processor works;
    (d)   describe how a computer can be set up as a word-processor.

2. When you type something wrongly you should
    (a)   return to the menu;
    (b)   type delete;
    (c)   press a key labelled delete;
    (d)   check that everything is connected to the computer.

3. When can you start typing what you want to print?
   (a) After pressing ESCAPE to leave the menu.
   (b) As soon as you have typed *W.
   (c) As soon as all the parts of the computer are connected.
   (d) When the menu is visible on the VDU.

4. When you press 6:
   (a) the printer switches itself on;
   (b) you see what you have typed on the VDU;
   (c) your mistakes are all corrected;
   (d) you get a printed copy of what you have typed.

'Some scientists have claimed that there is a correlation between your intelligence and the amount of sleep you need. The higher your intelligence, the less sleep you need. Intelligence reaches its peak in the early twenties and most great scientific discoveries have been made by under thirties. It has been shown that the two best ways to keep your intelligence at its youthful strength are to drink no alcohol and to continue studying throughout your life.'

5. Which of these statements is suggested by the passage above?
   (a) It has been proved that intelligent people need less sleep.
   (b) It is not certain that intelligent people need less sleep.
   (c) It is argued that less intelligent people need less sleep.
   (d) There is no connection between intelligence and sleep.

6. Most scientific discoveries:
   (a) were made by a very small group of people;
   (b) were made by people who have drunk very little alcohol;
   (c) were made in the first part of this century;
   (d) were made by young people.

7. You can stop your intelligence deteriorating if:
   (a) you rarely drink;
   (b) you go to university;
   (c) you always try to keep learning;
   (d) you never drink when you are studying.

8. This text probably comes from:
   (a) an article in a popular magazine;
   (b) an anti-alcohol pamphlet;
   (c) a psychology textbook;
   (d) a lecture for medical students.

For each of the questions 9 and 10 below, choose the answer that is closest in meaning to the original sentence. Note that several of the choices may be factually correct, but you should choose the one that is the closest restatement of the given sentence.

9. Can't you make do with that blouse for another day?
   (a) Can't you finish making that blouse tomorrow?
   (b) Can't you wear that blouse one more time?
   (c) Can't you mend that blouse before you wear it again?

      (d)   Can't you wear another blouse today?

10.   He said he'd help me repair my car as long as my son agreed to fix his roof.
      (a)   He agreed to help me with my car at the same time as my son mended his roof.
      (b)   He asked my son to repair his roof, reminding me that he'd helped me with my car.
      (c)   He agreed to help me with my car provided that my son helped him with his roof.
      (d)   He said he would help with my car when my son had finished helping him with his roof.

3.

The **RSA CUEFL** and the **Oxford** exams test your ability to skim through a lot of text and to pick out answers to questions. The best way you can practise for the reading part of these exams is by reading English newspapers and magazines because the texts used are usually taken from this kind of original source. There is no space here to reproduce material of the length you are given in these exams and so the practice question here asks you to look at the last chapter in this book and to answer the following questions on it.

Spend ten minutes now skimming through **Chapter 17**. Do not try to read it fully. Try to get an impression of the content of the chapter and a picture of its layout. Now answer these questions.

Allow yourself one hour to do them.

1.   Look at section A. This chapter is useful for:
      (a)   revision purposes
      (b)   would-be teachers
      (c)   careless students
      (d)   exam practice
   Put a tick (√) beside every point that is mentioned in section A.

2.   In section B why is it suggested you should check the question paper as well as your own work?
      (a)   You may have answered too few – or too many – questions.
      (b)   You may not have answered all the different parts of a question.
      (c)   You may have misunderstood a question when you first read it.
      (d)   You may have written too long an answer.
   Put a tick (√) beside every item that is mentioned in section B.

3.   In section B you read about VSPs. What are the two things that V, S and P can each stand for?

      V . . .
      S . . .
      P . . .

4. It is better to check your work immediately after writing it.

   YES
   NO
   DON'T KNOW (the answer is not in the text)

5. At the end of section B what are you recommended to do?
6. How many questions are there in section C?
7. What should you do before beginning question 1?
8. Which question has a special focus on prepositions?
9. How many spelling mistakes are there in exercise 5?
10. How many words is the student asked to write in question 7?
11. Look at question 1 and the answers to it. Correct these forms if necessary.

    (a) Jimmy suggested us to spend
    (b) My mother is teacher
    (c) they used to work hard
    (d) He's got difficulties to understand

12. Look at the notes on question 5 in section D. Are these points about spelling correct?
    Mark them YES, NO or DON'T KNOW (i.e. the answer isn't in the text)

    (a) E before I except after C.
    (b) The adverbs from 'economic' and 'economical' are identical.
    (c) If you know where the stress falls on words like 'prefer' and 'happen' it can help you to spell the past tense correctly.

13. Are these words spelt correctly? Put a tick (√) beside those that are. Write the correct spellings beside those words that are incorrect.

    (a) foreign
    (b) bycicle
    (c) adress
    (d) development
    (e) embarassed
    (f) wieght
    (g) received
    (h) planing

14. Read the punctuated text in question 6.
    What is the name of the newspaper where this story first appeared?
15. In this story what did the buses stop doing?
16. Why did they stop doing it?
17. Would the composition given in question 8, section D get good marks in an exam?

    YES
    NO
    DON'T KNOW (the answer isn't in the text)

18. In this composition, does the student answer the question asked?
    YES
    NO
    For the last three questions look at section E.

19. What is suggested as one of the best ways of learning?
    (a) Explaining something to someone else.
    (b) Looking at someone else's mistakes.
    (c) Just talking generally in English.

20. Which chapter should you read again just before you take your exam?

21. Is a black cat lucky or unlucky in Britain?

4.

Here is another example of a reading comprehension with multiple-choice questions. It comes from a Pitmans Higher Intermediate specimen paper. Note that in practice this exam does not necessarily include this kind of question but it is nevertheless good practice for this and for any other intermediate EFL exams and particularly for those which use multiple-choice questions.

> 'There are few places in the world today that have not been spoiled by industrial development and pollution. The air we breathe is more often than not polluted by the smoke from factory chimneys and the exhaust fumes of motor vehicles, while chemical waste poisons our rivers, lakes and seas. And by covering more and more of the earth's surface with buildings and roads, we are erecting huge barriers of concrete between ourselves and nature. It would appear that we are purposely cutting ourselves off from nature and destroying wildlife as we do so.'

In the following questions only one of the sentences is correct according to the preceding passage.

Example:
The passage is mainly about:

(a) the earth;
(b) pollution;
(c) rivers;
(d) buildings.

Answer (b) is correct

1. The passage states that:
   (a) Industrial development and pollution have spoiled most parts of the world.
   (b) Industrial development has only spoiled some parts of the world.
   (c) Industrial development and pollution have not spoiled many parts of the world.
   (d) Industrial development has not spoiled nature at all.

2. The passage suggests that:
   (a) Factory chimneys are poisoning the air we breathe.
   (b) Factories are poisoning the water of our rivers, lakes and seas.
   (c) Factories and cars are the main causes of our air pollution.
   (d) Factory smoke causes more air pollution than exhaust fumes.

3. According to the passage:
   (a) We are definitely destroying wildlife by isolating ourselves from nature.
   (b) We are intentionally destroying wildlife and isolating ourselves from nature.
   (c) We have completely destroyed both nature and wildlife.
   (d) We are accidentally destroying both nature and wildlife.

5.

In the **Trinity College Intermediate** written exam the examiners try to kill two birds with one stone by asking you to make up the questions as well as answer them. This question is taken from a summer 1984 paper.

Read the following passage. In your answer booklet write down the words to complete the questions at the end of the passage. Only ONE word is missing in each case.

'Edna left home early that day because at nine o'clock she was going to start work at an office in the city. She was only sixteen and this was her first job. But the traffic was so dense that she arrived a few minutes late.

She caught the lift up to the eighth floor and went along the corridor to the office where she was to work. She tapped on the door, but there was no reply. Then she heard the sound of someone's voice from the room next door. She opened the door and looked in. There was the manager, speaking to the people in the room in an angry voice. Then he turned round and left the room. Later that day Edna found out what had happened. Apparently the manager came to the office as a rule about nine-thirty, because he lived out in the country and came up by train every day. That morning, however, he happened to catch an earlier train, and when he arrived, not a single person was working. They were all standing around, smoking, chatting and telling jokes.'

1. What made Edna . . . late?
2. Why do you think there was . . . reply when Edna knocked on the door?
3. What kind of building . . . you think the office was in? What suggests this?
4. Why was the . . . angry?
5. If the manager . . . not caught an earlier train, what would have been one of the results?

D. TUTOR'S NOTES AND ANSWERS

(a) Read the notes to each answer before you try to do the question yourself.
(b) Then do the question.
(c) Compare your answer with that suggested below.
(d) Check to make sure that you understand your mistakes.

1.

To do this question well you need to know both the words underlined and those given in the choices offered. Either you will know the words or you won't. There are not many clues in the sentences. Usually there is not enough information for you to make a sensible guess from the context as you would usually be able to do in a longer piece of text. So, if you have no ideas about the answer, make a guess and move quickly on to the next question. Don't leave any blanks – remember you have a one in four statistical chance of guessing right even if you know none of the choices offered. However do use your time where you can use it most productively, i.e. where you know at least some of the words, so that thinking hard will really give you a better chance of making the right choice.

Answers

1 (c); 2 (b); 3 (a); 4 (b); 5 (d); 6 (a); 7 (c); 8 (b); 9 (c); 10 (a); 11 (d); 12 (b); 13 (a); 14 (c); 15 (c); 16 (a); 17 (b); 18 (a); 19 (d); 20 (c); 21 (a); 22 (b); 23 (b); 24 (d); 25 (b); 26 (c); 27 (d); 28 (b); 29 (c); 30 (a).

2.

In the **TOEFL** exam you will have thirty questions of this type rather than ten. The texts are usually on a scientific, or at least academic theme. The questions require an exact understanding of what has been read. It is best then to read the texts two or three times until you feel sure you understand it fully. Only then look at the questions. Read the questions equally carefully; do not be misled by something which you know to be true from your general knowledge. Is it actually what the text either states or suggests?

Answers

1 (b); 2 (c); 3 (a); 4 (d); 5 (b); 6 (d); 7 (c); 8 (a); 9 (b); 10 (c).

3.

Remember to use your preparatory reading time well. How many sections are there in the chapter? What does each section seem to be about? If you can work this out you will save yourself lots of time by being able to find the necessary parts of the material quickly.

You need to work quite fast in this exercise to finish all the questions. So work through them as quickly as you can. Don't waste time reading anything that isn't relevant. Don't waste time using your dictionary unless it's really necessary. If you find one question very difficult, leave it and go on to the next one. You may well have time at the end to think about the difficult questions more calmly.

1. (a), (b) and (d).   2. (a), (b) and (c).   3. Very and Verbs, Special and Spelling, Problems and Prepositions.   4. No. 5 To look back at mistakes you've made in your written English.   6. (8).   7. Look back at the twelve rules listed in Chapter 3.   8. (4)   9. Twenty. 10. 120–180.   11. (a) Jimmy suggested our spending (or we spent); (b) My mother is a teacher. (c) He's got difficulty in understanding. 12. (a)NO; (b)YES; (c)YES.   13. (a), (d) and (g) are correct; bicycle, address, embarrassed, weight and planning are the corrected spellings.   14. The Daily Echo.   15. Picking up passengers.   16. So that the buses could keep to the timetable.   17. NO.   18. NO. 19. (a).   20. Chapter 2   21. Lucky.

4.

As you do each question find the part of the text that it refers to. Question 1 refers to the first sentence, question 2 to the second and question 3 to the last.

Eliminate any alternatives that are clearly impossible. It is surely immediately clear that choice (d) is not possible for question 1.

Question 2 is probably the hardest of these questions. Think about these points.

Choice (a): are factory chimneys the only cause of air pollution?
Choice (b): what exactly does the passage say causes water pollution? Are factories the only things that are to blame for this?
Choices (c) and (d): does the text suggest which is more to blame for air pollution – cars or factories?

For question 3 look at the last sentence carefully. What is it that we are doing intentionally? What is happening as a result?

1 (a);   2 (c);   3 (a).

5.

Choosing the right word for the questions tests both an understanding of the text and of English structure. In questions 1, 2 and 4, use the words that you will find in the text itself. When you give your answers to the questions, do not feel that you need to change the words in the original text. It is all right to talk about dense traffic in question 1, for example. If you know a synonym for dense that you are sure goes well with traffic, then by all means use it. Keep the structures of your answers simple if possible so that you do not lose unnecessary marks. Also make sure that you don't misspell any words in your answer that are there in the text. It is amazing how often examiners see this happen!

1.   arrive
     The heavy traffic made Edna late for work.
2.   no
     There was no reply because everyone was in another room.

3. do

It was a skyscraper. We know that because Edna's office was on the eighth floor.

4. manager

He was angry because people were talking instead of working when they didn't expect him to arrive at the office.

5. had

If he hadn't caught an earlier train he wouldn't have realised that people didn't work when he wasn't in the office.

E. BEYOND THE COURSEWORK

The possibilities for extending your reading practice in English are endless. If you want exercises to check your comprehension of what you've read then there are lots of books available which will give you this. Longman, for example, have published *What the Papers Say* by Geoffrey Land. Other publishers also have good materials – *Meet the Press* and *Authentic Reading*, both published by CUP, are very useful books at this level.

If you want to read fiction for pleasure but feel that 'real' material is too difficult for you, why not try some of the readers in Longman's *Simplified English* series? Once you have got into the reading habit by reading some of these, you should probably soon find that you can manage 'real' stories. Here is a list of fiction in English which I have found that students can enjoy even when their English is not at a very advanced level. Perhaps start with some short stories?

Roald Dahl: *Kiss, Kiss; Someone Like You; Switch Bitch* (macabre short stories)
Agatha Christie: anything (detective stories)
George Orwell: *Animal Farm; 1984*
Gerald Durrell: anything (humorous stories about the experiences of a field zoologist).
James Herriot: anything (humorous stories about the life of a vet).
Monica Dickens: *One Pair of Hands; One Pair of Feet*
Richard Gordon: *Doctor in the House* (humour – life of a medical student).
Eric Segal: *Love Story*
Ernest Hemingway: *The Old Man and the Sea*
Somerset Maugham: *Short Stories*

Newspapers and magazines are also a very good thing to read regularly. Is there somewhere near you where you can occasionally buy a British or American newspaper? If so, buy one now and then, and see how much you can understand. If you often read newspapers in your own language, then you will probably not find it too difficult. If you buy the same newspaper regularly you will notice that it very quickly gets very much easier to read as the same vocabulary is used time and time again.

As we said before in Chapter 2, it is a very good idea to buy a book or magazines about any subject that you are particularly interested in. In that way you'll learn not only more about your own subject but also more about English.

Reading a lot in English is important for the kind of exam question discussed in this chapter. Above all, however, it is important for improving your general feel for English. You will find that your vocabulary increases by leaps and bounds and that your feeling for the structure of the language also improves dramatically. If you choose something to read that you enjoy, then you are improving your knowledge of vocabulary and grammar in an extremely pleasant way.

Chapter 10

From reading to writing

A. GETTING STARTED

This chapter deals with those exam questions which test both reading and writing skills. In other words, it is concerned with questions where you have to read quite a long text and then show your understanding by doing some extended writing. The types of questions covered by this definition are quite varied. The main ones which we shall look at in this chapter are:

(a) Summarising a text.
(b) Writing about a set book.
(c) Replying to a letter or responding to an article.
(d) Translation.

All of these tasks can be part of the **FCE** Exam although translation is an optional paper. The set-book question is only one of five composition possibilities in **FCE**. You have to do two compositions and so it is quite possible to ignore the set-book option if it doesn't attract you. If you find it useful to study a set book, then you can not only write a composition on it but you can also say that you would like to talk about the book in the oral part of the exam. The particular books to be studied for **FCE** change each year and you have a choice of three.

The **Oxford** and **RSA CUEFL** Exams have questions of type (c) and practice in summary will also be useful for you if you are doing these exams.

The **British Council Test** provides you with a booklet of materials relating to your own specialist subject and in the writing part of the test, you have to give answers based on your reading of this booklet. Again questions of types (a) and (c) are the ones you need to practise.

Summarising and translation are skills that you need for the **Institute of Linguists Grade II Certificate**. Translation is a compulsory part of the exam. So is summarising, although it is not a matter of going from reading to writing. You have to summarise a written text orally and you have to write a summary of something that you hear. The summarising and translation sections of this chapter will be useful for you if you are doing this exam.

Summary is also necessary for the **Pitman Exam (Syllabus L)** although again the summary is not of a written but of a spoken text. Practice in type (c) questions will be useful for you if you are taking **Pitman Exam (Syllabus C)**.

If you are taking the **Trinity College Spoken English** exam, you have to prepare yourself to talk about a chosen book. Here you may find the advice given relating to questions of type (b) helpful in your preparation.

Questions of types (a) and (c) involve useful skills. Even if you are not doing an exam with questions of this type, you may find it helpful to do the practice relating to these skills in this chapter. Writing about books and translating are much more specific skills and you need to decide for yourself whether they are really necessary for you.

B. ESSENTIAL PRINCIPLES

In this section we are going to look in turn at essential principles relating to each of the four types of question mentioned in section A. First one general point can be made. These questions are for testing reading as well as writing. For many students writing is far more difficult than reading and so they rush immediately into the writing part of the question. In this way they lose marks unnecessarily because they did not pay enough attention to the text to be summarised, commented on or translated.

Make sure you do not make this mistake. Spend time reading. Understand the text fully before you begin writing. A bit of simple equipment can help you here. Have a highlighting pen – or, if you can't get one, an ordinary pencil – and mark the parts of your text that are particularly important for your answer. So, for example, highlight the main points of the text for your précis. If you have to comment on a text, highlight the parts of the passage that need comment. Sometimes the questions of this type are themselves long and complicated with lots of different elements for you to do. Highlight each part so that you do not overlook anything at the beginning and then check at the end that you have indeed remembered to do everything you highlighted.

SUMMARY

Summary is a difficult thing to do well. It is also usually not really very interesting to do but it is a useful thing to be able to do for 'real life'.

The aim of summary is to pick out what is important in a text and to convey its sense in brief. To be able to do this well, you need to be absolutely clear what the sense of the passage is.

- Read it several times first.
- Then go through the text highlighting or underlining the key ideas.
- Next write these ideas into a connected paragraph.

The question will probably tell you how many words you can use. Keep to this limit. You will lose marks if you exceed it no matter how good your English is. You may find it useful quickly to estimate how many words there are in the original text so that you have a clearer idea of how much has to be cut.

What kinds of things will you cut from the original? Most detail will go. So will specific examples. Often writers make the same point in several different ways to put their ideas across more clearly. In a summary the idea will only be stated once – in its briefest form.

Sometimes long expressions can be replaced by shorter ones giving the same idea. It is not necessary, however, to try to put the text into your own words. You can lift sentences – if appropriate – straight from the original text. Only change words if you feel it makes the summary better.

SET BOOK

Set books are useful in that you learn a lot of good English from reading them and you can prepare them thoroughly so that at least one part of the exam is not a horrible surprise. Do try to choose a book that you like enough to study it at length. Ask the advice of someone who knows the three set FCE books or their authors if you can. It will be much easier both to study and to do good exam answers if you are enthusiastic about what you have read.

For the Trinity College exam you have a free choice of book and so it should not be too difficult to find something that you like. Perhaps you know an English writer in translation that you like. Why not read one of that writer's books in the original? You can ask your teacher's advice. You can have a look in your local library or bookshop to see what books are easily available in your area. If you want some suggestions you can write to Trinity College at the address given in Chapter 1.

How can you best prepare your set book?

There are six main areas which you need to think about whatever book you are reading.

1. Plot
2. Setting
3. Characters
4. Style
5. Author's purpose
6. Own reactions

The questions you will have to answer in an intermediate exam will probably be about the simplest of these areas. They will probably be factual questions about plot or character. To know the book really well, however, it is worth considering each of the above six areas and making brief notes on all of them.

Plot

Make sure that the plot of the book is absolutely clear for you. When you have read the book, go through it chapter by chapter making notes on the important developments that each chapter brings. Make your notes in English, of course. This will give you a useful summary of the plot.

Setting	Then write something brief about the setting of the book, i.e. where the story takes place and when it takes place. Is it set in a nineteenth-century working-class district of London, for instance?
Character	Character is also important in most books. Make a list of all the main characters and then write a few notes about them. What kind of person is each one? What are the relationships between the characters? What role does each character play in the story?
Style	Make some notes too about the author's style. Does s/he write a lot of description? Does s/he use a lot of figures of speech (e.g. metaphor or simile)? Does s/he use mainly long or short sentences? Can any of the following adjectives be used to describe his or her writing – humorous, dramatic, complex, sensitive, romantic? Make a note of any examples from the book which illustrate any of the comments that you make about the author's style.
Author's purpose	Can you answer the question about what the author's purpose was in writing this book? Was it simply to amuse? Or did s/he perhaps want to change the readers' view of the world? Or perhaps the writer wanted to tell something about his or her own experience of the world. When you have decided what the author's purpose was in writing the book, think about whether he succeeded in achieving that aim. It may be interesting and useful here to try and find out a little about the author. If you can, write a few biographical notes on his life.
Own reactions	The final area to make a few notes on is what you yourself feel about the book. What exactly do you like about it? Are there aspects of the book that you don't like? What are they? Why don't you like them? If you do all these things with your set book you will know it extremely well and should have no difficulty in answering any questions on it either orally or in writing. Remember that by doing all this work on a set book you are not only preparing for a set-book question but are also doing work that will benefit all aspects of your English.

REPLYING TO A LETTER OR RESPONDING TO AN ARTICLE

This section covers a lot of questions in modern communicative exams. These questions give you a piece of everyday text to read – a letter, an advert, a newspaper article, for example – and then they give you a realistic writing task to do to show your comprehension of the text. So you may have to write an answer to the letter, an enquiry about the advertisement, a complaint about the article. Questions of this type are potentially very varied. You never know exactly what could appear in section B of the Use of English paper in the FCE, for example.

The main general advice that can be given about questions of this type is to read the question very carefully and to remember to base your writing closely on what you have just read. Highlight the parts of the text that are relevant and then plan your answer before you write. Make sure you don't forget anything relevant. You will be getting marks for specific points of content as well as for the quality of your writing.

TRANSLATION

Translation is a very difficult art but one that may give you a lot of pleasure.

If you are doing a translation it is very important that you first read the entire text carefully. Make sure you are clear what the whole passage is about before you begin to translate the first sentence.

When you translate, remember that you are aiming at writing something that sounds good in your own language. This means that it is quite impossible to translate word for word. Idioms, for example, will very rarely be translated literally. How would you translate 'The children were as good as gold' into your language? There's nothing about metal in your translation, I expect. Probably you've quite correctly translated it as something like 'The children were very well-behaved'. Similarly, one long sentence in English may be better as two shorter sentences in your language. English may use a verb where you use a verb with an adverb to convey the same meaning.

If you can, have a look at a story that you have a copy of both in English and in your own language. See where the translator moved away from a literal translation and think about why s/he has done so. Patterns may become clear. Which language needs more words? Does one language prefer longer sentences? Does one language use more adjectives for example? Do you notice anything else that is interesting?

Be careful about 'false friends'. There are very probably words in English which resemble words in your language but in fact have quite different meanings. 'Become' is quite different from 'bekommen' in German and English 'sensible' is quite different from French 'sensible'. As you read make a list of 'false friends' and check that you can translate them correctly. In the exam keep your eyes open for any of these 'false friends' and don't be misled by them.

Remember that English words often have a lot of different meanings and that the first meaning that comes to mind may not be the right one for the context. 'Her irises were a vivid blue' may be referring to her garden or her eyes, for example. The context should make it clear which is right in the circumstances.

You may be allowed to use a dictionary in the exam. If you are then use it to check anything that you are not sure of or that sounds strange. Remember to look at all the possibilities offered to see which one fits the context. If you are not allowed to use a dictionary but there are things in the text that you do not understand then make sensible guesses from the context using some of the tips discussed more fully in Chapter 4.

C. EXAM QUESTIONS

In this section the first two questions involve summary, the third relates to set books, the fourth to sixth are questions of type (c) and the last two are translation passages. It is not possible to give full answers to the translation questions but the notes on these questions in Section D are particularly full.

1.

This question comes from the Institute of Linguists Grade II Examination Summer 1979. In practice, in the exam the text would be read to candidates twice. Notes can be taken during the readings. A summary of 100 words must then be written. Anything in excess of 100 words will be ignored. The text is reproduced here in written form as it provides useful practice in summarising for all of you who need to be able to summarise.

Colleges and universities will be forced to close scores of courses as a result of the substantial increase in tuition fees announced by the Government according to the National Union of Students.

It is estimated that more than 100,000 students will be forced to drop out of higher and further education because they will no longer be able to afford fees which will rise to as much as £850 per year.

University students who receive automatic grants will not have to pay the higher fees because they will be paid for them by their local education authority; but there are thousands of students who pay their own fees and there are a further 200,000 students taking college courses on discretionary grants awarded by local councils. Because of the current cuts in local authority spending it is unlikely that these grants will be increased by the amount of the rises in tuition fees which are more than trebling for some students.

Those worst affected by the rises are the 45,000 overseas students who pay their own way through college and the 9,000 postgraduate students who are responsible for paying their own fees. Estimates are that one in three of these students will be forced to drop out, with the inevitable result that universities will have to close courses.

It is said that several courses at Liverpool University are in doubt and that Birkbeck College, London University, where 84 per cent of students are part-timers who pay their own fees, will face acute difficulties.

The Union is calling for a national 'day of direct action' and expects sit-ins and occupations to be staged in protest at the higher fees in large numbers of colleges. (276 words)

2.

This is not an actual exam question but it is the kind of thing that you could be asked in any of the exams that test your ability to summarise. Read the advice on translation in section B of this chapter, then write a summary of it, using not more than 150 words.

3.

This is the kind of question you might be asked to write on one of the FCE set books.

    Charles Dickens: *The Christmas Carol*

    Describe how and why Scrooge changed during this story.

4.

This is an example of a question from the RSA CUEFL Summer 1984 Written Exam.

Pringle

SWEATERS
at
DISCOUNT PRICES
100% Wool,
Machine-washable
Sizes 34–40
V-neck Long Sleeve Sweaters
Only £12.95

COLOURS AVAILABLE
White; Navy; Neutral; New Blue;
Black; Khaki; Beaver Brown;
Derby Grey; Ranger Green; Cobalt;
Rally Red; Hunting Yellow; Bone

ALSO AVAILABLE
V-neck Slipover at sizes 36–46
at only £11.95

**Add £1.30 p. and p. for one garment
2 or more – no postage charges**

Mail order enquiries to
John Reay,
High Street,
Kersley,
Coventry,
CV6 2ER

    While you're in the UK you want to buy something to wear that's typically British. You see the above advert and decide to buy yourself a Pringle sweater. Write to the company to order the type you want. Make sure you state the type, size and colour that you want. State how you are paying and the total value of your purchase including postage and packing (p. and p.). You are leaving your present address in just over three weeks. Stress to the company that what you have ordered must be with you before then. You also feel a bit uncertain about washing a woollen sweater in a washing-machine. Enquire about the precise details of washing instructions.

5.

This is an example of the kind of question you might find in the FCE in Section B of the Use of English paper.

Read the four advertisements below and then, using the information given, complete the four paragraphs (i)–(iv) which follow. Use about fifty words for each paragraph.

(a) 2-bedroomed luxury flat to rent, kitchen-diner, sitting-room, bathroom with shower, central heating, close to Tube station. Rent £150 per week plus bills.

(b) Professional girl or student wanted to share house with two others. North London. Own bedroom. Share kitchen, bathroom and bills. No pets. Rent £30 per week.

(c) House available to let. Easy access to Central London. Three bedrooms, two reception rooms, large garden. Rent £400 p.c.m.

(d) Fully-furnished maisonette for short let (3–4 months) in South London. 2 double bedrooms. Open-plan kitchen-living room. Separate bathroom and w.c. Carport and small garden. Rent £100 p.w. all inclusive.

(i) The best accommodation for a family with two small children would be

(ii) House (d) would suit

(iii) The best accommodation for me would be

(iv) I should not like to live in

6.

This is an example of a translation passage from the Institute of Linguists Grade II Examination, Summer 1981. You have 45 minutes to do this piece of translation.

Translate the following passage into your own language. Your translation should read like a piece of original writing in your own mother tongue.

An attractive three-bedroomed bungalow on the edge of a pretty hill-country village is waiting to be occupied by Mrs Enid Belfield and her farmer husband, Gordon.

The couple have kept its large garden neat and trim during their regular visits to the bungalow at Hogmaston, near Wirksworth, Derbyshire.

But after four years the bungalow they built only a few fields from thier 17th-century farmhouse-home in the Henmore Valley remains empty.

Mrs Belfield, 54, and her husband, 61, are the only farming couple who have still to leave their home in the valley which is destined to be engulfed in the £36 million Carsington reservoir scheme.

Yet they still cannot bring themselves to part with their home and a host of farmyard pets – including Mrs Belfield's favourite, Peppermint the pig.

'They say I am kicking against fate and the like, but I am determined I will not move until the water is lapping around the front step', said Mrs Belfield.

'The bungalow is nice and has a large modern kitchen and I suppose it's the kind of place most housewives would dream about. But if I had the choice I would stay right here. Apart from anything else, I have to think of Peppermint and the other animals. If we left now there would be nowhere for them to go and I would not like that to happen.'

7.

This is another translation from an Institute of Linguists Grade II Certificate exam. You have 45 minutes to do this piece of translation. The instructions are as for the previous question.

Young people in Europe today have greater opportunities than previous generations of acquiring at least a grounding in one or more foreign languages while they are at school. But opportunities of this kind vary immensely from one country to another. Whereas in one country the study of a foreign language may be compulsory for all pupils for seven years and instruction in a second foreign language available on a voluntary basis for three years, compulsory foreign language studies in another country may be limited to three years and may be organised in such a way that they seldom result in any communicative proficiency.

The comparison between generations demands closer comment.

Admittedly compulsory schooling today generally affords greater scope for foreign language studies than used to be the case. But schools today have to prepare young people for a very different world from that which awaited yesterday's school leavers. In some respects, internationalism has gathered speed and has had more far-reaching consequences than we have perceived or perhaps have been willing to perceive.

It goes without saying, therefore, that young people with a command of one or more foreign languages can become attractive to employers, which thus saves them from being out of work.

D. TUTOR'S ANSWERS

Read the notes introducing each answer before you try to answer the question.

Then compare your answer with what has been suggested here.

1.

What are the key points of this article? A quick word count will show you that the original text is about 275 words. It has to be reduced, then, by about two-thirds. The version I suggest is 98 words and includes the main points which are:

- What has happened
- Who is affected by this
- What may happen as a result
- What the NUS is suggesting

Answer

The National Union of Students has criticised the Government's decision to raise fees for university and college courses to up to £850. Many students will have to leave their courses because they cannot afford to continue. The students who will suffer most are British students who do not get an automatic grant but pay their own fees, overseas students and post-graduates and many part-timers. Some universities will have to close courses because many students from the above categories will no longer be able to study. The Union is calling for a national day of protest against the increases in fees.

2.

In the answer suggested below, there are 90 words. The original text is about 700 words long and so you have to cut it very drastically. It is really possible just to pick out the key sentences of each paragraph and to build a précis from them without adding many of your own words at all.

Answer

Read and understand the whole text before you begin to translate it. Often a literal translation may not be possible or it may not be very natural-sounding in the target language. It may be necessary to make one long sentence into two. Compare a text that is available both in

English and your own language and see what different patterns there are in the structures of the two. Be careful about 'false friends'. Remember that many English words have more than one meaning. If a dictionary is allowed, use it carefully. Otherwise guess meanings logically from their context.

3.

This question is like a summary exercise – as are most of the questions you are likely to be asked on set books. You have only room to write the most important points. This question falls naturally into three paragraphs.

- How Scrooge was
- How he became
- Why he changed

Notice that a natural tense to use when talking about literature is the present simple. A work of literature is always there for our pleasure and that is why we use this tense. You can also use the ordinary story-telling tense, the past simple. Just be careful to be consistent. Don't use the present simple in one sentence and the past in the next.

Answer

At the beginning of the Christmas Carol Scrooge is a very mean man. He is a hard businessman who thinks only of how to save more money. Human relationships have no importance for him. He has no sympathy for those who are poor or even for his own family. He hates Christmas and thinks that it is a lot of nonsense.

By the end of the story Scrooge has completey changed. He no longer thinks only of money. He helps his poor clerk and he enjoys the company of his own relatives. He understands the true meaning of Christmas.

Why does he change in such a dramatic way? He has visions of Christmas as it has been celebrated in the past, as it is being celebrated now and as it will be celebrated in the future. He sees into the homes of his poor clerk and of his nephew and he is moved by their love for each other and by their concern even for him.

4.

In this question you have to pay particular attention to the detail in the question and to make sure that you include all the points you are told to include. Put a line through the bits of the question as you cover them. For more information about letter-writing refer to Chapter 16.

23 Arbury Road
Camford
CX1 27Z

23rd June 1985

John Reay,
High Street,
Kersley,
Coventry.
CV6 2ER

Dear Sir,

Please could you send me a Pringle V-neck, long-sleeve sweater in size 38 in black. Enclosed is a cheque for £14.25 to cover the cost of the garment plus £1.30 p. and p.

On July 15th I am leaving this country and it is very important that I should receive the sweater before my departure. I should be very grateful if you could send it to me by return of post.

Your advert states that these sweaters are machine-washable but I wonder if you could let me have some more precise washing instructions. What is the best temperature to wash at? How can I best dry my garment?

Thanking you in anticipation.
Yours faithfully,
Tonya Riaz

5.

There is plenty of freedom in which accommodation you choose for each section of your answer although (b) would clearly not be suitable for a family. What is important is that you base your answers on the information in the adverts.

Answer

(i) *The best accommodation for a family with two small children would be* house (c) because there is a separate bedroom for the parents and each small child. A large garden is good for children too. House (d) might be a little small and everything open-plan can be difficult with small children. Flat (a) lacks a garden and (b) is suitable for a single girl only.

(ii) *House (d) would suit,* for example, a professor from abroad who has come with his wife to work at London University for a term. They would not need a large house nor a long-term let. The fact that the house is fully furnished would also be convenient for them as they would not want to bring much from abroad or to buy household objects in England.

(iii) *The best accommodation for me would be* house (b) because I am a student and a girl. I enjoy sharing accommodation and as I have not lived in London before it would be a good way for me to get to know people. It is also quite cheap and I could not afford a high rent. I do not have any pets and so the fact that they are forbidden would not be a problem for me.

(iv) *I should not like to live in* flat (a) because it is so expensive and I should be worried about how I was going to pay the bills all the time. As it is close to a Tube station perhaps it could also be a little noisy. Moreover, I do not really like kitchen-diners as I don't always want my guests to see my kitchen.

Notes

6.

No 'Tutor's Answer' can be given for the two translation passages in this chapter. Below you will find just some suggestions on how to approach the translation and a brief discussion of some of the things that may be problems. When you have done the translation, try and find a teacher who can correct it for you.

Read the passage carefully. What is it all about? A couple do not want to leave their old farmhouse to go and live in a smart new house? Why do they have to leave? Because their farmhouse is going to be flooded by a new reservoir.

Think about what style the text is written in. Where do you think it was taken from? It is quite a colloquial, everyday style and probably came from a local newspaper. Try to give your translation a similar flavour.

Before you translate, think carefully about these points – they may be easy to translate into your language but they will more probably cause some difficulties.

In your language can you make an adjective 'three-bedroomed' or will you need to use a phrase like 'with three bedrooms'? You may have the same problem with the English adjective 'hill-country'. Perhaps you'll need to use a phrase like 'in hilly countryside'. If you need to use phrases would it then sound better to make the first English sentence into two in your language? For example 'There is an attractive bungalow with three bedrooms on the edge of a pretty village in hilly countryside. It is waiting. . . .' What about the verb 'wait'? Can a house wait in your language? 'to be occupied' may be translated by a noun like 'occupation' in some languages.

The names in the second two paragraphs do not need to be translated, of course, except for the word 'Valley'. If you have to transliterate the names into a different script, remember that the county, Derbyshire, is pronounced 'Darbyshire'.

The fourth sentence makes it clear that there were other people in the area who have had to move too and they have all already done so. Your translation must make that clear too.

'Destined' and 'engulfed' are quite dramatic words in English. 'The valley which is going to be flooded' would sound much more ordinary and calm. Can you find equivalent dramatic words in your language too?

Again 'a host of' means the same as 'many' but sounds more dramatic. Notice that 'farmyard pets' is not the same as 'farmyard animals'. 'Pets' suggest that these animals are much more part of the family in the way that dogs and cats often are in English homes.

It isn't necessary but you might be able to translate the pig's name literally.

Do you understand the idiom 'kicking against fate'? It means protesting against something that is inevitable. Is there an idiom with the same meaning in your own language? If not, you will have to translate the literal meaning.

The verb 'lap' is quite unusual but its meaning is probably clear from the context. It means 'make a gentle sound like a cat drinking milk'. (The same verb is used for what a cat does with milk. It laps it up.) You may feel that it is best to translate it into your language as simply 'moving around' or 'touching'.

In the last paragraph 'nice' is a positive word, of course, but it is not very strong and so make sure you translate it with a weakish word rather than with something like 'lovely' or 'beautiful'.

You may perhaps need to make the last sentence more explicit in your language. What she really means is 'If we left now they would have to stay here alone and I would not like that to happen to them.'

When you have finished translating, wait a few minutes, if possible and then come back and read your translation. Does it sound natural? Can you make any improvements? There are sure to be some corrections that you want to make. Correct them with the white fluid that typists use if possible. Your work will look much neater and you won't waste time writing everything out again.

Notes

7.

Here again are some notes which I hope may help you translate this text.

Follow the same procedure. Read the text carefully until you are confident you understand what it is all about.

What is its theme? It talks about young people's opportunities to learn foreign languages today. It says that opportunities vary from country to country but that they are generally better than they were thirty years ago. It also points out that the needs of today's world are much more international and so knowledge of a language can be helpful in finding work.

The language of this text is much more abstract than that of question 6 and your translation will need to sound academic rather than colloquial.

The last sentence in the first paragraph is very long and quite involved. You may find it best to make it two sentences by saying 'In one country . . . In another country, on the other hand, . . .' – 'on the other hand' creates the same contrast that 'whereas' gives.

Do you understand the term 'communicative proficiency'? It means being able to communicate, to say what you want and to understand other people. Traditional language-teaching in English schools used to teach pupils grammar rules and irregular verbs but the children completed their studies without knowing how to speak to a waiter in a restaurant. Do you know the term that gives the same idea in your language?

In the second paragraph can you translate 'admittedly' by one word? If not, a phrase like 'It must be admitted that' will give the same idea.

What does 'afford' mean in this context? It has nothing to do with money, of course; it means 'provides' or 'gives'.

How do you understand the expression 'gathered speed'? It means 'has become faster and faster'.

What about 'have been willing to perceive'? 'Have wanted to perceive' gives the same idea.

The last paragraph also may perhaps be better as two sentences in your language.

Again leave your translation if possible for a short time before you check it. Then read it again as objectively as possible. Is it clear? Does it sound natural? Can you make any improvements? Make them with typing fluid as neatly as you can. Then find a teacher to check your work.

E. BEYOND THE COURSEWORK

Keep a notebook with details of all the books you read. Make brief notes under the headings – plot, character, setting, style, purpose, personal reactions – for any novel you read. Write a synopsis of any non-fiction work you read. This will give you practice in summarising as well as helping you to consolidate what you have learnt from reading.

You may like to keep a similar notebook for films or plays. Write a little about each film or play you see. What was it about? What did you think about it? Write in English but write about any film you see even if it is not in English.

For translation get a story that is available both in your language and in English. Try translating parts from the English into your own language before you look at the professional version. Where did you do it differently? Which version do you prefer? Why?

Chapter 11   **Blank-filling**

A. GETTING STARTED

A number of exams test you by using gap-filling techniques. These are questions in which you have most of the words of a passage but have to decide what some missing words must be. Questions like this are said to be a very accurate test of how good your English is.

Some exams like the **FCE** give you a text with blanks for you to fill in. Others like **TOEFL**, British Council **ELTS**, and **Trinity College** offer you a choice of different possibilities to fit the blanks and you have to decide which alternative fits best. The **JMB** doesn't tell you where the blanks are – you just know that there is one word missing from each line and you have to decide where there must be a word missing and then you have to work out what that word could be.

B. ESSENTIAL PRINCIPLES

Let's think first about questions where you have complete freedom in deciding what to put in the blank. Usually these tests do not expect you to put difficult words in the blanks. They usually look for grammatical items. Most commonly you have to fill in things like articles, prepositions, auxiliary verbs, conjunctions, relative pronouns or simple verbs or adverbs.

You can only do this kind of test well if you understand what the text is about. The most important thing is to read the whole text through thoroughly until you feel you have a clear understanding of its content. Then it should not be too difficult to see what is necessary to make the text hang together grammatically.

In this section we shall do some exercises which focus on three types of grammatical items which are often tested by this kind of test. The actual exam questions practised later in the chapter will each cover a range of different points, of course.

You will find the answers to these exercises at the end of section B.

Here is a question of the FCE type. Here, however, all the words missing are prepositions. Work out what the correct answers are, check them with the answers given at the end of this section and then write down in your notebook the words and the prepositions they are associated with, e.g. to walk through a wood

Fred was walking (1) . . . a wood (2) . . . the rain one day when he suddenly noticed a strange object (3) . . . the middle of a small clearing. He went (4) . . . the object and carefully picked it (5) . . . . It was a parcel wrapped (6) . . . brown paper. He decided to open the parcel (7) . . . several different reasons, the most important (8) . . . which was simply his curiosity. (9) . . . the parcel he found a book (10) . . . George Orwell, a photograph of a girl (11) . . . an enormous hat and a large cup (12) . . . a hole (13) . . . the bottom. He was looking (14) . . . this cup and wondering what it could be used (15) . . . when suddenly he heard a yell (16) . . . anger. "What are you doing (17) . . . my parcel?" A little boy was standing (18) . . . him trembling (19) . . . rage. Fred was so startled that he dropped the cup and it broke (20) . . . pieces. He said he was sorry (21) . . . what he had done and told the small boy that he would pay (22) . . . the damage. (23) . . . that moment the small boy's big sister appeared. "(24) . . . goodness sake, Jimmy," she said. "It's quite impossible to look (25) . . . you if you won't stay near (26) . . . me. I've been looking (27) . . . you (28) . . . ages." Fred took the opportunity (29) . . . escaping (30) . . . the angry little boy. He ran away as fast as he could.

Exercise 2

This next exercise concentrates on verbs – and particularly on auxiliaries and modals.

I have been (1) . . . to swim since I was six but I never (2) . . . to like swimming in the swimming bath very much. I preferred the river although my mother (3) . . . like me going there alone. She was afraid I (4) . . . go too far from the bank and then (5) . . . into difficulty. I knew I (6) . . . not to go there without my parents but one day I decided not to (7) . . . attention to their rules. I (8) . . . been out with my older sister who (9) . . . me to swim all the way across the river. I jumped into the water and (10) . . . swimming as hard as I (11) . . . when I heard my sister (12) . . . from the bank. "Mummy's (13) . . .!" I (14) . . . decide what to do – to swim forwards to the other bank or to go back and then I realised I was (15) . . . carried downstream towards some large rocks in the middle of the river. I (16) . . . screaming. Mother quickly jumped into the water and soon (17) . . . to pull me out. She (18) . . . very crossly both to me and to my sister. "You (19) . . . have drowned!" she said to me and "You (20) . . . have known better!" to my older sister.

Exercise 3

This exercise concentrates on connectors – on words and expressions that are used to link sentences and parts of sentences together. They are very important in good written English and you will only be able to choose the right one if you fully understand the meaning of the passage to be completed.

Exercise 3	Stephen very much wanted to get married (1) . . . he was tired of living alone. He asked Mary and she said she would marry him as (2) . . . as he promised never to love anyone else. He felt he couldn't make a commitment like that and (3) . . . Stephen and Mary didn't get married. (4) . . . he proposed to Celia but she said she wouldn't marry him (5) . . . he gave her a Rolls Royce. That's far too mercenary, thought Stephen, and he decided not to marry Celia (6) . . . loving her very much. Next he asked Rosalind to marry him. She said she would marry him as (7) . . . as she finished her university course. (8) . . ., Stephen decided that he couldn't wait that long and he next proposed to Julia. She agreed to marry him (9) . . . that they could live in London. Stephen couldn't agree to that (10) . . . he hated London. "(11) . . . that we lived in London in the winter and in the country in the summer, would that suit you?" he asked. "Sorry, no," Julia replied. "I haven't been able to stand the country (12) . . . I was a child. I had no sooner arrived at my aunt's farm once (13) . . . I was bitten by a dog. Hardly had I recovered from that (14) . . . a horse kicked me." Stephen, who loved the country, (15) . . ., decided that they were incompatible too, (16) . . . was probably a good thing as the following day he met a girl (17) . . . appearance and personality he found very attractive. (18) . . ., she was equally attracted to Stephen. "You are everything (19) . . . I have always dreamt of," he said to her. She said she would marry him (20) . . . she was the only girl he had ever proposed to.

Now let's think about those questions where you are given a choice of possibilities and you have to choose the best one. This type of question is used to test your vocabulary, your grammar and your reading and listening comprehension. Reading and listening comprehension are discussed in separate chapters. Here we'll think about grammar and vocabulary.

- When doing this kind of question first read the basic question and decide what could fit the blank before you look at the alternatives suggested. If your first reaction is one of the possibilities suggested, then it is almost certainly the right answer and you do not even need to think about the other suggestions.
- If that doesn't help you, how can you eliminate the wrong alternatives? Look at what comes immediately before or after the blank.
- If there is a preposition there, it is usually a very important clue. Which alternative fits with this preposition?
- If you have to decide which verb form fits, then time expressions before or after the gap should indicate which alternative is best.
- If a noun is involved it is important to think whether it should be countable or uncountable. If there is 'a' or 'an' before the gap, then you need to look for a countable word.

- If, after looking at all the clues you still are not sure, make a guess. You have at least a 25 per cent chance of being right and if you are sure that one or even two of the alternatives are wrong then your chances are even higher.

Finally, let's think about the JMB kind of question where you have to work out where the blank is as well as to fill it. Here again the kinds of words that are missing will be little words like auxiliary verbs, prepositions, articles, relative pronouns, conjunctions and that particularly important little word, 'not'. You must again read through the text first to make sure that you understand the gist of what it is about.

Some missing words may be immediately obvious. Mark them at once. Remember that there is one word missing per line. Then check each sentence. Is the verb complete in each case? Are any prepositions or connectors needed to complete the sense of the sentence? If the sentence seems grammatically correct, perhaps not or never is necessary – the meaning of the text should make it clear if that is the case.

ANSWERS TO EXERCISES IN SECTION B

Exercise 1

(1) through; (2) in; (3) in; (4) up or over to; (5) up; (6) in; (7) for; (8) of; (9) Inside; (10) by; (11) in; (12) with; (13) in; (14) at; (15) for; (16) of; (17) with; (18) behind; (19) with; (20) into; (21) for; (22) for; (23) At; (24) for; (25) after; (26) to; (27) for; (28) for; (29) of; (30) from.

Exercise 2

(1) able; (2) used; (3) didn't; (4) would or might; (5) get; (6) ought; (7) pay; (8) had; (9) dared; (10) was; (11) could; (12) cry or shout or yell; (13) coming; (14) couldn't; (15) being; (16) started or began; (17) managed; (18) spoke; (19) might or could; (20) should.

Exercise 3

(1) because; (2) long; (3) so; (4) Next or Then; (5) unless; (6) despite; (7) soon; (8) However; (9) provided; (10) as; (11) Supposing; (12) since; (13) than; (14) when; (15) therefore; (16) which; (17) whose; (18) Fortunately; (19) that; (20) if.

C. EXAM QUESTIONS

(a) Read the notes on each question in section D before attempting to answer the question.
(b) Write your answer.
(c) Compare it with the answer given.
(d) Make sure that you understand your mistakes – if you made any!

1.
Here is a question of the FCE type. You have to fill each blank with one word only.

A man walked into a bank and asked to speak to the manager. Shown into that gentleman's office he asked if he (1) . . . have a loan.

When the manager heard that his visitor was (2) . . . one of the bank's clients, he explained that loans (3) . . . made only to customers (4) . . . accounts. "Why not open (5) . . .?"

"But I only want two pounds," said the man, "in return (6) . . . which I am prepared to offer my car (7) . . . security." (8) . . . examined the car the manager agreed (9) . . . the loan (10) . . ., as he pointed out, the proceedings were slightly unusual. The stranger left and the car was placed (11) . . . the bank's garage.

Two months (12) . . ., the customer entered the bank and asked for the return of his car, (13) . . . the manager the two pounds he (14) . . . borrowed. The manager pointed out that (15) . . . was interest to pay: the sum of fourpence. (16) . . . the customer paid. As he was leaving the manager asked (17) . . . he only wanted to borrow two pounds.

"Where (18) . . . would I be (19) to garage my car for two months (20) . . . fourpence?" said the man.

2.

This is another form of blank-filling question which is sometimes used by the FCE. Here the focus is on vocabulary. You are given a hint about the kind of word that is needed but alternatives are not suggested.

Fill each space with one word that means a way of cooking.
(a) Heat some oil in a pan and then . . . the bacon.
(b) Put the potatoes in some water and then . . . them for about twenty minutes.
(c) She's particularly good at . . . bread and cakes.
(d) If you want to . . . the chicken, put it in the oven with a little butter or bacon fat and it'll take about an hour and a half.
(e) Sausages taste delicious . . . on the barbecue.

3.

The FCE also tests your vocabulary in a blank-filling set of exercises. Here you are given a sentence with a blank and four alternative suggestions for filling that blank. You must choose which of the four suggestions is the correct one. In the exam there are twenty-five sentences of this type. This exercise is also good practice for the first part of the reading comprehension paper of the TOEFL exam which we looked at in Chapter 9.

1. You should . . . more attention to what the teacher says.
   (A) make   (B) pay   (C) do   (D) put.

2. It can be very difficult to find a (n) . . . in this country at the moment.
   (A) work   (B) career   (C) job   (D) employment

3. I washed my woollen sweater in hot water and it has . . . .
   (A) tightened   (B) shrunk   (C) decreased   (D) reduced

4. I wrote a telegram and sent a letter to the same . . ..
   (A) purpose   (B) intention   (C) effect   (D) idea.

5. It won't make much . . . whether you go today or tomorrow.
   (A) change   (B) problem   (C) matter   (D) difference

6. My grandmother is a(n) . . . of information on all sorts of subjects.
   (A) mine   (B) encyclopaedia   (C) wealth   (D) library

7. He doesn't much . . . for television.
   (A) interest   (B) care   (C) regard   (D) respect

8. Some people . . . up the language very quickly when they live in a new country.
   (A) brush   (B) pick   (C) make   (D) bring

9. Hello, is that the Town Hall? Please can I have . . . 345?
   (A) extension   (B) addition   (C) line   (D) supplement

10. You must be very careful if you . . . a bicycle in England.
    (A) drive   (B) go   (C) take   (D) ride.

11. Take your umbrella . . . it rains.
    (A) or else   (B) in case   (C) for perhaps   (D) if not

12. He agreed to take part in the play . . . he wasn't very enthusiastic about it.
    (A) despite   (B) while   (C) although   (D) however

13. I'm so cold that I can't stop . . . .
    (A) shivering   (B) trembling   (C) chattering   (D) twisting

14. The television is far too loud. Could you turn it . . . a little, please.
    (A) off   (B) back   (C) out   (D) down

15. Most people do not realise just how much work goes on . . . in a bank.
    (A) under the table   (B) behind the scenes   (C) outside the door   (D) over the moon

16. Are you sure you can . . . with all that luggage?
    (A) carry   (B) succeed   (C) do   (D) cope

17. . . . I were able to help you.
    (A) If only   (B) I hope   (C) I would like   (D) I wanted

18. I think we'd be quicker to walk. There's a terrible traffic . . . .
    (A) congestion   (B) stop   (C) jam   (D) block

19. Is there any . . . why he can't pay?
    (A) reason   (B) answer   (C) purpose   (D) cause

20. I think you'd better . . . to a different school.
    (A) to attend   (B) go   (C) moved   (D) leaving

21. You must get some fresh bread for our visitors; this loaf is terribly . . . .
    (A) crusty   (B) crisp   (C) stale   (D) ancient

22. Could you pass me some oil, please. I want to . . . these eggs.
    (A) boil   (B) poach   (C) scramble   (D) fry

23. Tell the chairperson if you want to . . . any points at the meeting.
    (A) rise   (B) raise   (C) rouse   (D) arouse

24. Chess is one of my favourite . . . .
    (A) games   (B) plays   (C) leisure   (D) hobby

25. We had some coffee before . . . .
    (A) going home   (B) to leave the restaurant   (C) ask for the
    bill   (D) paid for the meal

4.

This is the style of question that you have to test your grammar in the
TOEFL or the British Council ELTS test.

    You have to choose which of the four alternatives given fits the
space.
1. We spent a lot of money . . . souvenirs when we were on
    holiday.
    (A) for   (B) at   (C) on   (D) by

2. Although I've worked in New York for years I . . . in such an
    enormous city.
    (A) used to live   (B) can't get used to living   (C) am not yet
    used to live   (D) am getting used to live

3. In American schools the US flag . . . every morning.
    (A) is raised   (B) is risen   (C) is raising   (D) raises

4. I'll help you fix your car . . . you help me when mine breaks
    down.
    (A) whenever   (B) as soon as   (C) as long as   (D) unless

5. In the demonstration at the University last night the Prime
    Minister . . . .
    (A) had an egg thrown at him.   (B) was thrown at by an
    egg.   (C) had thrown eggs at him.   (D) was thrown with eggs.

6. She went to France . . . .
    (A) for learn French   (B) for learning French   (C) for to learn
    French   (D) to learn French

7. When we arrived, the auditorium was empty. All the
    audience . . . .
    (A) were leaving   (B) had left   (C) left   (D) had been leaving

8. Teacher blamed the boy's parents . . . not setting him a good
    example.
    (A) of   (B) by   (C) for   (D) with

9. If Shakespeare . . . born in Italy, he'd have written in Italian.
    (A) had been   (B) would have been   (C) were   (D) was

10. Hurry up, children. It's high time you . . . to bed.
    (A) to go   (B) went   (C) are going   (D) would go

11. If he wants to pass the exam he'd better . . . harder.
(A) to work   (B) working   (C) to working   (D) work

12. . . . . he isn't handsome, he's still very attractive.
(A) In spite of   (B) However,   (C) In case   (D) Despite the fact that

13. You really ought . . . . It's very bad for your health.
(A) stop to smoke   (B) to stop to smoke   (C) to stop smoking   (D) stop smoking

14. They say that the older you get . . . .
(A) the wiser you get.   (B) the more you get wise.   (C) you get wiser   (D) you get the wiser.

15. He suggested . . . to tomorrow's air display together.
(A) us to go   (B) we went   (C) we shall go   (D) we to go.

5.

This question comes from a Trinity College summer 1984 examination.

Read the following passage and select from each set of words in the numbered brackets the word or words you consider the most appropriate. Write the bracket number in front of each answer.

He had (1. a, some, few) difficulty in getting the mule into the hut. Then he (2. lifted, climbed, raised) up to the top of the hill and (3. laid, lied, lay) there, watching. The desert seemed empty, but he knew that it was not so. Someone was there, waiting. He went back to the house. Maquita brought some food (4. at, in, to) the table. As he ate, Jesse was thinking deeply, taking little (5. attention, notice, regard) of the lady. Her face was small and covered with dirt and dust. Her hair was (6. sort of, kind of, a sort of) dirty golden colour, tied up with bits of string. Jesse hardly looked at her as she sat there at the table, yet he felt (7. secure, safe, sure) that she was glad that he had stayed. The meal was finished; they left the table. She (8. round, turned, revolved) as if to look at him: "Jesse, how old are you?" "That's a strange thing to ask me," he said. "No woman (9. ever, dared, dare) asked me that before. I think I'm about eighteen." They were now standing quite (10. closed, close, next) to each other. Jesse had been travelling (11. during, since, for) weeks in the dry, waterless desert: he carried with him the (12. sniff, smell, perfume) of those unwashed places. "Jesse," she said, "you seem to think that there's nothing (13. rather, ever, quite) as important as gold – don't you? Well let me tell you that there are things which are (14. lot, so, far) more important. Cleanliness is one of them."

He was so surprised (15. as, that, than) he could find no answer. "Over there by the door, Jesse, we keep a pot of water for use in (16. cause, case, event) of any great need. I think this is one."

He began to understand.

"What!" he said, "waste water in this way – in washing!" It was (17. like, so, as if) she had asked him to do some terribly wrong thing.

He (18, had been borne, had born, had been born) in the desert; he had lived all his life in the desert where every drop of water was counted; a cupful of water might be a matter of life or death. But he did what she (19. told, said, did). When he had finished, she used the last few cupfuls of water to wash (20. up, clean, away) the dust from her own face and neck.

6.

This is a question of the JMB type in which there is a word missing in each sentence. You have to mark in the passage where the word is missing and then to write at the side of the page the missing word.

'Some writers like to type up own work – or
have – if they don't have a secretary to hand.
Most professional journalists come into category, for instance;
they are used to at a typewriter, typing as
they go. If you already work this you'll love a word-processor.
It gives you infinitely freedom to revise and adapt your work.
But at the time, you'll have special needs you must consider when
choosing your machine. If you're part of writer/secretary team,
which the person who originates the document
is the person who, when it is completed,
will typing it in, then you'll have different requirements. You
probably won't so concerned about skipping around from
page to page of a document. You'll want system on which
you run off rough copies for review, quickly
and cheaply, producing a final, perfect version.'

D. TUTOR'S NOTES AND ANSWERS

(a) Look at the notes introducing the answer to each question before you answer the question yourself.
(b) Then write your answer.
(c) Finally compare your answer with that given below. If your answer is wrong, use your dictionary, grammar book and teacher to help you work out why your answer is not correct.

1.

Remember to read the text all through first. If any answers seem immediately obvious, fill them in. Think about where a preposition is necessary. Which one fits? Check that each sentence has a subject and a complete verb to go with that subject. In one place in this exercise 'not' is the necessary word. Can you see where?

Answers

(1) might or could
(2) not   (6) for
(3) were   (7) as
(4) with   (8) Having
(5) one   (9) to

(10) although
(11) in
(12) later
(13) giving
(14) had
(15) there
(16) This
(17) why
(18) else
(19) able
(20) for

2.

If the FCE has a question like this, it will appear in the Use of English paper. The questions here can vary quite a bit from year to year and so it is particularly important to read the instructions to the questions very carefully.

Here you have to decide on the right word. You also have to think about what form it should be in. In (c) what form of the verb will follow 'at', for example? Don't spend too long on questions like this. Probably you either know the word or you don't and there is no point in wasting a lot of time trying to think of a possible answer.

Answers

(a) fry   (b) boil   (c) baking   (d) roast   (e) grilled

3.

In questions like this remember to look at what surrounds the blank. The meaning of the whole sentence may give you a clue about what can fill the gap. Or perhaps more important clues may be found in what comes immediately beside the blank. Is there a preposition nearby? If so, that will determine what can fit the gap.

The same words tend to be tested quite regularly in these exams. Practice from test books and old papers can help you – as long as you really try to make sure you understand why the alternatives given are right or wrong.

Answers

1 (B);   2 (C);   3 (B);   4 (C);   5 (D);   6 (A);   7 (B);   8 (B);
9 (A);   10 (D);   11 (B);   12 (C);   13 (A);   14 (D);   15 (B);
16 (D);   17 (A);   18 (C);   19 (A);   20 (B);   21 (C);   22 (D);
23 (B);   24 (A);   25 (A).

4.

This question tests many of the favourite points of English examiners. Before you do the test, check that you are sure about these points:

- Used to / be used to / get used to
- Constructions with blame, stop and suggest
- It's time
- Had better
- Raise / rise
- The basic patterns of 'if' sentences

Now try to answer the questions. If you aren't sure about why anything is right or wrong, check in a good reference book.

1 (C);   2 (B);   3 (A);   4 (C);   5 (A);   6 (D);   7 (B);   8 (C);   9 (A);   10 (B);   11 (D);   12 (D);   13 (C);   14 (A);   15 (B)

5.

The notes which follow may help you to decide which answers fit some of the blanks.

The text is laid out in this book as it is in the exam and you probably find it is quite difficult to read. Try to read it without looking at all the alternatives in brackets. You may find it helpful to highlight what is in brackets; then it should be easier to ignore those parts when you read. This will help you to understand what the text is about.

2 and 3.   Do you need a verb which takes an object or not?
5.   What verb is associated with 'attention'?
9.   What form of the verb would follow 'dared'?
12.   What kind of smell is 'perfume'?
15.   What word is always associated with 'so' in sentences like this?
17.   'Like' should not be used as a conjunction – it is a preposition.
19.   'Told' must be followed by the person she told it to.

Answers

1 some;   2 climbed;   3 lay;   4 to;   5 notice;   6 a sort of;   7 sure;   8 turned;   9 ever;   10 close;   11 for;   12 smell;   13 quite;   14 far;   15 that;   16 case;   17 as if;   18 had been born;   19 said;   20 away.

6.

First of all, read through the passage. What is it about? Do you agree that it's about choosing a word processor to fit your needs?

Read through the guidelines given in section B again before you try to answer the question.

Answers

up their own
have to – if
into this category
to working at
this way you'll
infinitely more freedom
the same time
of a writer /
in which
is not the
will be typing
won't be so
want a system
you can run
cheaply, before producing

E. BEYOND THE COURSEWORK

You could practise the FCE or JMB type of blank-filling exercises by working with a friend and testing each other by reading out sentences from an English book but missing out one word. You must choose the words you miss out carefully so that they are of the types of words which would really be omitted in the exam i.e. not difficult vocabulary items.

You could even do this yourself if you have a text that you can disfigure. Use Tippex to paint over some appropriate words. A few days later you can check to see if you can work out what the words were. It is a good idea to make a note of what you have Tippexed when you do it, just in case you can't remember!

Doing this is one way of focusing on the structure of the English language. It will also help you answer those exam questions where you are actually given alternatives to choose from even though you don't give yourself or your friend alternative choices.

As with all questions in written English exams the best way to prepare yourself is by reading as much as possible and in a way that is as attentive as possible.

Chapter 12

Listening comprehension

A. GETTING STARTED

Most of this chapter is concerned with techniques of doing listening comprehension. This book does not have an accompanying cassette and so you will have to find your listening practice material elsewhere. The chapter will give you some ideas about where you can find it. In sections C and D you will find transcripts of some questions from the listening comprehension components of different exams and some suggestions about how you could make use of them.

Listening comprehension is a part of all the exams considered in this book except for the **Oxford Higher Certificate** and the **Trinity College Written** examination. In the **Trinity College Spoken** exams and the **ESB** exams listening comprehension is not directly tested but it is an important skill in carrying out the conversation and other tasks required by these exams.

Listening comprehension is tested in different ways by the different exams. In the **FCE**, the **RSA CUEFL**, **Pitman's Syllabus C** and the **ARELS** exams you have to listen to more or less realistic bits of spoken English. These are often taken from real or simulated radio broadcasts. Having listened to a cassette you then have to answer questions. Usually but not always in these exams you hear the listening excerpts twice each. The questions in these exams may take different forms. You may have to:

- answer in a few words
- decide whether statements about what you have heard are true or false
- mark a diagram
- fill in a form
- select the best answer from a set of multiple choice items

In the **JMB** exam you listen to talks on slightly technical subjects – planning a garden and removing stains from bottles are topics that have been used in the past. In this exam you hear each recording twice. You then use what you hear to do things like:

- complete diagrams
- label illustrations
- identify statements that correspond to what you hear

The **TOEFL** listening test like all the other parts of the TOEFL exam depends on multiple-choice questions. First you hear a lot of short statements and answer a question relating to each. The multiple-choice answers are printed for you but the question itself is recorded like the statements. In the second part of the TOEFL listening test you hear slightly longer bits of English, with two or three questions on each. In this exam you only hear each item once.

The **British Council ELTS listening test** is similar in form to the TOEFL listening test.

The **Pitman's Syllabus L** exams use dictation as a means of testing your listening comprehension. They also read another text to you twice and then in the **Intermediate** exam you have to answer questions on what you have heard. In the **Higher Intermediate** exam you have to write a summary of what you heard. Unlike all other exams, notes may not be made while the texts are being read to you.

In the **Institute of Linguists Grade II** exam you also have to give a written summary of something that has been read to you twice.

Whether there is a listening component in your exam or not and whatever form it may take, listening is a skill which is very important to any learner of a foreign language. It is much easier to develop your listening skills if you have the chance to visit an English-speaking country. The ideas which follow should be especially useful for you if you are not studying in an English-speaking country, but they should also help you if you are in Britain or the USA or another country where the main language is English.

B. ESSENTIAL PRINCIPLES

When you are listening to something in English you are usually listening either for specific information or for the general meaning of what is being said. In either case it is not necessary to understand every word that the speaker says.

The best way you can train yourself both to make sensible guesses about meaning when listening and not to panic when you just can't understand something is by listening to as much English as possible. This should ironically not only convince you of the fact that it isn't actually necessary to understand everything in order to understand what is important, but it should also give you a much greater chance of understanding everything because, as we say in English, 'Practice makes perfect'.

How can you best give yourself this listening practice? It is not as simple, perhaps, as to practise your reading or writing but there are plenty of things you can do.

First you can listen to radio broadcasts in English anywhere in the world. The BBC World Service and the Voice of America are the two major stations which broadcast worldwide in English, but you may find that you can tune in to other stations too. If you don't have a friend or a teacher who knows what the appropriate wavelengths in your local area are, you can find out by writing to your local British or American Embassy or to:

BBC World Service
Bush House
The Strand
London
WC2B 4PH

Try to listen at least to the news in English every day. You will probably find it hard the first time but the same kind of vocabulary comes up again and again and so it will soon become familiar. Also you can later listen to or read the news in your own language and this may clarify points that you weren't sure about in English.

If you have a radio-cassette recorder you could also record the English news broadcast and listen to it several times to try to work out exactly what the newcaster is saying.

The material for the listening questions in the **ARELS** exams is usually mainly taken from the radio. Try to listen not only to the news but also to the kind of programme where an interviewer chats to someone about his or her job or an unusual hobby. This will be particularly good practice for the ARELS exam but it will also help for the FCE and the RSA which can use a similar type of material. Most important of all, it will train you to understand the kind of English which you will hear when you go to an English-speaking country or meet English-speaking people.

A cassette or record player will help you in lots of ways. Many students feel they learn a lot of English from listening to songs. Try to find some recordings of songs where the words are reasonably clear (folk or country songs and slow love songs are usually reasonably clear) and play something as you get dressed each morning. This will help to accustom you to the rhythms of spoken English, to the way little words are scarcely pronounced, and you may learn some new vocabulary too. Remember, however, that the grammar of songs may not always be exactly what you learn in your textbook – English and American people are allowed to make occasional grammar mistakes when they speak or sing but, if possible, try not to copy them in this. Nevertheless, when listening to a song, sometimes discipline yourself by trying to write down its words.

You can buy cassettes or records not only of songs in English but also of plays, short stories and poetry. These can also be a very pleasant way of practising listening comprehension. The text of what is on the recording will also probably be available. Try to listen several times without reading the text. Later check your comprehension by listening and reading at the same time.

Then there are lots of cassettes which are produced for students of English. These often go with books and have sets of exercises helping you to train your ear to listen more effectively to English. Longman have published a series of listening materials with workbooks. *Listening to Maggie* and *It Happened to Me* should be the right kind of level for you. Many other publishers of English as a Foreign Language also have good materials which you could use. These cassettes are rather expensive for an individual student but perhaps you can listen to them in school or you could club together with a group of students to buy one.

You can exploit your cassette recorder in another interesting way if you have an English-speaking penfriend. Instead of always sending each other letters, why not occasionally exchange cassettes on which you have recorded your news for each other in English? This will give you good practice in speaking as well as listening, of course.

You will find it easier if you listen to something where the content is already familiar, for example, lectures on a subject you are particularly interested in or talks about your own country. Find out if there is anything like this going on in English in your own area. It may be that there are lectures in English at your local university or college which you might be able to attend or there may be talks aimed at tourists which you could also go along to.

Indeed if you live in an area where there are a lot of foreign tourists, you may find that they can be a good source of spoken, as well as listening, practice. Can you think of any ways in which this would be possible in your area?

LISTENING FOR SPECIFIC INFORMATION

Some questions require you to listen for specific information. This often involves writing down names or numbers. You must be quite sure of the names of the letters of the alphabet in English and of how to pronounce numbers so that you can recognise them quickly and easily when they are said to you in English. In Chapter 6 you will find some help with this. Practise with a friend, spelling things to each other and dictating phone numbers, prices and large numbers as fast as you possibly can.

LISTENING FOR THE GIST

Most questions, however, require you only to listen for the gist, in other words for the general idea of what is being said. The main thing is to practise guessing things from context, just as you do when you are reading.

Imagine yourself at the airport where announcements are being made in your own language. Often there is so much noise that the announcements are not very clear. But if you are travelling to Rome and you hear "mm mmmm mm mmmm mm Rome mmm mm mmmmm m Gate 14", you probably feel confident that this is the call for your flight and you immediately make your way to Gate 14. It is the same with English – you should not expect to understand every word and you should not panic when you hear something that you do not understand. Just listen calmly for what comes next and it may well clarify what you didn't understand. If it doesn't, don't worry, perhaps it wasn't very important anyway.

OTHER TYPES OF LISTENING COMPREHENSION QUESTIONS

Listening comprehension is tested in other ways by some exams as we saw in section A.

Dictation is used by the Pitman's exam. You will find an example of this in section C and some guidance with doing dictation in section D.

Multiple choice questions are also used to test listening. Here the questions may test understanding of both gist and specific information. Read the questions through first if you have a chance, concentrating on the stem of the question rather than the four 'distractors'. If you can't decide which is the right answer, don't forget to make a guess. There is always a 25 per cent chance you will guess right.

Understanding of the importance of **stress** is tested in the ARELS exams. Question 2 in section C is an example of this. You can practise for this kind of question by practising stressing sentences in different ways yourself.

Can you read these sentences so that the correct word is stressed each time?

(a) The French student doesn't speak English very well but the French teacher does.
(b) The French student doesn't speak English very well but she speaks Spanish well.
(c) The French student doesn't speak English very well but she writes English well.
(d) The French student doesn't speak English very well but the German student does.
(e) The French student doesn't speak English very well but she speaks it quite well.

In each case, you are stressing in the final part of the sentence the word that contrasts with something in the early part of the sentence.

C. EXAM QUESTIONS

There are just three questions in this section. They are included to give you some idea of the kind of question you may come across. The best ways to practise for a listening exam, however, is to do some of the activities mentioned in section B.

Practise these questions by working with another person, if possible. Read each other the material that you would hear in the exam and test each other in that way.

1.
This is an example of a dictation question. Try it even if you are not planning to take the Pitman's Higher Intermediate exam – from a past paper of which this particular dictation has been taken.

Ask a teacher or friend to read you this passage following the instructions given.

1. Read the passage through at normal speed to give the Candidates an idea of the contents.
2. Dictate slowly and clearly in short groups of words, as indicated by the strokes. All punctuation should be given in English.
3. Read the passage again at normal speed after telling the Candidates that they make any corrections during this final reading.

Motoring really has become a nightmare nowadays. / To begin with, / the cost of a new car, / regardless of size, / makes it virtually impossible to buy one / unless you happen to be lucky enough / to command a high salary. / Secondly, the chances of purchasing / a new car which proves to be / comparatively trouble-free / are daily becoming more remote. / Manufacturers are even known / to call in a specific model / for certain modifications, or occasionally, / to make something perhaps as vital as / the steering completely safe. / Then, of course, there is the annual burden / of the licence and the ever-rising insurance premium, / not to mention the high price of petrol / and soaring maintenance costs. / Lastly, the motorist has to endure / not only traffic congestion / especially at those times when / he needs to drive to work / or back home, / but also badly neglected road surfaces, / which are probably too costly to repair.

See the notes in section D for some comments about potential problems in this dictation. The text of the dictation is not reprinted there.

2.

One of the best listening tests in the ARELS exam is one that tests your understanding of the importance of stress in English. Here is an example. You will have to ask a native English speaker to read it for you, if possible, so that the meaning intended by the exam is clear; the words in darker print should be stressed. (ARELS Higher Certificate 35)

In this question we want you to finish some sentences. Any suitable sentence in good English will score marks. Listen to these examples.

> I don't want a **blue** coat. I want a red one.
> I don't want a blue **coat**. I want a blue hat.

Now you do the same. Do the examples first for practice.

(1) I don't want a **blue** coat. I want . . .
(2) I don't want a blue **coat**. I want . . .
(3) I don't want an **English** dictionary. I want . . .
(4) I don't want a bottle of **wine**. I want . . .
(5) I don't want a **fried** egg. I want . . .
(6) I don't want a **chocolate** cake. I want . . .
(7) I don't want a gold **ring**. I want . . .

3.

This is a test of listening for gist. It comes from ARELS Higher Certificate AH35.

In this question you will hear a telephone call and you'll be asked to pass on a message to someone else. You will only hear the call once and you may take notes if you like. This is the situation. You are staying with an English couple called John and Susan. You are alone in the house when the phone rings. You answer it. Listen.

Susan: Look, it's Susan here. Isn't John there yet? Oh dear, well could you take a message for him? I'm stuck in the office. There's a sales meeting going on and it looks as if we'll be here for another hour. There's no way I'm going to get home in time to do dinner, so I think the best thing is to eat out somewhere. When John gets in, tell him what's happened and ask him to ring up a restaurant and book a table for us. I don't mind where so long as it's not too expensive. I suggest the Greek restaurant in the High Street – the Spartan – but I'm not fussy. But he'll have to book a table or we won't get one. I'll be back at about seven. OK? See you then. Bye.

A few minutes later John comes home. You have fifteen seconds to give him Susan's message. Start now.

D. TUTOR'S NOTES AND ANSWERS

1.

Dictation used to be a common way of testing listening comprehension in exams. It is now used only in the Pitman's exams. Dictation may not be something that you will ever need to do in real life unless you are going to be a secretary but it can still be quite a useful way of training your ear.

If you are doing an exam where dictation is involved you will need to know the names of the punctuation marks in English. Can you match up these marks with their names. If you're not sure, use a dictionary to check your answers.

!	question mark
" "	full stop
'	asterisk
( )	comma
–	hyphen
,	dash
.	apostrophe
?	exclamation mark
;	semi-colon
:	inverted commas
*	brackets
-	colon

When doing a dictation it is very important to think about the meaning of what you are writing. Read your work through carefully at the end. Does the text seem to be correct grammatically? Is the meaning clear? If so, then the chances are that you have not made many serious mistakes.

2.

The important thing here is to listen carefully for the stressed word and then to say something that contrasts with that word.

(3) I don't want an **English** dictionary. I want a French one.
(4) I don't want a bottle of **wine**. I want a bottle of beer.
(5) I don't want a **fried** egg. I want a boiled one.
(6) I don't want a **chocolate** cake. I want a cream one.
(7) I don't want a gold **ring**. I want a gold chain.

3.

Although the instructions say that you can take notes in this exercise, it is probably not a good idea to do so. If you write something it is very easy to lose concentration and to miss the next bit of what is being said. Only make a note of numbers or names or something that you might easily forget. The important thing here is to listen for gist. You can repeat Susan's message, using any words that you like but you must get across the basic points.

Record your answer if possible, not speaking for more than fifteen seconds, and then check what you say with the answer given below.

Answer

Seven marks are given for this answer, one for each of the points listed below:

- Susan is at a (Sales) meeting at her work
- She'll be back late
- At about 7 o'clock
- There won't be time to prepare dinner
- John should ring a restaurant and book a table for dinner
- She suggests the Spartan but she's not really fussy

E. BEYOND THE COURSEWORK

Section B dealt with many ideas for developing your listening skills far beyond the immediate needs of an intermediate exam. Here is one final suggestion for those of you who have the chance to visit an English-speaking country. While you are there, eavesdrop as much as possible. Do you know the word 'eavesdrop'? It is probably something which you were told not to do as a child. We tell English children: 'Eavesdroppers never hear good of themselves'. But you can eavesdrop with the worthy aim of improving your English. It means listening to other people's private conversations. You can do it on buses, in cafés and pubs and in English queues. You will probably find it quite hard at first but keep trying. You may hear some quite amusing things.

Chapter 13

Presenting a point of view

Chapter 13

A. GETTING STARTED

This chapter deals with the language of presenting a point of view. It covers language that will be useful when you need to present an opinion in a logical way, either when you write or when you speak. It is a skill which is tested by many exams.

FCE, Oxford, RSA, JMB, The British Council, The Institute of Linguists, Pitmans, Trinity College all test your ability to present an opinion in *writing*. **ARELS, The Institute of Linguists** and the **ESB** all test how well you can present your opinion *orally* and they let you have time to prepare your presentation. The **RSA** and **Trinity College** also require you to express opinions but in an unprepared and less extended way.

Apart from being necessary for exams it is something that you may well find useful in the future – particularly if you are going to use English in your job or if you are going to travel much in English-speaking countries.

Giving your opinion is a very personal thing. Exactly what you say is not so important from an examiner's point of view but the way that you say it is very important. For this reason this chapter gives more space to section B than some other chapters and only two model compositions and two model talks are given.

For exam purposes it is recommended that you follow the advice given in section B even if you feel that it limits you. It is – sadly, perhaps – risky to be too original in exams. It's better to keep to the formulae that examiners like.

B. ESSENTIAL PRINCIPLES

PLANNING YOUR PRESENTATION

It is very important to plan your presentation well and time spent planning is certainly not time wasted.

Firstly, note down all the ideas which a subject brings into your head.

Secondly, organise these ideas into a logical plan.

A student of mine had to write on the subject 'My First Impressions of England'. The ideas which she noted down first were:

(a) Small identical houses with little gardens
(b) Queues
(c) Litter in streets
(d) Pubs on every corner
(e) Lots of parks
(f) Bus conductor called me 'love'
(g) Friendly landlady with six cats
(h) First meal – delicious!

She decided to organise her composition in this way:

1. Arrival in England – first time abroad alone – all very strange
2. Bus journey from airport – bus conductor 'love' – houses – parks
3. Arrival at landlady's – friendly – cats
4. First meal – expected it would be terrible as everyone had warned me at home – delicious
5. Walk after dinner – litter on streets – queues for cinema – lots of pubs – went into one in a side street – people joked with me
6. Conclusion – didn't like lots of things about the surroundings of England but immediately liked the people – and the food! Now after a month feels much the same.

She spent at least twenty minutes planning her composition in this way but then she was able to write an excellent piece of work in a relatively short time.

Now you try it. Write down the ideas that come into your head when you think of each of these subjects and then try to organise them into a clear plan for each essay.

(a) The joys and problems of learning English
(b) Keeping pets
(c) The changing roles of women today

WRITING YOUR COMPOSITION OR GIVING YOUR TALK

When you come to write your composition or to give your talk it is very important to make it clear to the reader or the listener what the stages in the development of your presentation are. This will make it very much easier for others to follow your thoughts and so they are more likely to be impressed by what you say. This is particularly important if you are trying to argue a case. Certain phrases help to clarify the logic of your argument, for example:

- The subject of this composition/talk is . . .
- There are those who maintain that . . .
- It can also be argued that . . .
- On the other hand, . . .
- Moreover,
- In conclusion,

Notice the pattern which these phrases give. Firstly some points are given for one side of the argument. Then some points are given for the other side. Then there is a conclusion in which the writer will probably make his own position clear. Notice that the useful phrases suggested above do not include 'I think' and 'in my opinion'. Do not use these too often. It is better to keep to the more impersonal phrases listed.

The phrases above give a typical formula for writing a discursive composition in English. Using all the above phrases in the order in which they are given, try some practice in presenting a point of view. Write or speak on the subject 'Smoking should be made illegal'. Now try 'Television is more of a bad influence than a good one'. Now how about 'Air travel versus train travel'? The framework given by these phrases may not be very original but it helps both you to clarify your thoughts and your audience to see where you are going in a way that they will find reassuring.

If you plan well you will probably not make the mistake of failing to answer the question. If you are asked to write on 'The Joys and Problems of Learning English' you must be sure to refer to some joys as well as to the problems. Note, however, that if you are asked to discuss a controversial subject like 'Smoking should be made illegal' it does not matter whether you decide in favour of or against the subject, as long as you argue your point clearly.

If you plan well you will also probably avoid the other common mistake of going off the point. You will lose marks if you talk, in a composition on 'Keeping pets', as much about your boyfriend as your dog. When you are giving a talk too, you must keep to the point. Is it relevant to talk about, for example, football for the whole of a one- minute talk on 'English food'? It is hard to imagine how it could be made relevant and the examiner will think that you have done it because you know a lot of football vocabulary and no food vocabulary – even if this is not the case.

Look back now to the beginning of section B and try this exercise. Check to see whether I have made my points clearly enough. What do you think are the four main points I have been trying to make so far? Write down what you think they are in this space

1.

2.

3.

4.

Then look at the answers on the following page.

Do you agree that the four main points I was trying to make are the following?

1. Spend time planning.
2. Make your plan clear for your reader or listener.
3. Answer the question.
4. Keep to the point.

If you did not get all these points, was it because I didn't express myself clearly enough? How could I have made it clearer for you? (Any suggestions happily accepted!)

Having looked at planning and presentation, let us now turn to other aspects of expressing an opinion. I should like to point out that what we're going to look at is quite advanced and is really only for you if you are already writing accurate English and want to consider ways of improving your style. If you still find it very difficult to express yourself in English, do not worry too much about the quite complex things we discuss below. We shall look at these three areas:

(a) useful expressions;
(b) beginnings and endings;
(c) making it interesting.

USEFUL EXPRESSIONS

When you are presenting an opinion in writing or in a formal spoken way you may well find some of the expressions used in the twenty sentences below useful. I have put the expressions into a complete sentence as this may clarify meaning and usage for you. I have given sentences which relate to the general topic of twentieth-century problems.

- **I should like first to consider** the problem of unemployment.
- **I intend to limit this composition/talk to** a discussion of inflation in my own country.
- **It depends on how we define** women's liberation.
- **On the whole I agree with the statement that** 'Travel broadens the mind' but I feel that it would be more accurate if modified slightly.
- **Perhaps it would be more accurate to say** that travel broadens the minds of those whose minds are open.
- **There are two main reasons why I am opposed to/ in favour of** compulsory military service.
- The microchip **has already brought us many advantages**.
- **It cannot be denied**, that computers have created certain problems for society.
- **It goes without saying that** not all football fans are hooligans.
- **I should like to concentrate on two main points**.
- **Several factors must be taken into account** when trying to decide what makes the ideal school.
- **The main drawback of** air travel is that you do not have time to adjust to the change in your surroundings.

- **On the one hand**, women now have more freedom than ever before; **on the other hand**, they also have greatly increased responsibilities.
- **There is an increasing tendency towards** violence in our society.
- **Let me illustrate my point with the following example.**
- This policy **has a serious effect not only on** the health services **but also on** education.
- **The main problem is that** we do not really communicate with one another.
- **Having discussed** the causes of unemployment, **let us now turn to a consideration of** its consequences.
- **All things considered**, I remain firmly in favour of disarmament.
- **To sum up, the advantages of** television **far outweigh its disadvantages.**

Why not practise these expressions by trying to use as many of them as possible in a composition or talk on 'The Influence of the Computer on Life Today'?

BEGINNINGS AND ENDINGS

First and last impressions are extremely important and so try particularly hard to start and finish your talk or composition in a way that is:

(a) accurate;
(b) interesting.

Note that the former of these is perhaps more important. An elementary mistake at the very beginning will make the examiner feel that you are not a good student and you will have to do very well later on to compensate for this first impression. It is also certainly important to begin in an interesting way. It will not help you to start – as students quite often do – by saying 'I don't really know very much about this subject'. It may be honest but it does not encourage the examiner to look forward to hearing what you have to say.

As the beginning of a composition is especially important, you may find that it is easier to leave half a page blank and to write the middle of your composition before you do the beginning. The middle is often easier to write and by the time you have done it, you will not only have got into the swing of writing but you should also have a clearer idea of what you want to say in your first paragraph.

Sometimes you may be able to think of an original and striking way to begin. Don't waste time trying to do this if it doesn't come easily. Use one of these standard formulae:

1. *A general statement of the problem to be discussed*:
    Air travel has brought society both advantages and disadvantages.
    OR
    This is one of the most important problems facing the world today.

2. *A statement of your position*:
    I am a committed supporter of the women's liberation movement.
    OR
    It is hard to agree with the statement that 'Television has done society more harm than good'.

3. *A definition of the topic to be discussed*:
    Blood sports can be defined as those sports which centre on the killing of some animal.
    OR
    First of all, it is necessary to define what we mean by terrorism.

4. *A statement of what you intend to do in your talk or composition*.
    In this talk/composition I am going first to describe the nature of the energy crisis as it affects my country. I shall then examine the causes of the crisis and, finally, I shall look at some ways in which we may be able to overcome energy problems.
    OR
    In this talk/composition I shall limit myself to discussing the work of just one modern English poet, namely John Betjeman.

Endings are almost as important as beginnings. Once again there are standard formulae which may help you if you have no more original ideas. The best thing to do is simply to summarise what you have said and to draw a conclusion. For example:
In conclusion, although television has its drawbacks, I consider that it has done society far more good than harm.
OR
To sum up, the women's liberation movement has already achieved a great deal but there is still much more that remains to be done before women can really consider themselves liberated.
OR
All things considered, the energy problem is one of the most pressing issues in today's world and we must do all we can to solve it without delay.

MAKING IT INTERESTING

In this section I want to suggest a few ways of making the presentation of your opinion more interesting and therefore more forceful.

1. You may find it useful to insert questions into your talk or composition e.g.:
    * Why do I believe this?
    * What are the reasons for this state of affairs?
    * How can we solve this problem?
    Questions make your reader or listener stop to think and they give life to your style.

2. Dramatic inversion is also a good structure for presenting an opinion in a forcible way. Check in your grammar book if you are not sure how to use this rather advanced structure. Examples of it in practice are:

- Nowhere is the problem more serious than in France.
- Only under certain circumstances can this solution be applied.
- Never did he write more powerfully than in his autobiography.

3.   Another structure which gives strength to your argument is this one:
- It is shocking that people should be allowed to live in such conditions.
- It is disgraceful that nothing should have been done to solve this problem.
- It is surprising that so many people should still be so afraid of computers.

4.   Use concrete examples to illustrate your point. In other words, don't always talk or write in abstract terms. Being specific will make your work both clearer and more interesting for the examiner. When you discuss pollution, for example, refer to any particular instance of pollution you have read about or have personal experience of. Not only will this be more interesting for the examiner but you will also probably find it easier to write good English when you are being specific rather than abstract.

Bear these essential principles in mind when you are trying the exam questions in section C. You will probably not be able to use all the advice given in each of the questions as the length of work required at this level is usually very short.

C. EXAM QUESTIONS

(a)   Read through the notes introducing each model answer.
(b)   Then write your own composition.
(c)   Read the Tutor's answer.
(d)   Compare your answer with the tutor's. Where is yours better?
(e)   Where is it not so good?
(f)   Can you now rewrite your composition or talk so that it is better than it was at first?

1.
This is a question of the FCE exam type.
What are the advantages and disadvantages of the telephone?
Write between 120 and 180 words.

2.
This is a question from the Oxford Higher Certificate exam of May 1982.
Answer in about 400 words.
You have been to a club to listen to a talk on a subject which you found very interesting. The secretary has asked you to write a report for the club journal.

3.

In the ARELS Higher Certificate you have to talk for two minutes on a topic. You can choose from a list of five subjects and have about fifteen minutes to think about your talk. If you wish, you may make notes when you are preparing but you are not allowed to use your notes when giving your talk. Here is a set of five subjects which was used in the ARELS Exam AC29.

(a) People should take their leisure as seriously as they do their work.
(b) Aggression is a necessary part of human behaviour.
(c) People caught driving while drunk should lose their driving licence for life.
(d) Politicians are never free to do what they want to do.
(e) Money spent on space exploration is wasted.

4.

Here is an example of a question from the Institute of Linguists Summer 1981 Exam (Grade II Certificate). You have 20 minutes to prepare to speak for 3 minutes in English on any one of these topics. You may write down the headings of your talk but not detailed notes and may refer to the headings during the talk.

(a) An experience I will never forget
(b) Inflation
(c) Summer sport in Britain
(d) The Conservative Party
(e) The prospects for peace in the '80s
(f) The South of England

D. TUTOR'S NOTES AND ANSWERS

1.

In the FCE exam you have one and a half hours in which to write two compositions. You need to allow at least a quarter of an hour to check your work at the end and so that gives you about thirty-five minutes per composition – after you have made your choice of subject. I would allow five to ten minutes for planning. Do you remember the process I suggested in section B? First, write down all the ideas that come into your head

telephone rings the moment you've got into the bath etc . . . can take you by surprise and you waste time . . . can pass on news quickly . . . can speak to someone the other side of the world . . . new telephone technology . . . many uses in business

What ideas can you add to these? Can you organise them into a logical composition? You may not want to use all the ideas. Even 180 words is not very much. Try writing the composition yourself before you look at my suggestion below. Before writing, remind yourself of the points that we made in section B.

The Advantages and Disadvantages of the Telephone

The telephone always seems to ring just when I've made myself comfortable in the bath. It frequently rings when my favourite hot meal has just been put on the table. In other words it rings at all the wrong times.

A second disadvantage of the telephone is that it takes you by surprise. When a friend unexpectedly phones from Australia, it is only too easy to find yourself talking about the time and the weather. As soon as you've hung up you remember that you should have told her that your sister was getting married.

On the other hand the telephone has many enormous advantages. You can speak to those you love even when you are a long way apart. You can get an answer to a business inquiry in seconds instead of days. You can organise your social life with the greatest of ease. You don't have to depend on unreliable postal services.

All things considered, I must admit that, although I sometimes curse the telephone, I really would find life much more difficult without it.

2.

This question is very open. Don't spend too long choosing your topic. Choose something that you can write about quite easily – either a subject that you could yourself give a talk on or something that you have actually heard a talk on or perhaps watched a programme about on TV recently. A very suitable choice would be a talk on your own country. Then plan your article. Remember that you are writing for a club journal and so you have to give certain facts about where and when the meeting was held for the records. What kind of style would you expect for this kind of writing? It shouldn't be too formal. Firstly, you are writing for a small group of club members and, secondly, you are reporting on a talk which would probably have been delivered in a fairly informal way.

Suggested answer

On Saturday April 1st Mr David Mowat gave a very interesting talk on Scotland in St Margaret's School Hall. Mr Mowat is a teacher by profession but he is intending to stand as a candidate for the Scottish Nationalist Party in the next elections. About seventy-five club members were present and we all enjoyed his talk very much.

Firstly, he told us a little about the geography of Scotland and he illustrated this part of his talk with the most beautiful slides. We saw magnificent views of lochs and mountains and many of us immediately decided to spend our next holidays on the West Coast of Scotland. Mr Mowat had particularly spectacular pictures of the Northern Isles and of the Borders. These are the areas where his own relatives come from.

He continued by giving us some basic information about the history of Scotland. We learnt about the age-old hostility between England and Scotland. Now we all have a much clearer idea of just who William Wallace, Mary Queen of Scots and Bonnie Prince Charlie really were. The Scots were also not really united among themselves and we learnt about the clans and the rivalries and the conflicts that there have always been between them. Mr Mowat told us about the Highland Clearances too and we now understand why there are so many Macs to be found in Canada, New Zealand and the United States.

The final part of his talk dealt with Scotland today. The oil which has been found off the Scottish coast has brought a lot of money but Mr Mowat says that many Scots feel bitter that this money is not staying in Scotland. The oil industry has certainly not solved Scotland's economic problems. Although traditional wool and whisky industries are still strong, other industries like fishing and ship-building are dying. Unemployment is a major problem in many Scottish towns.

We then had a break for tea and Mr Mowat's wife gave us some delicious Scottish food to enjoy with our tea. We had lovely shortbread and some very rich home-made Dundee cake.

After tea there was time for some questions. Members were particularly interested in the reasons why Mr Mowat is a member of the Scottish Nationalist Party. He explained that, for him, this party offers the only way for Scotland to become the prosperous country that it deserves to be.

Mr Mowat gave us much interesting and useful information about Scotland. We hope very much that he will be able to come back and talk to us again next year.

3.

Make your choice of subject carefully. The examiner marking your tape will be giving you three marks:

(a) (out of 12) Holding the listener's attention (by the *interest* of what the candidate has to say and the skill in which he says it).
(b) (out of 12) *Fluency*.
(c) (out of 6) *Accuracy* of all aspects of the candidate's English.

How can you get better marks for each of these areas? You will get better marks for *interest* if you:

- Speak in an organised way;
- Speak clearly and with an intonation that is not flat and monotonous;
- Say something that is a little bit different from everyone else's – perhaps by adding something from your personal experience.

You will get better marks for *fluency* if you do not hesitate too much when you speak – plan well and try not to finish more than a second or two before the minute is up (use your watch if you can without it distracting you too much).

You will get better marks for *accuracy* if you choose your subject carefully – take a topic where you know the vocabulary you will need.

I have chosen here to take the last of the five topics because I felt that it was not too difficult to think of enough clear points which I could make. What would you say on this subject? You are free to agree or disagree with the statement as long as you make your points clearly. Think about what you would say for fifteen minutes, then time yourself speaking for two minutes. If you have the chance, make a recording of your voice and listen to yourself critically afterwards. Then look at my suggested answer below.

The little talk below lasts about two minutes when given at normal speed. Think about how you would assess it for "Holding the listener's attention (by the interest of what the candidate has to say and the skill in which he says it)". Remember that part of holding the interest depends on speaking clearly and with an intonation that is not monotonous.

Suggested answer

I cannot agree with the statement that money spent on space travel is wasted. On the contrary, I feel that space research does bring mankind real benefits.

Firstly, there are all sorts of by-products of space research. Space research has improved the quality of life in all sorts of areas which do not seem to be directly concerned with space. Thanks to space research, we have, for example, better medicines, better air travel, better technology in the kitchen and the office.

Secondly, it is exciting for people to think of space travel. It is thrilling not only for small boys but also for adults to think of exploring the stars. It seems to meet some need in the human spirit for adventure. Throughout history man has aspired to go out to seek the unknown. Most corners of the Earth have now been discovered and so we are turning our sights even farther afield.

Thirdly, who knows when we will actually have a real need of space? The world is steadily becoming more and more over-populated. In addition, the resources of the world are being gradually used up. We may find that our children are actually having to make use of any living-space and resources that can be found in space.

For these three reasons given above I feel quite strongly that money spent on space research is money put to good use.

4.

In the Institute of Linguists' Grade II Certificate you will have three topics to choose from that relate to British life and three that are more general. Again it is important to choose the topic you can answer most easily, even if this may not be such an interesting topic. As this chapter is concerned with presenting an opinion we are going to practise with topic (e) 'The prospects for peace in the '80s', but remember that the first topic could be just as easy. In this exam you get marks for three main things:

- confidence of delivery;
- content of talk;
- quality of English.

Try to think of all these things when preparing. Note down headings to give yourself a logical, well-organised talk. When you speak, expand each heading fully. Here are my suggested headings. Can you make them into a talk? When you have tried, compare your talk with mine. How many of the pieces of advice which I gave in section B did I manage to use? What about you in your talk?

- Introduction – the importance of the topic
- The twentieth century – world wars and other wars
- Potential danger of modern weapons
- The world situation – its tensions
- What some people are doing for peace
- Conclusion – fears for the future

If I speak clearly, confidently and not too fast this talk lasts about three minutes.

Suggested answer

I have chosen the topic 'Prospects of peace for the '80s' because it is the most important issue facing the world today. Even fundamental social issues like equality and unemployment, inflation and pollution seem insignificant in comparison. Is it not true that all ordinary people, in all countries of the world, desperately want peace for themselves and their children?

In the twentieth century we have seen two terrible wars which have involved most of the nations of the world. The Second World War is often referred to in Britain as 'the last war' but this is not really accurate. Since the Second World War there have been wars in many places, including Korea, Vietnam, The Middle East, Afghanistan and the Falklands. This does not really suggest that the prospects for peace in the 1980s are in fact very good.

It cannot be denied that war has always been dreadful but it is even more terrifying to think of war today. The kinds of weapons which mankind has developed are powerful enough to destroy the whole world many times over. One so-called 'small' bomb is enough to kill hundreds of thousands and to injure and deform many more.

In the past, on the whole, only soldiers died in wars. This, of course, was bad enough. With modern weapons, however, things are even worse. Children, women, old people, all perish and in unbearably horrible ways. It is indeed unthinkable that there should be another world war or major military conflict between the superpowers.

What is the political situation in the '80s? Does it suggest peaceful prospects for the future? Unfortunately, it certainly does not. There seem to be at least as many tensions as ever before. NATO and the Warsaw Pact distrust one another and the arms race between them seems to know no end. All sorts of conflicts are arising in the Third World as new nations become aware of their rights. The Middle East has many complex problems. There is hardly any corner of the world that can truly be called peaceful.

Most people fear the possibility of war – they understand the terrible potential of the new weapons and they are afraid because of all the problems which they see around them in the world today. The movements for peace are growing stronger and stronger in many nations of the world. People of all political parties and religions are joining together to work for peace. Women are often particularly active in the struggle for peace. In Britain, for example, large numbers of women have organised camps and demonstrations in an attempt to persuade the British government not to let the Americans use Britain as a nuclear base.

In conclusion, I must say that the prospects for peace in the '80s do not seem to be good. There are tensions all over the world. Arms are produced with greater power and in larger numbers than ever before. We can only hope that common sense and the peace movements will win in the end and that there will be no major military conflict either in the '80s or indeed ever again.

E. BEYOND THE COURSEWORK

Read and listen to other people's presentation of their opinions. Look at a British or American newspaper and analyse how the editor gives his opinion in the editorial articles. You may be able to see English-speaking politicians making their case on television. If you can't listen to them, you will at least be able to read their speeches in the papers. Ask yourself the following questions about what the editor or the politician says. You may be able to learn from these people who have got to the positions they are in now largely because they use language well.

- What favourite phrases do they have?
- Do they use lots of abstract words?
- Do they use concrete examples or statistics to make their points more firmly?
- Do they vary their sentence structure?
- Do they refer to their opponents' arguments?
- Do they make use of repetition or any other 'tricks' of style like metaphor, rhetoric questions or dramatic inversion?
- Can you notice anything else that is special about their style?
- Do they use any expressions that you feel you might want to use yourself?

Chapter 14

Narrative and dialogue

A. GETTING STARTED

Telling stories and writing dialogue is something that you have to do in a number of EFL exams. One of the choices of composition in the **FCE** Exam is to tell a story or to describe an experience. There is often an element of narrative in the written papers of the **Oxford** and **RSA CUEFL** Exams. **Pitmans** and **Trinity College** both have composition papers giving you the opportunity to write a story or a dialogue. In the **ARELS Higher Certificate** you do not have to write anything, of course, but you may find some of the things that we practise in this chapter useful for section five of the exam when you have to tell a story based on pictures. In the oral part of the **Institute of Linguists** exams you usually have the chance to tell a story.

B. ESSENTIAL PRINCIPLES

WRITING DIALOGUE

Let's look first at writing dialogue. How do you do this? First note the punctuation of the piece of dialogue below:

JOHN: What's the weather like in Spain now?
INEZ: Fantastic! It's hot and sunny and hardly ever rains.

- How does this dialogue show who is speaking?
- What punctuation mark follows the name?
- Are verb contractions used?
- Would you use fantastic to describe weather in a meteorology textbook? Why is it possible here?

When you are asked to write dialogue, follow the same pattern. Write the names of the speakers on the left, followed by a colon. Use contractions and feel free to use the kind of informal words and structures that people use when they speak.

Some exams will ask you to write a full piece of dialogue. Most will not. However, including a bit of dialogue is a good way to make a composition more interesting. This is particularly useful if you have to tell a story. If you include dialogue in an ordinary composition, the punctuation will be different from that used above. It'll be like this:

"What's the weather like in Spain?" asked John.
"Fantastic!" replied Inez. "It's sunny and hot and hardly ever rains."

Notice that the inverted commas are all above the line and that they include all the natural punctuation of what the speaker says.

VIVID VERBS

If you use dialogue in your composition try to avoid always using 'he said', 'she said'. 'Said' is fine but boring if used all the time. There are lots of other much more vivid verbs you could use to give variety and colour. Do you know, for example, the following?

whisper
scream
stammer
exclaim
shout

What other verbs of speaking could you add to this list? Think about what mood a person would be in if he spoke in the ways indicated by these verbs?

Other verbs that you can vary in an interesting way are verbs of moving. Don't always use 'went'. Can you add to this list?

rush
stroll
march
crawl
trudge

Again think about how a person is feeling if he moves in this way.

TENSE OF SENTENCES

You can make storytelling more interesting if you add dialogue and if you use vivid verbs. You can also make it more interesting by varying your tenses and your structures. What is the natural tense for storytelling? I hope you agree that it is the past simple.

The present tenses – including the present perfect – are not usually used for dramatic effect in storytelling in written English in the way that they are in some European languages. But you can use the past continuous and the past perfect – if you can find good times to do so.

Use the **past continuous** for description of a scene at one particular moment of time.

It was mid-morning. I was reading a book while Fred was washing the dishes. The children were playing in the garden. The birds were singing.

This tense sets the scene. The reader will expect something to happen to interrupt this scene. What happens will, of course, be in the past simple, e.g.

Suddenly I heard a loud crash.

You can use the **past perfect** in the middle of your story to tell the readers about something that had happened before the incident you are describing. To return to Fred and the children and the birds:

Fred had never before washed up for us and so I was very happy.
It had rained all the previous week and so the children had had to play indoors.
I had heard a crash like that only once before in my life.

Varying the tense like this – even just a little – will make your writing seem much more professional.

SENTENCE STRUCTURE

Try also to vary the structure of your sentences. It is very easy to write a story like this:

He went to the shops. He bought some tomatoes. Then he took a bus into town. He got off at the city centre.

A string of simple short sentences like this will quickly become dull although occasional short sentences can certainly be very effective.

Here are a few ways of making the above sentences a little more interesting, I think. Try to identify what I have done in each case.

When he had bought some tomatoes, he took the bus into town. The bus eventually arrived at the city centre where Dan decided to get off.
At the shop on the corner Dan bought some beautiful but expensive tomatoes.
Feeling rather depressed, Dan thought he would cheer himself up by going into the city centre.

DESCRIPTION

You can also vary the pace of your composition by adding bits of description. You can describe the scene on the street. You can describe what Dan looks like and how he feels. You probably won't have time or space to do this at great length and it can also easily be overdone. However, a little description can make your story come to life.

When you are describing something, remember what you practised in Chapter 4 about avoiding 'nice'. What words can you think of now that could be a substitute for 'nice'?

BEGINNINGS, MIDDLES AND ENDINGS

Try also to begin and end your stories in a way that is interesting for your reader. You can perhaps get ideas for how to do this by looking at the beginnings and endings used by writers in the stories you read.

In practice in the exam you will probably find that the word limit given seems small. You could easily write more. It is very important, however, to keep to a word limit if one is given. To do this and still write a story with some form, I found it useful to have a ready-made plan for a story.

- Paragraph 1 – set the scene
- Paragraphs 2 and 3 – what happened
- Paragraph 4 – consequences of the incident described.

Paragraphs 1 and 4 must not be too long. They just give an introduction and a conclusion to the main point of your composition.

You may feel that a pre-plan like this is too rigid and, of course, it isn't always appropriate. Yet I think it can often be helpful for the kind of limited storytelling that exams allow you to do.

C. EXAM QUESTIONS

Work through these compositions in the following way:

(a) Read the question and think how you would answer it;
(b) Read the notes introducing the compositions suggested in section D;
(c) Write your composition;
(d) Read my composition.

In what ways do you think my composition is (a) better, (b) worse than yours?

Can you now modify my and/or your compositions in a way that improves them?

1.
This question comes from the Pitman's Specimen Higher Intermediate Exam.

Write, using about 100 words:
The exact words of a conversation between yourself and a friend whom you have telephoned to ask for help in choosing a mutual friend's birthday present.

2.
This question comes from a Pitman's Higher past paper. Write about 180 words:
How I met my friend.

3.
Sometimes you have to tell a story orally. This question comes from the Institute of Linguists' winter examinations of 1982. You have 20 minutes to prepare to speak for 3 minutes in English on the following topic:
A strange incident in which I was involved.

4.
This is a question of the FCE type. Write between 120 and 180 words:
A birthday I shall always remember.

5.

This is a question from the RSA CUEFL exam of November 1983. Narrative is only one part of this question but it is an important part:

> On holiday you met a very nice English couple at the first youth hostel you stayed at. They took some photographs of you and you want to see them. They gave you their address, so write a letter to them telling them about the rest of your holiday and ask them to send you copies of the photographs. You are happy to pay for the copies.

D. TUTOR'S NOTES AND ANSWERS

1.

Don't forget to lay out your dialogue in the way described in section B. Notice that you are asked for the exact words of a telephone call and so it is important to include all the formalities of a phone call – your friend must answer the phone, you have to say who you are, you must greet each other and you must say goodbye. All these things have to be done but you only have about 100 words and so you can't give too many of them to greetings and other formalities. The main part of the phone call is to be about choosing a birthday present. Your friend has to make suggestions. He or she should use nice informal suggestion structures like:

> Why don't you . . .
>
> How about . . .

Suggested composition

NADINE: 278934

ME: Hello, Nadine. It's Regina here. How are you?

NADINE: Fine, thanks, And you?

ME: Fine, thanks. I'm just a bit worried about what to get Rex for his birthday present. I hoped you might be able to give me some advice?

NADINE: Well, I've got him a Wham LP that I know he wanted. Why don't you get him a book? He loves reading.

ME: That's a good idea but it's difficult to choose a book for him when I don't know what he's already got.

NADINE: How about a book token, then? He can choose exactly what he'd like himself.

ME: Brilliant! I'll go and get him one immediately. Thanks a lot for your help.

NADINE: Not at all. See you at his party.

ME: See you. Bye.

NADINE Bye.

2.

This question also has a strict word limit. You may find this frustrating and it is certainly difficult to write anything so short that still has a clear form and answers the question set. In my composition I used a standard plan.

Set the scene – one paragraph
What happened – two paragraphs
Consequences – one paragraph

Remember that the middle two paragraphs are the most important ones. It is easy to spend too long setting the scene and discussing the consequences. Try to avoid the temptation to do this.

Suggested composition

It was my first time abroad without my parents and I felt both excited and a little nervous. I was travelling with a group of students to the Soviet Union. We had been in the train for two days, singing, drinking beer and looking at the flatness and immense forests of Northern Europe.

Early in the morning we drew in to Leningrad station. It was a sunny day and already quite hot. We were to be met by some Soviet students and there they were, carrying bunches of flowers for us in the traditional Russian way of greeting travellers.

"Does anyone here speak Russian?" asked one of their group.

"I do – a little," I replied timidly, speaking for the first time to a real live Russian.

"How many are there in your group?" he continued.

"Eighty," I answered and was alarmed at the look of horror on the Russians' faces. Fortunately I quickly realised my mistake as I always had found Russian numbers confusing. "Eighteen," I hastily corrected myself.

For the next week the Leningrad students showed us their magnificent city and I spent most of my time with the first one I had spoken to at the station. That is how, ten years ago, I first met my friend, my husband.

3.

I could not quickly think of any really strange incident in which I had been involved and so I took a real incident that happened to me – a burglary when I was staying with some friends – but changed the ending just a little to make it fit the title. This is a little riskier in an oral exam as the examiner may then ask you more questions about the incident and it may be harder to answer well if the situation is imaginary.

Suggested talk

A strange incident in which I was involved. This story takes about three minutes to tell.

It happened about three years ago, just after New Year, when I was staying with some friends in Birmingham. They had just moved into a beautiful new house in a cul-de-sac on a modern estate and no-one else had yet moved into the neighbouring houses. They had only moved about a week before my visit and they hadn't yet unpacked all their things. They hadn't had time to put any curtains or pictures up, for example, but all their basic furniture and their stereo equipment was in place.

I hadn't been in Birmingham for some time and they invited some mutual friends for dinner. It was difficult for the friends to make it as it had begun to snow very heavily and my friends' house was at the top of a very steep hill. We had a lovely evening with good food and wine and listening to our favourite music. If anyone had had a look in through the uncurtained windows from the snowy street outside we must have looked very cosy.

Soon after midnight our friends left and we all went up to bed. I was in the bathroom when I suddenly heard my friend shrieking. She was quite a temperamental girl and at first I thought she was just having a loud row with her husband. When I realised that she was screaming in fear not anger I opened the bathroom door and looked out – a little apprehensively, I must admit. I saw two men rushing up the stairs towards me. I immediately went back into the bathroom and slammed the door shut. It didn't yet have a lock and I had to push hard against it. I could feel the men trying to force it open from the other side. I don't know where I got the strength from to hold it closed against them but fortunately they fairly quickly gave up trying.

They left the door and I could hear them running back downstairs again. Then there was a loud crash followed by silence. After a few moments my friends called to me and I left the bathroom and went downstairs to find out what had happened.

My friend's husband had heard the doorbell ring just after we had gone up to bed. He had assumed that our dinner guests had returned for some reason. When he opened the door there was a strange man outside who asked for a bucket of water for his car. Harry gave it to the man who immediately threw it over Harry and rushed upstairs, closely followed by two other men. They ran into every room throwing my friend, Anthea, into the corner of the room.

Fortunately, she wasn't hurt although her glasses were broken as she fell.

The strange thing about this incident was that the men took nothing. They ran into every room but they ignored Anthea's handbag and my watch, for example, both of which were lying quite unprotected. They broke dishes in the kitchen and smashed a mirror in the hall. Then they tore the stereo out of the wall, threw it through the picture window – that was the crash I'd heard – and then jumped through the hole in the glass and ran off across the snowy garden into a park at the bottom of the garden. The stereo was left lying in the snow just outside the window.

Why had they come? What were they looking for? They could have seen through the uncurtained windows that there was only basic furniture in the house. Why did they break things? Why didn't they take the stereo or our handbags with them? We'll never know now, I suppose, and, thank goodness, the house has proved a happy one for my friends despite this strange start to their life there.

4.

Again this composition follows the set pattern described at the end of section B. This actually did happen to me on my birthday but you could of course write about any memorable day in your life and call it your birthday, imagining a few birthday details. There is an English proverb that says 'All's fair in love and war'. Perhaps we could add exams to love and war.

N.B. Cheating is of course not fair in exams – or indeed love or war either, I suppose.

Suggested composition

Every year in my childhood we used to spend our summer holidays in the Shetland Islands, far to the north of Scotland. We used to go there because my father was very interested in archaeology. He liked to take us and a party of students to a remote island to excavate a ruined church there.

On my eleventh birthday, the adults were digging as usual and I was playing in a rockpool when suddenly someone cried out, "Look what I've found!" We all rushed over and saw a glint of greenish metal. Slowly and carefully, they began extracting objects. Eventually there were about eight bowls and six brooches lying on the ground. I remember picking one up and it fell to pieces in my hand.

It turned out they were made of silver and had probably been hidden in the church when Vikings attacked the islands centuries ago. Now I fully appreciate the excitement of this find. However, on the day itself I remember mainly feeling upset that everyone was too thrilled to come and eat my birthday cake.

5.

Don't forget the conventions of letter-writing. Look at Chapter 15 if you are unsure of how to lay out a letter. This letter is more than just narrative but it does involve narrative skills. The better you are at telling stories, the better you will be at writing letters to friends.

The outline plan of my letter is the following:

- Paragraph 1 – greetings + request for photos
- Paragraph 2 – general summary of holiday
- Paragraph 3 – description of interesting person met
- Paragraph 4 – description of incident
- Paragraph 5 – friendly wishes

Suggested letter

10 Pig Street
Frogburton
10th August 1985

Dear John and Isabel,

It was lovely to meet you on holiday last month. I hope you enjoyed the rest of your trip as much as I did mine. How did the photos you took of us all together come out? I should love to have some copies. Would it be too much trouble for you to get some copies done for me? I enclose a five pound postal order and would be very grateful if you could have copies of some of them done for me.

After I left you I drove to the south-west corner of Wales and spent nearly a week there. The weather was heavenly and I did a lot of walking although I also found time just to lie on the beach.

I gave lifts to some very interesting people. One was a huge red-haired New Zealand student with a flowing beard. He'd been travelling around the world for nearly three years. Lucky thing! Every now and then he'd do some work – usually on farms – to get the money to go on further. His next stop is the Lake District. I gave him your address. I hope you don't mind. I'm sure you'd like him.

I only had one disaster. That was when my car ran out of petrol. My petrol gauge must have stopped working. It happened in a very remote place on a Sunday, of course. It was also the one day when it rained! I had to walk for about six miles before I came to a house with a phone. A garage fortunately agreed to bring me some petrol but it was certainly the most expensive petrol I have ever bought.

It would be lovely to hear about your adventures. Perhaps you'd be able to come over here for a weekend and we could catch up on all the news. You'd be more than welcome to stay at my place if you don't mind a mattress on the floor.

With all good wishes,

Anna

E. BEYOND THE COURSEWORK

An important way of improving your storytelling skills is to read "with your eyes open". Whenever you read a story in English, notice the way the author writes. If he uses a phrase that you like, mark it in pencil. When you've finished the story, go back through it and write down in a notebook all the things that you marked. Don't be afraid to use these phrases yourself later.

It is also a good idea to write a brief summary of the story and how you felt about it in your notebook. This helps you to remember what you have read but it also gives you practice in basic storytelling.

Chapter 15

Writing letters

A. GETTING STARTED

This chapter looks at letter-writing in English and at the kind of letters you may be asked to write in examinations. The exams only ask you to write letters which any foreign learner of English might really need to write some day, particularly if he or she is living in an English-speaking country.

The kind of letters we shall consider are:

1. Informal letters to friends
2. Formal letters to a government or tourist office, for example.

We shall not deal with business letters as these are not covered by the exams we are concerned with.

B. ESSENTIAL PRINCIPLES

Choosing to write a letter in an English exam is a good idea. You will get marks simply for writing the date and address in the correct way and for opening and closing your letter as English people do. It is not difficult to learn how to do these things properly.

TYPES OF LETTERS

Many of the conventions of letter-writing depend on whether your letter is **formal** or **informal**. This is a matter of your relationship to the person you are writing to. Are you writing to someone in an official position? Then your letter will be formal. Are you writing to a close friend or relation? If so, your letter will be informal.

There are degrees of formality and informality. Could you arrange these letters along a formality/informality continuum?

(a) Letter to your sister telling her about your new boyfriend.
(b) Letter to the Home Office in London asking for an extension of your British visa.

(c) Letter to an aunt thanking her for a birthday present.

(d) Letter to a lawyer asking whether he hasn't made a mistake with his bill.

(e) Letter to a friend's parents congratulating them on their silver wedding.

Do you agree that the order on the formality scale is (b) – (d) – (e) – (c) – (a)?

ADDRESS

English people do not usually write their address on the backs of envelopes. Instead they put it at the top of the first page of their letters. You must do the same in both formal and informal letters. Write your address (but not your name) in the top right-hand corner of your letter. The order of the parts of the address are important and may be different from that used in your language. On the top line you put first the house number followed by the name of the street; this is followed by the name of the town; next comes the name of the county; the postal code comes last and may or may not be put on a separate line. Some people put a comma at the end of every line except the last; others do not. You can choose which you prefer.

46 King Street
Newmarket
Suffolk
NT7 4XU

In other words – apart from the postal code – you **start** with the **most specific** piece of information and **finish** with the **most general.** Thus:

- Where do you think a flat number or a house name would go, if they are needed for your address?
  They would be the top line of the address.
- Where would you put the name of the country if your letter was going abroad?
  On the last line of the address.
  Write your own address here as it would be written on an English letter.

The date is often put immediately under your address.

If you are writing a very formal letter, for example to an official or a company, write the name and address of the person **you are writing to** on the left-hand side of the page, often one line lower than the date, e.g.

172 Cherry Hinton Road
Cambridge CB4 1AN

12th June 1985

The Principal
Cambridge Eurocentre
62 Bateman Street
Cambridge CB4 6ZU

There is sometimes some variation in the way dates and addresses are arranged in modern letters. If a formal letter is very short, for example, some people will put the name and address of the addressee in the bottom left-hand corner of the letter. Some people prefer the date on the right-hand side of the page. It is a good idea to learn the set of conventions suggested above for your personal use. You can be sure that they are right.

DATE

As we have seen the date usually goes in the top right-hand corner under your address in both formal and informal letters. You can write it in a number of different ways:

12.6.85 (US usage for the same date is 6/12/85)
12 June, 1985
June 12 1985
12th June 1985
June 12th, 1985

You can choose whether you want a comma before the year or not in the last four examples.
Write today's date in five different ways.

OPENING

Almost all English letters begin

Dear ———,

Write this on the left of the page – not in the middle.
If you do not know the name of the person you are writing to, but you think it is a man, you write:

Dear Sir,

If you think it is a woman, you write:

Dear Madam,

If you are not sure, you can write:

Dear Sir or Madam,

If you are writing to a company, you can begin:

Dear Sirs,

If you know the name of the person you are writing to, you begin:

Dear Miss Fitzherbert,

OR

Dear Annabelle,

The first line of the main part of your letter begins:

    (a) with a capital letter
    (b) below the comma after the salutation

CLOSING

The closing of your letter must also follow certain conventions. First, your closing phrase should be written in the middle of the page. Like the opening salutation, it must start with a capital letter and finish with a comma. If your letter begins:

Dear Sir,

OR

Dear Madam,

finish it with:

Yours faithfully,

(Your signature)

If you know the name of the person you are writing to, but are writing quite a formal letter, you will finish with:

Yours sincerely,

If you are writing an informal letter you can choose from different endings:

Yours,

OR

Love,

OR

With best wishes,

OR

With kind regards,

OR

With lots of love,

STYLE

It is important for the middle – as well as for the opening and the closing – of your letter that you decide whether you are writing a formal or an informal letter.

In **formal** letters do not use contractions or colloquial vocabulary. You should try particularly hard to be polite. Your own personality does not show through – different people's formal letters on the same theme will be extremely similar.

In **informal** letters, on the other hand, you write to your friend more or less as you would talk to him. You use contractions, possibly even abbreviations, and colloquial vocabulary is common. Your personality is usually well illustrated by your informal letters.

Can you decide whether the following phrases come from formal or informal letters?

1. Thanks for your nice letter.
2. Thank you very much for your letter of the 15th January.
3. Give us a ring soon.
4. Perhaps it might be possible for you to telephone me.
5. I'd never call him a nice guy, would you?
6. He is, in my opinion, not completely reliable.
7. I'll pick you up at 7, O.K.?
8. Would it be convenient if I arrived at 7 p.m.?
9. Looking forward to hearing from you soon.
10. I look forward to hearing from you at your earliest convenience.

I hope you agree that the odd numbers come from informal letters and the even numbers from formal ones.

COMMON EXPRESSIONS	Here are some expressions that we use frequently in English letters. You may find it helpful to learn them.

For formal letters

- I apologise for the delay in replying to your letter but . . .
- I should be very grateful if you could . . .
- I wonder if you could tell me . . .
- I was interested/disturbed/shocked to read your article on . . .
- I should very much appreciate an early reply.
- I look forward to meeting you at your earliest convenience.

For informal letters

- I'm terribly sorry not to have written sooner but . . .
- Many thanks for your lovely long letter.
- How's life? I hope things are going well with you.
- Do write soon.
- Remember me to your brother.
- Give my regards to your parents.
- Looking forward to getting together again soon.

Now we have discussed the essential principles of letter-writing in English, can you answer the following questions?

1. Do you write your name at the top of your letter?
2. Where do you write your own address?
3. What comes first when you write the address and what comes last?
4. Can you begin a letter: Hi, pal!
5. Can you write the first three words of a typical thank-you letter? Remember to punctuate them correctly.
6. How do you begin a letter to a businessman when you don't know his name? Remember punctuation.

7. How would you finish your letter to that businessman? Remember punctuation.
8. Which prepositions go in these phrases?
   Thank you . . . the delicious dinner.
   I'm looking forward . . . . . . your party next week.
   I apologise . . . not replying promptly.
9. Put these words in the right form and add any necessary prepositions:

   I – look – forward – hear – you – soon.

Answers

1. No
2. In the top right-hand corner
3. Flat or house number; postal code or town or county or country.
4. No!
5. Dear Mary,
      Thank
6. Dear Sir,
7.   Yours faithfully
8. for
   to
   for
9. I look forward to hearing from you soon.

C. EXAM QUESTIONS

Here we have chosen some typical examples of letters which students have been asked to write in recent exams. The Oxford Higher and the RSA examinations tend to give a much more detailed brief than the FCE but the types of letter which you need to know about are the same for all the exams:

- thank-you letters
- invitations and their acceptance or refusal
- complaints
- enquiries, particularly about holidays or accommodation
- apologies
- job applications
- requests
- letters asking for or giving advice
- letters introducing yourself to someone
- narrative letters

Tackle each question like this.

- Read the question carefully.
- Briefly answer questions (a), (b) and (c) below. This will make sure you identify the key points you need to know when you come to write the letter.
  (a) Who is the letter to?
  (b) What is it essential to say in the letter?

(c) What tone is appropriate?

- Check your answers to these three questions with the answers given in section D in the introductory notes on each question. Read any other notes given there but do not read the complete letter suggested.
- Draft out your letter. Remember to write the address and date correctly and to open and close your letter as English people do. Write in paragraphs where appropriate.
- Where possible, check your answer against the suggested answer given in section D. Suggested answers are provided for only the first four questions in this section.
- The suggested letter is just one of many possible answers. Make sure that your letter covers all the vital points and conveys the right tone. Check the address, layout, opening and closing. If you are not happy with your letter, rewrite it.

After each of the exam questions in this section there is space for you to answer each of the three key questions and to make notes on how you would approach this question in an exam. It is also helpful to underline or highlight those parts of the question which have particular relevance for the way you develop your answer.

1.

You have been given permission to stay in England for six months by the Immigration Authorities, but now you find you need to extend your stay for at least a further six months to complete the work/studies you are involved in. Write a short letter (100–120 words) to the Home Office (Immigration Dept.), Lunar House, Wellesley Road, Croydon CR9 2BY, explaining the situation and asking for an extension of stay. Make sure you give all the relevant facts. Write address(es) on the letter as appropriate. (RSA CUEFL May 1982)

Answer these questions in only two or three words each.

- Who is the letter to?
- What must it say?
- What are the relevant facts?
- What is the appropriate tone?
- Underline relevant points.

2.

You recently bought a radio cassette alarm through a special-offer advertisement in a magazine. It was faulty, so you returned it, and have now received the replacement. When you tried to use this replacement, you found a number of the same faults and poor packaging had meant that it was also damaged. You know that a friend of yours is thinking of buying the same machine from the same company.

Write two letters, one to the company from whom you bought the machine (Scottoe Ltd, 29 Upper Sheep Street, Westpool, Powys) complaining about the replacement you have been sent, and the other to your friend, telling him or her about your experience.

Figure 14.1 represents the replacement machine, showing the faults you found.

(Each of your letters should be between 100 and 200 words)
(Oxford Higher, May 1983)

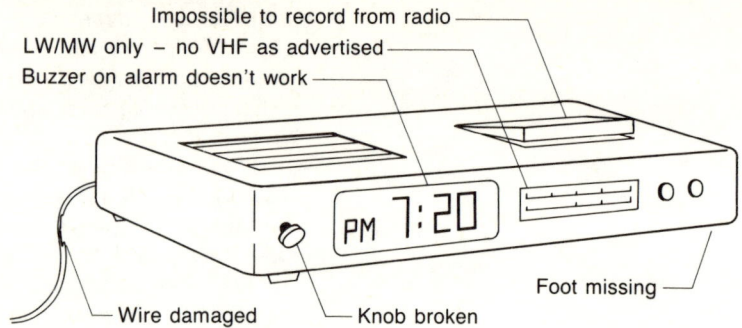

Impossible to record from radio
LW/MW only – no VHF as advertised
Buzzer on alarm doesn't work
PM 7:20
Wire damaged
Knob broken
Foot missing

Notes for letter to company

- Who to?
- What do I want to say?
- Tone?

Notes for letter to friend

- Who to?
- What do I want to say?
- Tone?

3.

You are the Honorary Secretary of a Club. A guest speaker has been invited to talk to the Club, and he has written to you accepting the invitation and asking you fo find him a hotel for the night after his evening lecture. The Club is very short of money and will be unable to pay for the hotel room, but will pay the nominal fee of £25 for the lecture, as well as for the travelling expenses.

   (i)   Write a letter, correctly set out, to the guest speaker, Dr E. Adams, University College, Cardiff 1CF 2DL, explaining the situation to him.

  (ii) Write a letter, correctly set out, to the manager of the Old Lodge Hotel, 20 Rodney Place, Bristol BS8 2LR, provisionally booking a single room and explaining who will be responsible for payment.

 (iii) Write a note to the Chairman of the Club, explaining what you have done and why.

You are advised to spend about 50 minutes on this question.
(Oxford Higher, May 1984)

                                        i   ii   iii

- Who to?
- What to say?

- Tone?
- Underline relevant points.

4.

Questions 4 to 7 have not been taken from actual exam papers but they are of the type used in the FCE.

Write a letter to thank an English friend for a weekend which you spent at his or her house and which you enjoyed very much. You should make the beginning and the ending like those of an ordinary letter, but the address is not to be counted in the number of words. Write 120 to 180 words.

- Who to?
- What to say?
- Tone?
- Underline relevant points

5.

Write a letter to a friend in England asking for advice about how best to spend a two-week holiday you are planning to spend in Britain next year. Ask about such things as where to go, what to take and how to travel.

Make the beginning and ending as for an ordinary English letter, but do not count the address in the number of words. Write 120 to 180 words.

- Who to?
- What to say?
- Tone?
- Underline relevant points.

6.

Write a first letter to a new English penfriend. Introduce yourself, telling about your studies, interests, home town and family. Make the beginning and ending as for an ordinary English letter, but do not count the address in the number of words. Write 120 to 180 words.

- Who to?
- What to say?
- Tone?
- Underline relevant points.

7.

Write a letter inviting a friend to come to a party at your house. Your friend has never been to your house before. Explain exactly how to get there. You should make the beginning and ending as for an ordinary English letter but the address should not be counted in the number of words. Write 120 to 180 words.

- Who to?
- What to say?
- Tone?
- Underline relevant points.

8.

This is part of a letter you have received from a friend.

> not the only bit of good news either. I've just been offered a job teaching English in your country, and what's more – you'll never believe it – it's at your own school! I'd like to accept the job but I thought you could give me some ideas before I do. What kind of problems do you think there would be? If any, of course. And what kind of things will the job demand? And do you think I'll fit in? Am I really the right sort of person? So – could you tell me what you think about all this, and anything else you think I should know?

(This extract from a friend's letter was hand-written not typed in the original exam.)

Write your reply using about 300 words. You are advised to spend about 55 minutes on this question. (Oxford Higher 1984)

- Who to?
- What to say?
- Tone?
- Underline relevant points.

D. TUTOR'S NOTES AND ANSWERS

In this section you will find notes and suggested answers for questions 1 to 4 only. These suggested answers are enough to give you a range of types of letter – formal, semi-formal and informal; friendly, angry and businesslike. My letters are only suggestions and there are many variants which would be equally good.

1.

Who to? Home Office
What must it say? Who I am, what I want
What are the relevant facts? Where I come from, where and what I'm studying, what I want and why
What is the appropriate tone? Formal, polite
The relevant points are those below:

> . . . permission to stay in England for six months . . . now need to extend stay . . . to complete the work/studies . . . short letter explaining . . . asking for extension of stay

In this letter include all the important points but nothing extra. It is not worth telling the Home Office exactly what you feel about life in Britain, for example.

9 Norfolk Road,
Aberdeen,
AB1 6JR

June 28th 1985

The Immigration Officer,
The Home Office,
Lunar House,
Wellesley Road,
Croydon,
CR9 2BY

Dear Sir,
  Your ref. PY48720
  I am a Brazilian doing a post-graduate course in Scottish history at the University of Aberdeen.
  When I arrived in the UK in April this year I was given permission to stay here for six months. I now find that my dissertation will take me another six months to complete as many of my source materials have to be translated from Gaelic.
  My father regularly sends me money from Brazil to cover all my expenses here. I hope very much that you will be able to extend my permission to stay here until the end of April next year.

Yours faithfully,

Maria da Silva

2.

Notes for letter to company

Who to?   Company
What do I want to say?   Complain, ask for money back
Tone?   Angry

Notes for letter to friend

Who to?   Friend
What do I want to say?   Don't buy it
Tone?   Angry

The relevant points in this question are all the notes on the diagram and the following things from the question:

   radio cassette alarm . . .replacement . . .same faults . . .poor packaging . . .damaged

   In the letter to the company it is appropriate to include all the faults noted in the diagram. The faults there are described in note form and when you describe them in your letter you must be careful to add any necessary articles and auxiliary verbs. You must show your anger without being rude.

In the letter to your friend there is no need to give all the details of the problems and you can express your anger far more outspokenly.

Suggested answers

62 Bateman Street
Cambridge

Dec. 1st 1985

The Manager
Scottoe Ltd.
29 Upper Sheep Street
Westpool
Powys

Dear Sir,

Recently I ordered one of your radio cassette alarms through a special offer advertisement in the Sunday Times. It took six weeks to arrive and, when it eventually came, it did not work. I returned it to you and a replacement reached me yesterday.

However, when I tried to use this machine, I found that it had at least as many problems as the first one. Some of the difficulties are the same: it is, for example, impossible to record from the radio with this machine, just as was the case with the previous one you sent me. Moreover, the radio operates on only long and medium waves; it does not work on VHF although this was advertised.

In addition to these technical faults, the replacement machine you sent me was badly damaged in the post because it had been inadequately packaged. One of its feet was missing, wires were damaged and the on-off knob was broken. To crown it all, even the buzzer on the alarm does not work.

I had thought your company was a reputable one and I am very disappointed in these low standards. I am now returning this machine also and this time I should be grateful if you could refund my £25.99. I shall buy a Japanese model instead.

Yours faithfully,

James Wilson

62 Bateman Street
Cambridge

Dec. 1st 1985

Dear Nelly,

Thanks a lot for your letter. It was good to hear your news and I'm sure you'll soon get used to the new job.

You write that you are thinking of taking up that Sunday Times radio cassette alarm offer. Don't do it! I got one and it has been a total disaster. I am furious. First, they sent me a defective machine which I returned and then they sent me another defective machine! It could have been the same one, of course, except that it was even more badly damaged than the first.

The radio didn't play VHF, the recorder wouldn't record from the radio and the alarm wouldn't go off. It is terribly disappointing as the advert made it sould such a great machine. If I were you, I'd look around at what there is in the shops rather than order something through the post.

Let me know if you find something good.

Looking forward to hearing from you again before too long,

Love,

Jim

3.

	i	ii	iii
Who to?	speaker	hotel manager	chairman
What to say?	thank, explain	book room provisionally	inform
Tone?	tactful, formal	formal	informal, brief

Relevant points

Club . . . guest speaker . . . accepting . . . asking . . . hotel . . . Club short of money . . . unable pay for hotel . . . pay nominal fee . . . travelling expenses.

These three letters show a range of style and different degrees of formality and politeness and this must be clear in the letters and note written.

47 Smith Place
Bristol BS8 2KP

3rd October 1985

Dr E. Adams
University College
Cardiff 1CF 2DL

Dear Dr Adams,

Thank you for your letter. We are delighted that you are able to come to speak to us on the 5th of November and are very much looking forward to your lecture.

You ask me to book you a hotel room for that night which I shall do with pleasure.

Unfortunately, the Club cannot offer to pay for your accommodation. Our funds are low and we can only afford to give our speakers the nominal fee of £25 plus travelling expenses. Perhaps you would like to stay at the home of one of our members?

There are a number of us who would be more than happy to put you up if that were convenient for you. I shall, however, provisionally book a hotel room for you but shall not finalise arrangements until I hear from you.

Yours sincerely,

Eve Biggles

47 Smith Place
Bristol BS8 2KP

3rd October 1985

The Manager
The Old Lodge Hotel
20 Rodney Place
Bristol BS8 2LR

Dear Sir,

I should like to make a provisional booking for a single room for the night of 5th November. It is for Dr E Adams from University College, Cardiff. Dr Adams is coming to Bristol to speak at the Vintage Cars Society of which I am the secretary, but he will be paying his own bill. I shall confirm the booking within the next two weeks.

Yours faithfully,

Eve Biggles

Fred,

Here's a copy of Dr A's reply. Have written to him pointing out we can't afford to pay his hotel bill and have provisionally booked him a room at the Old Lodge. John says he can stay at his place if he prefers.

See you Wednesday,

Eve

4.

Who to?   Friend
What to say?   Thanks
Tone?   Friendly

Relevant points
    thank . . . weekend . . .enjoyed

Suggested answer

10 Rotton Park Road
Birmingham

20th March 1986

Dear Jane,

Thank you very much for the wonderful weekend we had together. It was lovely to see you again after so long and I thoroughly enjoyed everything that we managed to do.

Didn't we do a lot? My new shoes already need resoling after all that walking but I now feel I really have quite a good idea of what London is like. I didn't expect it would be so varied or that the cafes would be quite so good. Whenever I think about that delicious Chinese meal we had in Soho, my mouth starts watering.

I do hope you'll be able to come and see me in Birmingham soon. We won't be able to look at so many interesting museums and stylish shops here but the countryside roundabout is very attractive and quite easy to get to.

Give my regards to your flatmate,

Lots of love,

Renata

---

5 to 8.

To check whether your answer to any of the remaining questions in this chapter is a good one, ask yourself the following questions:

1.   Does it say everything the question asks it to say?
2.   Have I written the address(es) and the date correctly?

3. Have I chosen an appropriate opening and closing and have I punctuated them correctly?
4. Have I written in a style that is good for (a) the context and (b) the person I'm writing to?
5. Have I obeyed the general rules for written work in English exams which were outlined in Chapter 2?

If you can safely answer 'yes' to all these questions then your answer should get a good mark.

E. BEYOND THE COURSEWORK

To take your coursework a step further with letter-writing, there are two things you can do – read letters and write them. A number of the activities suggested below combine both sides of the art of letter-writing but some concentrate on just one side. The aim of these activities is to show you English letters in a real context and so to increase, it is hoped, your own enjoyment and skill in writing them.

READING LETTERS

1. If you are studying in a class ask any student who can to bring in an informal letter in English from someone the rest of the class do not know. The other students look at the letters and find out as much as possible from them about the personalities of the writers – clues will be found in what the person says, in how he or she says it and also, perhaps, in handwriting. The student who knows the writer of the letter in question can confirm or deny the detective work of the other students. If you are working alone, you may be able to adapt the idea by asking anyone you know to lend you a letter or by analysing a letter to yourself. It is an interesting activity in that it makes very clear how much we reveal of ourselves, or suggest of ourselves, in our letters.
2. This activity can only be done if you are working with a teacher. Ask your teacher to bring in a whole range of letters in English written to him or herself. Read these letters and this time work out as much as you can about the personality, interests and experience of your teacher. This is an idea of Mario Rinvolucri's which I saw him do in a very successful class.
3. Alone or in class you can organise a project to look at the leters in English newspapers. Collect letters from one newspaper or from contrasting newspapers – perhaps *The Times* and the *Mirror*. What are the letters about? Who are they from? What mood was the writer in when he wrote the letter and why?
4. Problem pages from women's magazines can also be an interesting source of letters. You can also do the activity suggested here alone or in class. Cut up a problem page separating the problems from the advice given. Read the letters first. What advice would you give? Find the advice that the journalist gave. Do you agree? Why (not)?

WRITING LETTERS

5. Write a letter to an English newspaper. You may know what you would like to write about but possible ideas are:

(a) how you as a foreigner see British life;
(b) how the British press treats your country;
(c) comment on any topical issue;
(d) comment on a recent article in the newspaper.

6. Write a letter to a famous person. If you are lucky, you will also get a reply to read. You could:

(a) Write to an author whose work you have enjoyed. You might just want to say how much you have enjoyed it or you might want to ask something about his or her work.
(b) Write to your local Member of Parliament, if you are living in Britain, or to the British Ambassador, if you are elsewhere. Give your opinion of a topical issue.
(c) Write to the Prime Minister of Britain or to the President of the United States. Say what you feel about any relevant issue that is important to you.
(d) Write to anybody you admire in sport or entertainment. Say why you like their style.

If you write to the Queen, the right way to open your letter is:
May it please Your Majesty,
and the right way to close is:
I have the honour to remain, Madam, Your Majesty's most humble and obedient subject.

READING AND WRITING LETTERS

Having a regular correspondence with someone in English is a very good way to practise your language and to learn more.

7. Find a penfriend in an English-speaking country. Perhaps you have a teacher or a friend or colleague who could help you find someone suitable. Or perhaps you could find someone through a special-interest club or magazine if you have some particular hobby. You can also ask for a penfriend by writing to the following address, enclosing an international reply coupon.

International Youth Service
PB 125
SF 20160
Turku
Finland

8. If you have a teacher or a friend who is also studying English why not agree to write to each other in English. This should develop both your English and your friendship.

9. Finally, why not write to me telling me whether you found the advice in this book helpful. Perhaps you could give me some more hints which I could pass on to other students? I shall do my very best to reply to your letter.

| Chapter 16 | # Communicative writing tasks |

A. GETTING STARTED

This chapter will deal with the skills you need to do many of the more realistic writing tasks which modern exams often ask you to do. Modern exams often call their questions 'communicative' which means that they ask you to do things that you might really want to do in English at some time. The kind of things we shall look at are:

- forms
- postcards
- telegrams
- instructions
- notes and messages
- advertisements
- reports

If you come to an English-speaking country it is quite probable that you will need to do some of the things which these exam questions require you to do and so I recommend you to think of this chapter not just as exam preparation but as being potentially very useful for 'real life' too.

B. ESSENTIAL PRINCIPLES

The tasks we are looking at here are realistic and you will probably write much better answers and spend less time thinking what to write if you really imagine yourself in the situation. For example, if you are asked to write a note to an English friend who is in hospital, think of a real friend and what you would write to him or her in those circumstances. If you are writing a description for the police of a suitcase of yours which has been stolen, think of one of your own suitcases and describe it. Look ahead to section C and questions 5, 7, 9, 11, 14 and 15 and think about how you could use your own experience in giving your answer.

Don't, of course, be so rigid over this that you try to write something that you are not sure of. Use your own experience as a prompt but feel free to lie in order to show off what you know or to hide what you don't know. Can you think of places where you would want to modify what you might have said in questions 5, 7, 9, 11, 14 and 15? How could you modify your answers in order, firstly, to show what you know well and, secondly, to hide what you're not sure of.

As always the **instructions** for these questions are very important. The instructions are often quite detailed and you must take care not to overlook anything. You might find it useful to use a highlighting pen to emphasise all the important parts of the instructions. For example, don't forget to use block capitals if you are asked to do so – and remember that you are usually asked to do this in questions where you have to fill in forms or to write telegrams.

The instructions will also make the **register** of your answer clear. Are you writing to someone you know well or to a friend? This will affect the style you write in. With a friend you write more as you speak – with contractions, colloquial language, even slang, and it is not necessary to be quite so polite to a friend.

Politeness is frequently important in these tasks. You will often be asked to write a note refusing an invitation, for example. It is not polite in English simply to say that you cannot do something; you have to give some reason why you cannot do it. Politeness is possibly more important than truthfulness – at least as far as exam marks are concerned.

You often have to write quite **briefly** in these tasks particularly if you are writing a telegram or a classified advertisement. In this style of writing what words are usually missed out? Look at question 6 for an example of a telegram. You should notice from that that all articles, auxiliary verbs and prepositions are missed out. The meaning is still clear and the payment for the telegram is less. You may find two standard telegram abbreviations useful:

ETA = Expected Time of Arrival
ASAP = As Soon As Possible

Can you decipher this telegram?

ETA LONDON 14.00 THURS. CONTACT ME RITZ ASAP FAROUK

In standard English it would be 'I expect to arrive in London at 2 on Thursday afternoon. Could you please contact me as soon as possible after that. I'll be staying at the Ritz Hotel. With best wishes from Farouk'.

C. EXAM QUESTIONS

(a)   Read through each exam question
(b)   Then look at the notes introducing the answer to each question in section D.
(c)   Write your own answer.

(d) Compare your answer with that suggested in section D.
(e) Does the answer in section D give you any ideas for modifying your own answer to make it better?
(f) If so, rewrite your answer.

1.

This question comes from the RSA CUEFL Intermediate Exam, May 1984.

You are in the United Kingdom.
On entry into the United Kingdom you were not given permission to stay for as long as you need. Fill in this form to extend your stay for the period you require.

APPLICATION FOR AN EXTENSION OF STAY IN THE UNITED KINGDOM

You may use this form if you are at present in the U.K. and wish to apply for a longer period of stay.

Please complete all sections of the form clearly in ink. Put n/a if not applicable. For Section A use block capitals.

Section A

1. State Mr., Mrs., Miss, Ms., or Other Title

2. Family Name

3. Other Names

4. Date of Birth (write month in letters)

5. Nationality

6. Present Address
   (incl. daytime tel. no.)

Section B

7. Place of Birth: Town
                    Country

8. Occupation

9. Marital Status

10. Purpose of stay in U.K.?

Section C

11. How long have you been in the U.K.?

12. What period of extension do you require?

13. What evidence of funds can you provide?

14. Name and address of person willing to act as a referee on your behalf.

15. Home Office Reference Number (if known)

    Date of application

    Usual signature

2.

Here is another typical example of a question where you have to fill in a form. This question is taken from the RSA CUEFL Exam of May 1983.

> You urgently need somewhere to live while you are in the UK. Fill in this form to register with 'Flat-U-Rent', a nation-wide agency for rented accommodation.

"The flat we find is the flat you rent"

FLAT-U-RENT

APPLICATION TO JOIN OUR RENTED ACCOMMODATION REGISTER

Please answer all the questions. Do not leave a blank. Put n/a if not applicable.

1. Surname (block capitals)

2. Mr/Mrs/Miss/Ms

3. Other Names

4. Address for Correspondence

4b. Postcode   4c. Tel. No. (incl. area code)
                        i. Work
                        ii. Home

5. Age

6. Occupation

7a. Nationality

    (if not a British National give place of birth. Specify town and country)

7b. Town   7c. Country   215

8a. Marital Status   8b. No. of Children

8c. Ages of Children   8d. Pets

Details of Accommodation Required (Please specify the following)

9a. Preferred Location

9b. Type of Property

9c. No. and Type of Rooms

9d. Furnished or Unfurnished

10. Expected Duration of Tenancy∗

11. Maximum Weekly Monthly Rental (incl./excl. rates)

12. Name and address of Bank/Employer/other suitable person to whom reference can be made

13. How would you wish Weekly/Monthly payments to be made?

14. Special requirements

15. Date by which accommodation required

16. Date of Application

17. Usual Signature

∗No short lets: 3 months minimum.

(FLAT-U-RENT is a registered accommodation agency. All agreements are entered into subject to the provisions of the appropriate Housing Acts.)

3.

This is another example of a form-filling question from an RSA CUEFL Exam. This one is taken from the exam set in November 1984.

The Society for International Friendship (SIF) is a society for people who want to meet people from other countries. The idea of the society is to help people learn about and understand the customs and ways of living of other nationalities.

Each year the society has a conference in a different country. Next year the conference will be in Brighton, a seaside town on the South coast of England, so the language used will be English.

You are a member of SIF and are going to the conference, but do not worry, you do not need to know about SIF or conferences to be able to answer the questions. Good Luck.

SIF 17th Annual Conference

Langfords Hotel, Hove

4th–6th January 1985

Applicants should complete this form and return it to the Conference Organiser together with a deposit of £20 if UK member/£40 if overseas member.

Please answer all the questions

Put N/A if not applicable.

A.   *Personal Details. Please use block capitals for this section*

1.   Surname or Family Name

2.   First Names in Full

3.   Sex

4.   Date of Birth

5.   Age

6a.   Place of Birth: Town
6b.   Country

7.   Nationality

8.   Present Address

9.   Address for correspondence if different from above

B.   *Hotel Information*

10.   Double/Single Room
(please state preference)

11.   Are you willing to share a room?

12.   Bath/Shower (please state preference)

13.   Approximate arrival time at hotel

14. Will you require parking facilities?

15. Special dietary requests

C. *For Conference Organiser's Information*

16. Languages spoken

17. Countries visited

D. *Administration*

18. I enclose a deposit of

19. Signature

20. Name of Parent or Guardian if under 18

21. Date

4.

In the next two questions you have to write postcards.

This question comes from the June 1984 Intermediate CUEFL exam.

You had planned to babysit for some English friends one evening next week. Now you realise you won't be able to do so. They aren't on the phone. Write a card to them, explaining the situation, apologising for not being able to do it and offering them similar help in the future. Ask them to let you know if they'd like you to babysit for them after next week.

Write the message and their address on the card below.

5.

Here is an example of a postcard question from the Oxford Higher Exam of May 1984.

(You are advised to spend about ten minutes on this question)

Two friends of yours have taken an examination. One has passed with distinction, the other has failed dismally. Write a suitable card to each of them.

6.

In your exam you may be asked to write a telegram in English. Here is a question from the RSA CUEFL Exam of June 1981.

You receive the following telegram from the college to which you have applied for a place.

POST OFFICE TELEGRAM

5TXZ/9.56 83 LON
PLACE CONFIRMED. PLEASE STATE TYPE ACCOMMODATION REQUIRED.
CONFIRM ARRIVAL DATE, PERIOD, MAX. PRICE P./W., SPECIAL REQUIREMENTS. ANSWER NEEDED IMMEDIATELY REGISTRAR RSACO.

Write in the space provided below your telegram reply. Use block capitals. Your message should not exceed 25 words.

7.

Instructions are another example of a communicative writing task often tested in exams of all types. This, the first of three 'instructions' questions which we shall look at, asks you to write directions. This is a very frequent question. This particular example comes from the Oxford Higher Exam of May 1984.

(You are advised to spend about fifteen minutes on this question.)

Write clear directions to someone who is coming to visit you (not from abroad) and who intends to travel on some form of public transport.

8.

This 'instructions' question comes from the Oxford Higher Exam of May 1982.

The furniture is to be delivered for a study/bedroom.

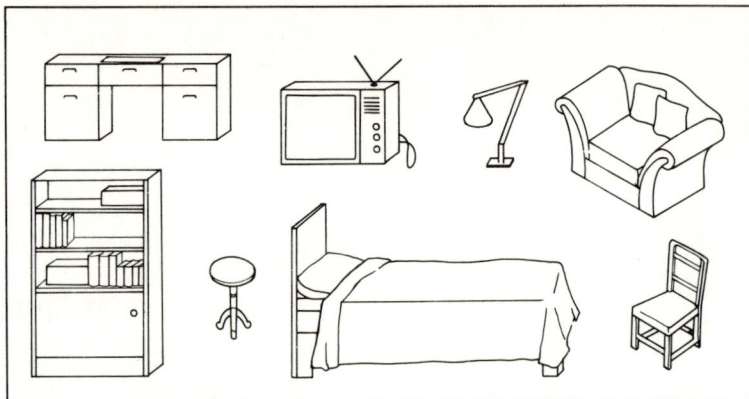

No one will be there when it is delivered but you want to be able to use the room as soon as you return. Write instructions for the delivery man. This is a plan of the room. (No more than 120 words.)

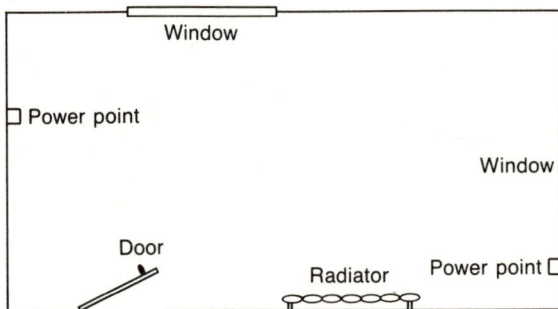

9.

The next three questions deal with notes and messages. The first example comes from the RSA CUEFL Exam of May 1984.

While you are away from home, some American friends are coming to stay in your house. You are leaving before they are due to arrive, so you decide to leave them a short note to help them with all the things they need to know while staying in the house. Your friends have never been to your country before so there is quite a lot of advice you need to pass on. Write your message on the notelet pad sheet below.

10.

Here is another example of a message question from the RSA CUEFL Exam of November 1984.

> You have met an English couple staying at the same hotel as you are. They have invited you to go shopping with them this afternoon but you are not feeling very well and want to go to bed. You 'phone their room but they are out. Write the note that you would leave for them at reception.

11.

This question comes from the Oxford Higher Exam of May 1982.

> You and some friends are going out for an evening on the town. One of the group can only join you later. Write a note to tell him where to find you.

12.

In this question you have to write an advertisement of the type often found in the classified adverts section of local newspapers. This question comes from the RSA CUEFL Exam of June 1984.

> You and a friend have decided that you want to live in your own accommodation for the final period of your stay in England. You have found a four-bedroomed house which is both comfortable and convenient, but you can't afford the rent at over £200 per

month. You decided to advertise in the local paper for two other people to share the house (and the bills) with you. The type of ad. you can afford limits you to a maximum of thirty words, one word per space on a standard form. The ad. must include your name and tel. no. Make sure you include all the relevant information.

13.

Here is an advert of a less public type for you to write. This question comes from the RSA CUEFL Exam of November 1984.

You see the following announcement in Brighton's local paper:

THEATRE ROYAL, BRIGHTON
RONALD LEIGH HUNT
HILDEGARD NEIL
RICHARD COLEMAN
in AGATHA CHRISTIE'S THRILLER
VERDICT

O.A.P.s £3.00 Thurs. and Sat

Mats. bookable now

You like the theatre and would like to go to the play this evening, but you would prefer to go with somebody. The conference hotel (see introduction to question 3 above) has an information board where you can put messages. Write the notice that you would put on the board.

14.

This question is another type of communicative task which is quite commonly found in modern exams. It is a report. This particular question takes the form of a statement to the police about lost property. It comes from the Oxford Higher Exam of May 1983.

> You have lost your wallet (or purse). The police have asked you to write a brief statement saying where and when you think you lost it, what it looked like and what was in it. Write the statement.

15.

The last question in this chapter is another example of a report. It is taken from the RSA CUEFL Exam of June 1981.

> You are involved in a traffic accident while on your way to meet a friend in the town you are living in. You have to write a report for an insurance company, giving details of the date, time, place, circumstances of the accident, other parties involved, who was responsible for the accident etc. Your report should be no more than 120 words long. Be brief, but include all relevant information.
>
> INSURANCE REPORT   IR/RSA/81/WPEL/9

D. TUTOR'S NOTES AND ANSWERS

It is a good idea to read just the notes introducing each question before you try to answer the question yourself. Then compare your answer with the answer suggested and think about whether you now want to change your answer in any way.

1.

Look back to question 1 and read the introduction to the question very closely. What does this make clear?

Firstly, that you are not a British national and, secondly, that you have already been in the UK for some time. Now look at the instructions at the head of the form. When do you need to use block capitals? Do you need to use them for all your answers?

Question 6 on the form – remember that you are in the UK at present. Question 9 on the form – what are the different possibilities for marital status? You can write either as single, married, divorced, separated or widowed. Make sure that you don't answer question 1 as Miss and then say that you are married in question 9. This is one reason why the first point in section B suggested that you imagine real circumstances for these questions. It is easier to be consistent.

Answer

APPLICATION FOR AN EXTENSION OF STAY IN THE UNITED KINGDOM

Section A

1. State Mr., Mrs., Miss, Ms., or Other Title MR

2. Family Name REAGAN

3. Other Names RONALD

4. Date of Birth (write month in letters) 6th FEBRUARY 1910

5. Nationality AMERICAN

6. Present Address (Incl. daytime tel. no.) 60 BANKS STREET LONDON SE 22

   TEL: 01 234 5678

Section B

7. Place of Birth: Town SAN FRANCISCO
   Country USA

8. Occupation Actor

9. Marital status Married

10. Purpose of stay in U.K.? Study

Section C

11. How long have you been in the U.K.? 2 months

12. What period of extension do you require? 3 months

13. What evidence of funds can you provide?

    Letter from Bank Manager enclosed

14. Name and address of person willing to act as a referee on your behalf.

    Margaret Thatcher
    (Member of Parliament)
    House of Commons
    Westminster
    London

15. Home Office Reference Number (if known) *Not known*

Date of application   *02 . 02 . 86*

Usual signature

2.

Approach this question in the same way that we approached question 1. Look closely at the introduction to the question. Then pay attention to the instructions at the top of the form. Again it is clear that the person filling in the form is not a British citizen and that he or she has been in the country for some time already. Again you have to use block capitals for some of, but not all of, the form. Look at the footnote before you answer question 10 on the form. In question 11 'rates' are a kind of local tax and your answer must show whether the rent you state is inclusive of this tax or not. In question 12 on the form you must indicate the position of the person whose name you give as a referee.

Answer

"The flat we find is the flat you rent"

FLAT-U-RENT

APPLICATION TO JOIN OUR RENTED
ACCOMMODATION REGISTER

Please answer all the questions. Do not leave a blank. Put n/a if not applicable.

1. Surname (block capitals)   *PEEP*

2. Mr/Mrs/Miss/Ms   *MISS*

3. Other Names   *Bo*

4. Address for Correspondence

    c/o Cambridge Eurocentre,
    62 Bateman Street,
    Cambridge.

4b. Postcode *CB2 1LX*   4c. Tel. No. (incl. area code)
                             i. Work   *0223 353607*
                             ii. Home   *0223 123456*

5. Age   19

6. Occupation   Shepherdess

7a. Nationality   Swiss
    (If not a British National give place of birth.
    Specify town and country)

7b. Town   Berne   7c. Country Switzerland

8a. Marital status   Single   8b. No. of children   n/a

8c. Ages of children   n/a   8d. Pets   one sheepdog

Details of Accommodation Required
(Please specify the following)

9a. Preferred location   village near cambridge

9b. Type of property   small cottage

9c. No. and type of rooms   one or two bedrooms,
living room, bathroom and kitchen.

9d. Furnished or unfurnished   furnished

10. Expected duration of tenancy*   6 months

11. Maximum weekly monthly rental (incl/excl rates)
     £120   incl. rates

12. Name and address of Bank/Employer/other suitable
person to whom reference can be made
       John Smith (Bank Manager)
       Lloyds Bank
       Gonville Place
       Cambridge

13. How would you wish Weekly/Monthly payments to be
made?   monthly by standing order

14. Special requirements   none

15. Date by which accommodation required
     as soon as possible

16. Date of Application   3rd February 1986

17. Usual Signature

*No short lets: 3 months minimum

(FLAT-U-RENT is a registered accommodation agency. All
agreements are entered into subject to the provisions of the
appropriate Housing Acts.)

3.

Again the introduction is important. It helps you to imagine the situation you are in. Often in forms you are asked not to leave any sections blank – as then the person receiving the form does not know if you forgot to answer the question or if it is not in fact applicable to you. What do the instructions ask you to do if the question does not apply to you? If you are not sure how to answer a question, e.g. no 15, the least risky way is simply to write N/A. Note that the instructions also tell you how much the deposit will be – and it varies depending on where you come from. How much will it be for you? In which parts of this form do you have to use block capitals? Remember to use capital letters for the languages you list in q. 16 on the form. Under countries visited it is better to write the names of the countries you know that you can spell than to be totally truthful.

Answer

SIF 17th Annual Conference

Langfords Hotel, Hove

4th–6th January 1986

Applicants should complete this form and return it to the Conference Organiser together with a deposit of £20 if UK member/£40 if overseas member.

Please answer all questions.

Put N/A if not applicable.

A. *Personal Details. Please use block capitals for this section.*

1.	Surname or family name	CLAUS
2.	First names in full	SANTA
3.	Sex	MALE
4.	Date of birth	25.12.0001
5.	Age	1985
6a.	Place of birth: Town	KILPISJARVI
6b.	Country	FINLAND
7.	Nationality	FINNISH
8.	Present Address	I SOUTH STREET THE NORTH POLE LAPLAND
9.	Address for correspondence if different from above	N/A

B. *Hotel Information*

10. Double/Single Room
    (please state preference)   Single

11. Are you willing to share a room?   Yes

12. Bath/Shower (please state preference)
    Shower preferred

13. Approximate arrival time at hotel
    midday 3rd January 1986

14. Will you require parking facilities?   No

15. Special dietary requests   none

C. *For Conference Organiser's Information*

16. Languages spoken Finnish, English, Arabic,
    Thai and Japanese

17. Countries visited most European countries

D. *Administration*

18. I enclose a deposit of   £40

19. Signature

20. Name of Parent or Guardian if under 18   n/a

21. Date   21. 11. 85

4.

Here you have to show that you can make an explanation, an apology
and an offer clearly and politely in English. To be polite you will need
to give a good reason why you can't do what you promised.
Remember that a postcard doesn't give you a lot of space to do all this
and so you will have to be fairly brief. You have to write the address
as well. Make sure you know the order of the parts of the address in
English. Why not use an address that you know in Britain – if you
have a penfriend there or are now staying in Britain why not use that
address. It will save time and you are less likely to risk marks. As you
are writing to friends with a baby, it is perhaps best to address the card
to 'Mr and Mrs . . .'

I'm terribly sorry but I won't be
able to babysit for you next
Tuesday. I had quite forgotten
that I'd promised to drive my
landlady to visit her mother in
hospital that evening.
I hope this won't cause you
too much inconvenience.
I hope that I shall be able
to babysit for you before
too long.
How about Tuesday week?
With all good wishes,
Anna

Mr and Mrs Hubbard
6 Shoe Lane
Brighton
BN2 6AS

5.

This question tests whether you can put your feelings into English. It is not always easy to do this kind of exercise in your own language; it will probably be easier if you remember the advice in section B and try to imagine that you are writing to real friends of yours – what would you say then? Pay attention to the time limit suggested. Don't spend more time than is recommended – the extra marks you may get will not be worth it.

Answer

Congratulations on doing so well in your exam! I was sure you would! Let's get together for a celebration drink this weekend. How about Friday evening in The Red Lion?
Love,
Franceska

I was so sorry to hear about your exam. Next time I'm sure you'll pass with distinction! Let's get together and drown our sorrows some time soon. Are you free on Saturday?
Love,
Franceska

6.

In telegrams remember that the ordinary rules of grammar do not apply – they are too expensive when you have to pay by the word (see section B for a reminder of what parts of speech are usually missed out in telegrams and classified ads). The telegram in the question means, in standard English, 'Your place has been confirmed. Please tell us the type of accommodation which you require. Please confirm the date when you are going to arrive and the period you are intending to stay for. We should also like to know the maximum price per week which you are prepared to pay and whether you have any special requirements. Please send your answer immediately to the registrar of RSACO.'

Remember to use block capitals and to give all the information requested. You will lose marks for exceeding the word limit.

Answer

ARRIVING 6TH SEPT STAYING THREE MONTHS ROOM WITH LANDLADY PREFERRED £30 MAX P/W NEAR COLLEGE ELENA SANTOS

7.

Make sure you can give directions – it is a very popular task with examiners and is something you will often need to do. Learn to do it accurately. Think about a real place when you answer this question and describe how to get there as clearly as possible but if you are not sure how to say something in English then change it to something you *are* sure of.

Answer

When you arrive at Cambridge Railway Station, walk straight down Station Road until you come to the traffic lights. Then turn right and cross the road at the pelican crossing. On the right you'll see the bus stop for the 186 bus. It's only about 300 metres from the station to the bus stop so it's not too far to walk, even with luggage. Take the 186 bus and ask for Milton Road Corner. It costs 35p and the journey takes ten to fifteen minutes. The stop where you get off is the first one after crossing the river. When you get off the bus, turn right and walk along Milton Road. Take the second turning on the left (there's a modern church on the corner) and then the first right. You can't miss it!

8.

Quickly draw how the furniture can go on the diagram given. Make sure you can name all the objects. You should then be able to answer this question quite quickly. Be clear and don't include any unnecessary information.

Answer

Please put the bed along the wall to the left of the door with the head to the window wall. I'd like the desk and the hard chair to go under the window on the right. Please put the lamp on the desk. The bookcase can stand to the right of the window opposite the door. Put the armchair near the radiator and the round table in the middle of the room. The television should fit in the corner by the power point on the right. I hope this will work out all right.

Many thanks,

Marco Polo

9.

In this question you have to write in a friendly way as well as to give a lot of information. Think about what you would really need to say in this situation. Be careful not to spend too long on this question – you will probably find there is a lot you could write but remember it is only one question in quite a long paper. You can write your information in the form of a list. There is no need to worry about carefully constructed paragraphs in this kind of writing.

Answer

Amy and Marty,

I hope you'll enjoy being here and look forward to hearing all about it when I get back in a couple of weeks' time.

Do make use of everything you find in the house. I've put clean sheets on the beds but you'll find more – and towels – in the cupboard outside the main bedroom.

The back door key is hanging behind the door in the cupboard under the stairs.

I've left instruction books for the washing machine and the video on top of the television – you probably know how to use them anyway.

Would you mind watering my plants once a week or so? Thanks.

Buses to the city centre go every half hour from the stop on the corner. If you want, you could hire bikes from a shop which you'll find a hundred yards down the road on the left.

I've left local guidebooks and maps on top of the television too. There's really quite a lot to see and do. I haven't cancelled the local paper which comes every evening – it'll tell you about all sorts of local entertainments. The corner shop sells most things you could want – it's open from 8 a.m. to 7 p.m. every day including Sundays. The people there are very friendly and will be happy to help you with anything you want to know.

If you have any problems you could also phone my friend, Suzanne. Her number is 345 7123 and she'll be ringing you soon anyhow to invite you for a meal at her place.

With all good wishes for a happy stay.

Jan

10.

You don't know these people very well so you need to apologise quite formally. You must tell them what you can't do, why you can't do it and you must make it clear that you are really disappointed. There is no need to write a lot as long as you do all these three things.

Answer

Charles and Diana,

I am terribly sorry but I have a dreadful headache and I think I'd better go to bed rather than go shopping with you this afternoon. I am so disappointed as I was looking forward to it very much.

Best wishes,

Ariadna

11.

Again look at the question and work out exactly what you have to make clear. You have to say where you are going to be and when. Be friendly but brief.

Answer

Johann

    We're meeting at the Green Dragon at 8-ish and will be there until about ten when we'll go to the Raj Belash in the Market Place. See you later.

Giovanni

12.

This kind of ad is like a telegram in that you pay by the word. So omit any words that are not essential for the meaning. When the instructions are quite long like this, it is a good idea to tick off on the question all the points as you write them. Then it is easy to check that everything has been included.

Answer

TWO GIRLS WANTED TO SHARE COMFORTABLE CENTRALLY-HEATED FOUR-BEDROOMED HOUSE NORTH LONDON WITH TWO ITALIAN GIRLS RENT £200 PER MONTH PLUS BILLS PHONE MARIA VISCONTI 01 246 8642 EVENINGS AFTER SIX

13.

There is no need to write much here. The only important information is what you'd like to see and when you want to go, as well as a way for interested people to contact you.

Answer

Is anyone interested in going with me to see Agatha Christie's VERDICT at the Theatre Royal tonight. If so please contact Luigi in Room 202.

14.

What are the points that this question asks for? Place lost, time lost, description and contents. Make sure you cover all these four things. The English you need will be formal – i.e. avoid contractions and slang. Make sure you describe the purse well enough for the police to identify it.

Answer

I have lost my purse. I think I must have lost it on a 151 bus going from Meadowlands to the City Centre at about nine o'clock last night, February 29th 1984. It is a brown leather purse with a zip and my initials – R.S. – in gold on one side. Inside there were some coins, about twenty pounds in notes, three or four safety pins and my Access card. Rosmarie Schneider.

15.

The language here will also be formal and must give a precise description that will help the insurance company. Again tick off the points as you deal with them so that nothing is forgotten.

Answer

The accident occurred on March 16th 1986 at the corner of High Street and Queen's Road in Westport, Sussex. It was raining heavily. I was on my bicycle and was turning right from Queen's Road into

High Street. My lights were on and were in good condition. A car was travelling at about fifty m.p.h. along High Street and its right-hand headlamp was not working. It hit my back wheel and I was thrown into the road. Fortunately I was only bruised but my bicycle – which I had bought for £150 only last month – was completely ruined. The car did not stop but an off-duty policeman witnessed the accident and was able to note the car's registration number. It was a dark-coloured Jaguar and its registration number was ABC 123A. The policeman and I agree that the driver of the car was totally responsible for the accident. Karl Jung

E. BEYOND THE COURSEWORK

If you are not staying in an English-speaking country you will find that you need to do a lot of this kind of task in your everyday life. When this happens ask a native speaker to check what you write so that you learn by your mistakes – if you make any.

Keep your eyes open. Look at notices in your local newsagent's window. Read the small ads in the newspapers. Notice what English-speaking friends write in their notes to you. Have a notebook with you always and write down anything you see that surprises you or that you particularly like.

If you are not staying in an English-speaking country you will find it useful here – as in many other aspects of learning English – to have an English penfriend or to read an English newspaper or magazine. When in your own language you have to do a task like those described in this chapter try to translate what you write from your own language into English.

Chapter 17

Checking and correcting

A. GETTING STARTED

An essential part of doing well in an exam is to check your work carefully. When you're working out your timing campaign for any written exam don't forget to allow time to check your answers very thoroughly. Don't hurry away from the exam room if you finish early; use your extra time to check again.

The aim of this chapter is to give you some practice in looking through work for errors and in correcting those mistakes. The chapter will also be a kind of revision for you of many of the points raised earlier in the book.

This chapter will not only be useful exam practice but it should also help any of you who think you may be teachers of English at some time as it will give you practice in correcting work.

B. ESSENTIAL PRINCIPLES

There are different aspects of checking work in an exam. First you must check that you have done everything that you should have done.

- Are you sure you haven't missed any questions out by mistake?
- Have you answered the right number of questions?
- Above all, have you done exactly what you were asked to do in the question?

It isn't at all difficult to forget to answer part of a question or to jump to the wrong conclusion about what the question wanted you to do. So, when you check your work, first read through the question paper again!

Then you have to check the language content of your answer.

- Have you used the right tenses?
- Have you got the right verb forms and endings?
- Have you used the correct structures required by particular verbs?

- Have you put in articles where they are necessary and left them out where they are not necessary?
- Have you chosen the right prepositions?
- Are there any words where you are worried about the spelling?
- What about your punctuation?
- Is your style appropriate?

If there are any points where you have serious doubts whether something is correct or not, perhaps you can express yourself in a different way, using words that you feel confident about. An exam is not a good time for experimenting with language. You may also want to add something that you know is correct if it is appropriate and you feel it will impress the examiners. If you can, for example, make correct use of any of the problem points that we have looked at in this book, you may well help yourself to make a good impression.

When you are making corrections like this you will find that some of the equipment we described in Chapter 2 comes in especially useful. I find typist's correcting fluid (Tippex) particularly good but some of you may prefer a good ink rubber. It will also make your work look better here if you have left lines between your writing where this is possible. This gives you a chance to correct your work without it looking too messy. Remember that if your work is very untidy and particularly if it is difficult to read, it will not help your position with the person marking your paper.

When you're checking your writing, look carefully at these VSPs, Very Special Problems or:

Verbs – tenses and forms
Spelling
and
Prepositions

If at all possible do not check your work immediately after completing it. You will usually find it easier to spot your mistakes if you first answer at least one other question and then return to check your first answer.

Remember the point that we made in Chapter 2 that you can learn by your mistakes. Look back now at work that you have done. What kind of mistakes did you make? Do you understand why they were not correct? If any of these points comes up in the exam, let's hope a little warning bell will ring in your mind and you will think particularly carefully about what you're going to write.

C. QUESTIONS

The questions in this section are not all exam questions. Their aim is to give you practice in error correction and to help you to revise some of the points made in this book.

(a) Read the question
(b) Look at the notes introducing the answer to the question in section D.
(c) Answer the question.

(d) Check your answer with that given in section D.

(e) Correct any mistakes.

1. TWELVE BASIC GRAMMAR RULES

In this first question look back at the twelve basic grammar rules listed in Chapter 3. Then try the following exercise.

Which of these sentences are correct and which aren't? If there is a mistake, can you correct it?

(a) Jimmy suggested us to spend an other day in the France before to go home.

(b) When we arrived to home, we were very shocked of a terrible news.

(c) My mother is teacher but she is soon going to stop to teach for looking for a new work.

(d) Before came to England they used to working hard.

(e) I liked very much that film; in fact it was one of the best film I've every seen.

(f) I don't mind to live by a landlady but I can't get used to not have a shower every day.

(g) He's got difficulties to understand English verbs and feels he'll never succeed to learn them.

2. VERBS

This question concentrates on verbs – their tenses, their forms and endings.

Read through the section of Chapter 3 which deals with verbs and then correct the sentences below where it's necessary.

(a) I am go to London but he going to Paris.

(b) He's already here for six months but he'll stay for a year altogether.

(c) Every morning I'm getting up at 6 o'clock.

(d) Last night I was watching some television, then I was writing some letters and, finally, I was going to bed at 11.30.

(e) After he left school, he had gone to university.

(f) If I would be a millionaire, I'll spend a lot of money on travel.

(g) Supposing he will fail the exam, what he will do then?

(h) I have first fallen in love when I were 18.

3. VOCABULARY

For this question look back at the section on Commonly Confused Words in Chapter 4. Then decide where there are mistakes in the sentences in this exercise.

(a) She made a very interesting travel to the Himalays.

(b) Can you borrow me five pounds?

(c) I don't really agree with the government's economic policy.

(d) I made many good experiences in London.

(e) Let's practice our verbs.

(f) He became a beautiful bicycle for his birthday.

(g) Are you agree with him about nuclear disarmament?

(h) I'm afraid I didn't have any opportunity to meet him last week.

4. CONNECTORS AND PREPOSITIONS

Before doing this question look back at the points made about connectors in Chapter 3 and at the points about prepositions made in Chapters 3 and 4. Then check these sentences carefully, thinking particularly about the use of connectors and prepositions. Some of the uses are correct and some are not.

(a) I saw him in the other side of the street because I pretended not to.

(b) English children start school with 5. However, they don't seem to learn any more than children who start with a later age.

(c) She got married with Charles despite she loved someone else.

(d) It depends of how much money we've got if we go to abroad this year or not.

(e) Please, phone me as long as you arrive back to the house.

(f) In that moment I knew I had to do it. Once I had made that decision, I felt relieved.

(g) The school is near from the railway station. Anyway, it's a long way from the bus station.

(h) He lived in France during ten weeks while he was trying to write his book.

5. SPELLING

This question deals with one of the things you should check quite carefully when looking through your exam. Spelling is particularly difficult in English. It often seems to bear little resemblance to pronunciation. As one Russian joke says, the English write 'Liverpool' but they pronounce it 'Manchester'. English and American spelling is often different. The American spelling is usually simpler. It doesn't really matter which spelling you prefer.

Can you find twenty spelling mistakes in the sentences which follow? Write out the words in their correct forms and you will have a list of some of the most commonly mis-spelt words in the English language. Learn the spellings of these words by heart. In section D you will find one or two basic spelling rules to help you.

(a) The foriegn student got on his byciicle and rode quite quickly off to his new acomodation.

(b) Can you tell me wether the current chairman of the comitee has moved to a new adress?

(c) The governement has dissappointed many of its supporters by stopping the plans for new industrial developement in the north of the country.

(d) I said I thought Italian girls were typicaly beautifull but he declared that he prefered Brazilians.

(e) I felt very embarassed when the nurse measured me to find out my hight and waight.

(f) I don't know wich of the to letters he recieved first.

(g) I belive he is planing to return to Britain soon.

6. PUNCTUATION

This penultimate question deals with something this book does not deal with at length elsewhere – punctuation.

The person who wrote the following passage has completely forgotten about punctuation. Can you correct it, putting in the punctuation marks and adding capital letters where necessary. In section D you will find some of the basic points to remember about punctuation in the notes introducing the answer to this question.

can any bus service rival the elchester to drayford route in england in may 1975 it was reported in the daily echo that the buses not longer stopped for passengers this had come to light when one of them mrs jane smithson reported that buses regularly sailed past queues of up to thirty people when questioned about this situation councillor william jackson said if these buses stop to pick up passengers theyll disrupt the timetable its a disgrace said mrs smithson im going to buy a bike tomorrow

7. EVERYTHING

Here is a final question to practise as many of the above points as possible. It is an answer to this possible FCE exam question: 'Write 120 to 180 words on Taking Exams Helps You Learn English'.

This subject is not interesting but I try to answer it. I am boring with exams. They make you to learn stupid things. They do not help you for studing. Perhaps you know very well something but it isn't time for writting everything in the exam. So you don't suceed to the exam. So I give an other student an advice. You'd better not to pass exams. It has people who likes to pass exams. This people makes lots of homeworks and at last they can make well the exam. But this people does not know really a lot. I have taken one exam last year. My teacher sais I know English good. The examiners have decided different. I am not understanding why. Everybody in my class have good marks. Now I make this exam which I am hopping I am going to succeed to it. You are agree, Mr Examiner, aren't you?

D. TUTOR'S NOTES AND ANSWERS

1.

There are 21 mistakes altogether in this question. Can you find them all? Do keep referring back to Chapter 3 if you're not sure if something is right or not.

Answer

(a) Jimmy suggested our spending (OR we spent) another day in France before going home.

(b) When we arrived home we were very shocked at some terrible news.

(c) My mother is a teacher but she is soon going to stop teaching to look for new work (OR a new job).

(d) Before coming to England, they used to work hard.

(e)   I liked that film very much; in fact, it was one of the best films
       I've ever seen.
(f)   I don't mind living with a landlady (OR at a landlady's) but I
       can't get used to not having a shower every day.
(g)   He's got difficulty in understanding English verbs and feels he'll
       never succeed in learning them.

2.

In this question remember to think first about what tense is needed in
the particular context and then about how to form that tense.

Answer

(a)   I'm going to London but he's going to Paris.
(b)   He's been here for six months but he's staying (OR he's going to
       stay) for a year altogether.
(c)   Every morning I get up at six o'clock.
(d)   Last night I watched some television, then I wrote some letters
       and, finally, I went to bed at 11.30.
(e)   After he (had) left school, he went to university.
(f)   If I were a millionaire, I'd spend a lot of money on travel.
(g)   Supposing he fails the exam, what will he do then?
(h)   I first fell in love when I was 18.

3.

Check that you understand the differences between all the commonly
confused words listed in Chapter 4 before you try to do this question.

Answer

(a)   She made a very interesting journey to the Himalayas.
(b)   Can you lend me five pounds?
(c)   Correct.
(d)   I had many good experiences in London.
(e)   Let's practise our verbs.
(f)   He got or received a beautiful bicycle for his birthday.
(g)   Do you agree with him about nuclear disarmament?
(h)   Correct.

4.

Connectors and prepositions are what you need to make your
sentences hang together well in English. Revise the relevant sections
of Chapters 3 and 11 before trying this question.

Answers

(a)   I saw him on the other side of the street although I pretended not
       to.
(b)   English children start school at 5. However, they don't seem to
       learn any more than children who start at a later age.
(c)   She got married to Charles despite the fact that (OR despite
       loving) she loved someone else.
(d)   It depends on how much money we've got whether we go abroad
       this year or not.
(e)   Please, phone me as soon as you arrive back at the house.
(f)   At that moment I knew I had to do it. Once I had made that
       decision, I felt relieved.

(g) The school is near (to) the railway station. On the other hand, (OR however,) it's a long way from the bus station.

(h) He lived in France for ten weeks while he was trying to write his book.

5.

You just have to learn the spelling of many English words individually, but here are a few rules that should help a little. How do you know whether to write occurred or occured, gallopping or galloping? It is a matter of stress. If the stress is on the final syllable of the root word, then the last consonant is doubled. If the stress occurs earlier in the word, then the consonant remains single.

Thus the correct forms are occurring and galloped.

The suffix 'ful' only has one 'l' in all adjectives, like cheerful, hopeful, graceful, etc. In the adverb 'ful' becomes 'fully', e.g. joyfully, gratefully, beautifully etc.

Adjectives that end in 'ic', e.g. comic, domestic, form their adverbs with 'ically', e.g. comically, domestically etc.

The sound 'E' in English can be spelt in a number of ways including either 'ei' or 'ie'. English children learn the rule 'I before E except after C'. This helps them to remember how to spell such words as believe and receive. The exception to the rule is the word 'seize'.

Make sure you are clear about the differences between two, too and to. Two is a number, too is also or excessively, and to is a preposition or part of the inifinitive.

Make sure you are clear about the differences between the words 'quite' and 'quiet'. They are pronounced quite differently and have quite different meanings. They are even quite different parts of speech.

The question and relative words in English with the sound 'W' all begin with 'wh' – where, which, who, what, why and whether.

Answer

foreign   bicycle   accommodation
whether   committee   address
government   disappointed   development
typically   beautiful   preferred
embarrassed   height   weight
which   two   received
believe   planning

6.

Here are some punctuation rules you should try to remember. These are just some of the rules about English punctuation – those that are most commonly forgotten by foreign students. For a more detailed set of rules refer to a full reference grammar.

You must use capital letters for

> the first letter in a new sentence
> names and titles of people, places, books etc.
> countries, nationalities and languages
> days and months

You must finish each sentence with a full stop unless it is a question. In that case put a question mark at the end of the sentence.

The rules about when to put commas are not so strict in English as in some languages. The general rule is to put a comma where you would naturally pause for breath.

An apostrophe often means that a letter or several letters have been missed out, e.g. he'd = he had or he would. Be especially careful wtih it's (= it is). The possessive of it, as in 'The cat won't eat its dinner', is written without an apostrophe.

The apostrophe can also indicate possession. Notice the difference between 'The boy's bicycles' and 'The boys' bicycles'. In the former there is one boy and in the latter there are at least two boys.

Inverted commas are used at the beginning and end of direct speech. They go above the line, e.g. "Hello," said Fred. "What are you doing here?"

Answer

Can any bus service rival the Elchester to Drayford route in England? In May 1975 it was reported in The Daily Echo that the buses no longer stopped for passengers. This had come to light when one of them, Mrs Jane Smithson, reported that buses regularly sailed past queues of up to thirty people. When questioned about this situation, Councillor William Jackson said, "If these buses stop to pick up passengers, they'll disrupt the timetable."

"It's a disgrace," said Mrs Smithson. "I'm going to buy a bike tomorrow."

7.

This composition is terrible from all sorts of points of view. Firstly, think about whether it actually answers the question asked. There is no need to argue in favour of the proposition but your arguments for or against must be made clearly. This certainly has not happened in this example. There are no paragraphs and there seems to be no plan. The beginning and the ending are weak and would make a very bad impression on the marker. Then there are masses of grammar and vocabulary mistakes.

How many of these can you spot? Here are just a few points to help you.

- What is the difference between bored and boring/interested and interesting/shocked and shocking etc?
- What is the difference between to take, to do, to pass and to fail an exam?

- What is the rule about verb and direct object?
- What is special about the word 'people'? What about 'everybody', on the other hand?
- What other mistakes can you find?

Answer

As the notes above make clear, this essay has mistakes of content, style and English. The paragraph that follows corrects the language mistakes but it still doesn't give an answer that would get good marks. The content would have to be made more to the point and the composition would have to be more neatly organised into paragraphs for that to happen.

This subject is not interesting but I shall try to answer it. I am bored by exams. They make you learn stupid things. They do not help you to study. Perhaps you know something very well but there isn't time to write everything in the exam. So you don't pass the exam. So I give other students some advice. You shouldn't take exams. There are people who like to take exams. These people do lots of homework and in the end they pass their exams. But these people do not really know a lot. I took an exam last year. My teacher says I know English well. The examiners decided differently; I cannot understand why. Everybody in my class got good marks. Now I am taking this exam, which I hope I am going to pass. You agree I should pass, don't you?

The composition is now without grammar mistakes but it still has serious mistakes of tone. It would be better if the first and last sentences were left out for a start. Better still, rewrite it totally. How would you write a composition on this subject?

E. BEYOND THE COURSEWORK

In practising error correction it may be easier for you to find the mistakes which someone else has made. Perhaps you can find someone else to work with. Check each other's work and try to decide together whether something is right or wrong. You will probably find that talking about language and trying to explain something to someone else is one of the best ways for you yourself to learn and to remember what you have learnt.

Now you should have worked through all the parts of this book which you need for your exam. It is probably getting near to the day of your exam. Read through again those parts of Chapter 2 which deal with the day of the exam itself. Then try not to worry about the exam – you should now be well-prepared to pass the exam. If you have any time left, just spend it reading an English book or magazine or listening to your favourite British or American record. On the day of the exam, I hope that a black cat crosses your path – this means good luck in England.

When your exam is over, do not stop using your English. Read, speak, write and listen to English as much as possible. You have learnt the language not just to pass an exam but to be able to meet new friends and colleagues and to enjoy other cultures.

Bibliography

These are just a few of the many books and magazines published in order to help you with your English.

GRAMMAR

Practical English Usage, Michael Swan, OUP
Basic English Usage*, Michael Swan, OUP
Basic English Grammar*, Mackin and Eastwood, OUP
Cassells Students' English Grammar*, Jake Allsop, Cassells

*With accompanying book of exercises.

DICTIONARIES AND DICTIONARY WORK

Longmans Dictionary of Contemporary English, Longman
Oxford Advanced Learner's Dictionary of Current English, OUP

Learning with LDOCE, Janet Whitcut, Longman
Use Your Dictionary, Adrian Underhill, OUP

WRITING

Writing Tasks, David Jolly, CUP
Writing Skills, Norman Coe *et al.*, CUP

READING SKILLS

Authentic Reading, Catherine Walter, CUP
Meet the Press, Janice Abbot, CUP

See Chapter 9 for a short list of novels, short stories and other books that you might enjoy reading in English.

LISTENING

Listening to Maggie, Lesley Gore, Longman
It Happened to Me, Roger Scott *et al.*, Longman
What a Story, Mary Underwood, OUP

SPEAKING	*Functions of English*, Leo Jones, CUP
	Partners, Language Teaching Publications
	Pair Work A and B, Peter Watcyn-Jones, Penguin

COURSEBOOKS	*Progress to FCE*, Leo Jones, CUP (has self-study guide)
	Longmans First Certificate Course, Roy Kingsbury *et al.*, Longman

MAGAZINES

English Today, CUP

London Calling, (For details write to:
P.O. Box 76
Bush House
The Strand
London
WC2B 4PH)

BBC English, (For details write to:
BBC English by Radio and TV
Meed House
21 John Street
London
WC1N 2BP)

Viewfinder, (For details write to:
ELA
21 High Street
Shrivenham
Swindon
Wilts
SN6 8AN)

The EFL Globe (For details write to:
P.O. Box 807
Bransholme
Hull
HU7 4FG
U.K.)

BOOKS ABOUT LANGUAGE *Our Language*, Simeon Potter, Penguin
The Changing English Language, Brian Foster, Penguin
Language Made Plain, Anthony Burgess, Collins

Index